ENGLISH GARDENS

English Gardens

From the Archives of Country Life

KATHRYN BRADLEY-HOLE

Foreword by The Duke of Devonshire

RIZZOLI
NEW YORK

New York · Paris · London · Milan

CONTENTS

PAGE 1 Mowing patterns in the quadrangle at Worcester College, Oxford.

PAGE 2 Courtyard at the Old Rectory, Naunton, Gloucestershire.

PAGE 4 Sunrise at Wudston House in Wiltshire. The garden was created by its owner in 2010, around a new house.

OPPOSITE The recently made reflective pool, amid irises under orchard trees at Bryan's Ground in Presteigne.

FOREWORD

THE DUKE OF DEVONSHIRE

Gardening has been a significant part of English and British culture for hundreds of years. This celebration of English gardens is a reminder that the cultivated space around people's homes is as important now as it ever has been. There are more people gardening and to a higher standard than ever before. Cottage gardens are thriving. The Yellow Book (of gardens open to visitors once or twice a year for charity) expands annually. The medium-to-large private gardens are now more numerous and better than ever before. The whole of gardening and horticultural life in the United Kingdom is prospering mightily.

The Royal Horticultural Society (RHS) is the leader in education and sustainability, two comparatively new responsibilities that it has embraced with remarkable vigour. The RHS also maintains the highest possible standards through its various shows. I was very struck by the reaction of Derbyshire people when the RHS announced in 2016 that its newest show would be here at Chatsworth. This was rightly regarded locally and beyond as an enormous compliment to Derbyshire—the key to this rejoicing was that the RHS differentiates our five-day show from the many other horticultural events by focusing on quality and well-informed innovation.

As in all matters cultural, fashion in gardening is a potent and ever-changing force. New styles of gardening are appearing with bewildering frequency. The skill of the plant breeders means that there is now a far wider choice of longer flowering, sweeter smelling, more disease resistant plants to choose from. Amanda and I have lived at Chatsworth for thirteen years, and in that time we have inevitably made a number of changes in the garden and the park. My parents did a magnificent job in saving, restoring, and enhancing the garden during their more than fifty-year tenure; we have taken a different route in one particular way.

After several years of clearing and thinning, and some only moderately successful new planting, we decided, with the complete support of Steve Porter, the head gardener, that, despite our great interest in plants and gardening none of the three of us had the ability to see the big picture and plan and plant accordingly. So for the past few years we have invited Dan Pearson and Tom Stuart-Smith to take on various parts of the garden,

OPPOSITE Chatsworth House in Derbyshire, principal home of the Duke of Devonshire. Formal gardens within the curtilage of the house lead out to the historic water features, encompassed by a magnificent landscape park. Created by Capability Brown from the late 1750s to 1765, it makes the most of its glorious setting, in the hills of the Peak District.

Reflected glory: Chatsworth House's Canal Pond, created between 1702 and 1703. The house appears to rise from the water, a trick achieved by setting the pond a few inches higher than the South Lawn.

redesigning and replanting them in their own individual styles. This has already made an enormous difference to the garden, and the changes will become more obvious and more successful as nature takes her course. Steve Porter and his brilliant team have enabled very significant projects to be planted and established in a remarkably short time, surviving even the rigors of the boiling hot of 2018 with very few losses.

This expansion of horticultural excellence at Chatsworth has shown me how many young people there are with a passion for gardening. The career structure for gardeners is at last beginning to improve. Historically, it was often the public local authority purse that enabled individuals to learn the many different aspects of horticulture required by parks and gardens departments up and down the country. Now it is more the private sector that has taken on this responsibility and, while the apprenticeship structure is a lot less formal than hitherto, there are plenty of places where the Paxtons of the twenty-first century could start their careers.

This book contains wonderful images of a very diverse selection of gardens, and I am delighted that the photographers have often included animals and children because in a family garden they are nearly always present but too often left out of formal portraits. Inevitably, both children and animals can cause painful conflicts to the gardener: dogs rampage, hens scratch up new sowings, and precious shrubs get used as goalposts. Nonetheless the pets and the children are a fundamental part of the point of having a private space, a garden, so we must learn to welcome them all. Certainly chickens, especially Buff Cochins, in the garden at Chatsworth, were one of the most popular sights with our visitors. Sadly the foxes and badgers have made it impossible to keep hens in the garden any longer.

The *Country Life* articles about gardens and gardening, written by sympathetic experts, have encouraged an international audience of tourists to visit the country's amazingly eclectic selection of gardens, and this is of enormous financial benefit to our country, especially to so many rural areas. The new wave of gardens and garden designers are extending the season for garden visiting and anyone who thinks the gardens aren't worth going to during the winter should go to see John Sales's winter garden at Anglesey Abbey—it is nothing less than magnificent.

What a book, what a legacy. I now have too many gardens that I must see throughout the year.

INTRODUCTION

KATHRYN BRADLEY-HOLE

OPPOSITE The stuff of life itself. Running water invigorates gardens with its presence; this fine old fountain at Badminton House in Gloucestershire creates a cooling atmosphere, surrounded by lush ferns.

Living where we do, within a little group of islands on the eastern edge of the North Atlantic Ocean, close to continental Europe but separated by a deep-sea channel, it is second nature to the English to be watchful of the weather. Hereabouts, its one consistent feature is fickleness. As I write this introduction on a warm, sunny day in mid-February, spring's bulbs are pushing their snouts out of the ground and small birds are singing lustily. The odd bee zooms by, foraging for pollen and nectar in the nodding flowers of hellebores. It's unseasonably warm, but only last week, a storm strong enough to have been dignified with its own name was blasting icy gusts through the bare tree branches and torrential rain was bouncing off the windows. T-shirt weather on Saint Valentine's Day is unusual but not unknown; yet snow might still return in time to wreck Easter or Whitsun.

BELOW At Mirehouse, in the Lake District, a carved-stone quotation from Virgil advises, "First seek a settled home for your bees." Today we need to find all sorts of ways to accommodate insect life in the garden. Virgil reminds us that bees themselves are valuable enough to require a priority in our thoughts; as pollinators alone, they are crucial.

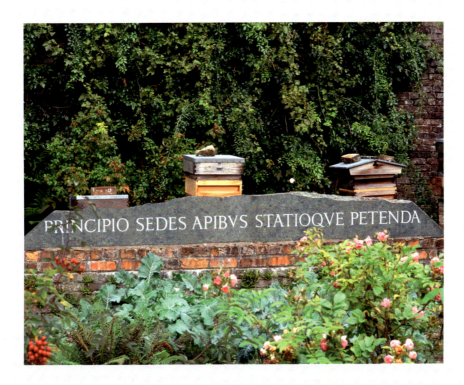

At Crewe Hall in Cheshire, W. A. Nesfield created a magnificent parterre, its pattern drawn with low box hedging. The spaces were infilled with gravel in shades of buff and blue.

That the English are a nation of gardeners as well as weather-watchers is well known; the two national obsessions are as intertwined as the honeysuckle and the hedgerow. Sowing seeds or planting a slip of something into the ground are acts of intention and hope. For the seeds to grow and flourish in the face of weather, wild creatures, weeds, and water (too much or too little), we have to take charge and nurture, to see things through the challenges they will undoubtedly face.

Consequently, for many people, gardening is therapy as well as a metaphor for life, with the rewards of beauty, food, creativity, and connection with nature. It's also important to the nation's economy. "The Economic Impact of Ornamental Horticulture and Landscaping in the UK," a report published in October 2018 by Oxford Economics, concluded that ornamental horticulture contributed £24.2 billion to national GDP in 2017 and accounted for nearly 600,000 jobs. It further concluded that gardens and parks are a major tourism draw for international visitors to the United Kingdom, accounting for some £2.2 billion in spending by visitors from overseas during 2017 alone.

This book is therefore a timely celebration of English country gardening as it is now, in the twenty-first century, illustrated via the unique archive of *Country Life*, a pictorial weekly journal that launched on January 8, 1897, the year of Queen Victoria's Diamond Jubilee. The magazine has long been deemed a national treasure, so a quick canter through some highlights of its history will be useful.

Aside from the sporting and artistic aspects of English life covered each week in the magazine, *Country Life*'s mainstay feature is the profile of a country house and a country garden, nearly all of them in the British Isles. More than 6,000 gardens across 120-plus years amounts to an enormous and diverse pictorial and textual archive. It has therefore frequently been invaluable to researchers and restorers, from academics to private owners, to the National Trust.

The magazine's early volumes contain an interesting potpourri of garden fashions, the legacy of the Victorian age recorded in clear, monochrome photographs. Spectacular rock gardens were photographed at Swaylands in Kent and Waddesdon in Buckinghamshire; by about 1900, ancient topiaries had morphed into weird shapes at Cleeve Prior in Worcestershire, and Campsea Ashe in Suffolk. Mid-Victorian swagger could be seen in the grounds of aristocrats and industrialists alike. The Marquess of

At Hardwick Hall in Derbyshire, the Victorian parterre with its E and S commemorated its earlier owner, "Bess of Hardwick" (Elizabeth, Countess of Shrewsbury). This design is long gone, although in dry summers, aerial photography has revealed that its pattern still lies beneath.

Northampton's lively parterres of seasonal bedding plants spread out over vast terraces at Castle Ashby were immensely high-maintenance statements of grandeur, dating from the 1860s but apparently still in full sail in 1897. Likewise, Nesfield's intricate *parterres de broderie* of low box hedging and multihued gravels, created in 1854, were still neat and thriving up to the early twentieth century at Stoke Edith in Herefordshire, although W. A. Nesfield's 1850s swirls and gravels laid out at Crewe Hall in Cheshire were looking somewhat threadbare by 1901. Lavish Italianate gardens crowded with carved stone balustrades, statues, and fountains were created all over the country in the confident boom years of the mid-nineteenth century, but often the grandeur would not last far into the twentieth.

For centuries, the houses and families at the heart of traditional country estates were supported by income from their farms, especially after the seventeenth – to nineteenth-century land grabs known as "enclosure." But in the 1870s, agricultural income took some severe knocks, owing to a blip in the weather that resulted in several years of poor harvests. Unable to pay their rents, tenant farmers departed to find work in the cities, or to emigrate. Cheaper food had to be imported from abroad—a situation that became irreversible. Consequently, agricultural land valued at £54 per acre in 1875 had fallen to just £19 per acre by 1897. Starting in 1894, increased and more effectively enforced death taxes added to the financial burden on landowners' households. Hundreds of mansions and thousands of acres were therefore put on the market by cash-strapped owners in the closing years of the nineteenth century. The situation carried on well into the 1920s, following the further crises of a devastating world war from 1914 to 1918 and the deadly flu pandemic that followed shortly thereafter.

The carving up of large estates enabled lesser mortals—especially those who had recently become very wealthy in business and industry—to buy into the life of a country gentleman. Finding somewhere to build a house and be surrounded by enough land to feel part of rural England, without the need for farm income to support it, became an achievable goal in the new, socially mobile society. Estate agents flourish in such times; so, too, do builders and furnishers, makers of glasshouses, and manufacturers of mowing machines. And so do those who can provide a platform for relevant advertising—of land, houses, things to put in them, and cars to make them accessible. *Country Life* therefore launched when it did because of an unmissable business opportunity: to serve the needs of countless people having a direct or indirect interest in selling, buying, or enhancing property.

With its niche audience and exceptionally high-quality photography and printing, the magazine's focus has always been high end, but it has also always been devoted to craftsmanship. And with the arrival of the twentieth century, a freer style was being championed alongside the confident Victorian gardens of rockwork, bedding plants, and Italianate terraces. Indeed, *Country Life*'s hands-on founder and proprietor, Edward Hudson (1854–1936), encouraged by the famous artist-gardener Gertrude Jekyll (1843–1932), wholeheartedly took up the cause of the Arts and Crafts movement—its objects,

BELOW Boulder dash: Magnificent rock work at Waddesdon Manor in Buckinghamshire. Baron Ferdinand de Rothschild engaged James Pulham and Son to build some rock features; most of it is made with "Pulhamite," a patented fake rock, realistic looking and enormously popular in mid- and late-Victorian gardens.

FAR LEFT The White Garden at Hidcote Manor in Gloucestershire in 1930. "It is possible that the idea came from Johnston's American novelist friend Edith Wharton, who is believed to have made one of the first white gardens," suggests Fred Whitsey.

LEFT The view out down the Long Walk at Hidcote, as seen from the interior of one of the twin gazebos that terminate the Red Borders. In creating the Long Walk, Johnston is believed to have been inspired by his time spent living in France.

PREVIOUS PAGES The Great Plat at Hestercombe in Somerset: arguably the finest work of the Lutyens and Jekyll partnership. Laid out from 1904 onward, it is surrounded by Lutyens's playful use of stone pavings and a magnificent long pergola.

furniture, architecture, and gardens. Articles on the vernacular-inspired houses being created by the talented young architect Edwin Lutyens (1869–1944), and the gardens Jekyll planned for them, made their way into the pages of the magazine, thereby attracting important new commissions for the design duo.

Jekyll's own garden at Munstead Wood, as well as Gravetye Manor, the garden of her friend William Robinson, the gardener-turned-publisher, were the two most famous Arts and Crafts gardens of the time. Conversely, Hidcote Manor, now widely regarded as the most influential garden of the twentieth century, didn't appear anywhere in print until 1930, by which time it had achieved maturity.

Hidcote was the creation of Lawrence (Johnny) Johnston (1871–1958), an Anglophile American who brought his rich, twice-widowed mother to live with him there, on a chilly north-Cotswolds hilltop, in 1907. To someone less determined than Johnston, the location might have seemed an unpromising place to make a garden. Today we continue to admire Johnston's clever layout and the arrangement of his garden's spaces, alternating from open and directional to enclosed and intimate, all of it enhanced by considered plantsmanship. "No garden made in the twentieth century has had a greater influence on the evolution of the art of garden design or home garden making," enthused Fred Whitsey, Hidcote's biographer, in 2007. Johnston's friend, the novelist Edith Wharton, who stayed there several times, described it as "tormentingly perfect." His donation of the garden to the National Trust in 1948, the first garden in its own right that the trust took on, has ensured its preservation and, crucially, access for visitors.

OPPOSITE The view to the manor and fine cedar tree. *Country Life*'s monochrome images of Hidcote Manor show the garden as it was in 1930. Tipping's two articles from that year announced the garden to the world for the first time.

As the twentieth century drew on, international modernism also had a presence in *Country Life*, albeit dropped in here and there among a more traditional fare. Modernist gardens of the mid-century tend to be pared-down affairs, perhaps with a squared-up, asymmetrical terrace and formal pool alongside the house, that led to an open expanse of lawn with sparse scatterings of trees (as at Bentley Wood in Sussex and Gribloch in Stirlingshire). Likewise, modernist houses set into woodland and sandy heath, as at Serenity and the Homewood, both in Surrey, required little more than their sylvan settings to feel complete; the comings and goings of birds, squirrels, and deer perhaps supplied adequate interest beyond the large windows. King's Head House in Buckinghamshire was unusual in showing a terraced in-town courtyard with a modern pool, art deco sundial, and bifolding doors that turned the house interior and courtyard into a single indoor/outdoor space—a device we like to think of as belonging to our own times, but the King's Head garden was photographed in the late 1920s. Much later, a very English preoccupation with plants was comfortably united with modernity in the gardens of designer-plantsmen, such as architect Peter Aldington at Turn End, from 1970 onward, and garden designer John Brookes at Denmans, from the 1980s (page 437), although neither was featured in the magazine before the millennium.

The story of plant collecting (page 207) is wide ranging, but in the decades of monochrome printing, it was difficult to make a collector's's garden or arboretum appear exciting. Spring bulbs, blossoms, or azaleas at peak bloom, so spectacular in real life, tended to translate as blobs of white and grey. Likewise, rock gardens filled with delicate alpine plants, although

BELOW LEFT Charters in Berkshire was a modernist house built in 1938, in a style reminiscent of public buildings in Italy in the time of Mussolini. The circular templelike structure and house are surrounded by "plant and leave" conifers; it was clearly not a gardener's garden.

BELOW RIGHT Bentley Wood in Sussex, completed in 1938: the house was built by the architect Serge Chermayeff for his own use. Fellow modernist Christopher Tunnard designed the garden, maintaining wide-open southerly views. Stepping-stone paths in the grass lead to a subtle, serpentine route through the birch trees.

fantastically popular in the first half of the twentieth century, were often too fussy to be reproduced in print.

After the Second World War, Margery Fish (1892–1969) was prominent in rekindling a love of cottage garden flowers via her instructive books, beginning with the best-selling *We Made a Garden* (1956). Her laissez-faire style, which allowed plants to self-sow through the garden, won many fans when staff shortages were acute and extra help expensive. As the queen bee of ground-covering species (a subject that preoccupied both amateur and professional gardeners of the time), she offered good advice for tricky locations, such as damp ground and dry shade. Her crown passed to a worthy heir in Beth Chatto (1923–2018) a generation later.

Key aspects of context and horticultural history introduce each chapter of this book, which, when added together, will furnish an overview and understanding of the multitude of styles, interests, and historical and visual references that combine to make up "the English garden." What will quickly become apparent to the reader is how extremely diverse English gardens are. Yet there is also a unified thread that runs through, the strongest of which, I believe, is the emotional connection that people have with their gardens. Often, this springs from a deep-seated love of plants and/or landscape, or memory. For many people, their garden is the main focus and outlet for their creative side. If you get the gardening bug, you'll never tire of it, since gardens are forever growing and changing, constantly presenting challenges as well as frustration and delight.

I was lucky enough to become gardens editor of *Country Life* in 2000, removing myself from the toil of weekly deadlines exactly eighteen years later. A whole generation had been born and grown up in that time, and it was an incredible journey for me, coinciding with a fortunate era of relative stability and abundance. At such times, people like to invest in their gardens,

ABOVE In the spirit of William Robinson's "wild gardening" style, spring in the woodland garden at Abbots Ripton Hall, with 'Pheasant Eye' narcissi spread through the grass among reawakening shrubs and young trees.

OPPOSITE, CLOCKWISE Four views of Beth Chatto's influential woodland garden in Essex, as photographed in spring 2000. Fifty shades of pink in *Primula japonica*, relishing damp soil. Ostrich-feather fern *Matteuccia struthiopteris* with orange *Meconopsis cambrica var. aurantiaca*, the Welsh poppy. Bleeding heart *Dicentra spectabilis* joined by creamy-white flowers of *Tiarella cordifolia*. The enchanting primrose-yellow peony, *Paeonia mlokosewitschii*.

A Jekyll revival in the 1980s stimulated a vogue for colour-themed borders. The most extreme colour theory exponents were Sandra and Nori Pope, at Hadspen House's walled garden in Somerset. This planting of Oriental poppies, *Centranthus ruber* and *Astrantia* 'Hadspen Blood' is from 2006–7 at Littlethorpe Manor in North Yorkshire.

ABOVE Purple haze: a detail in the 2.5-acre walled garden at Holme Hale Hall in Norfolk, redesigned by Arne Maynard. Globular flower heads of *Allium hollandicum* 'Purple Sensation' are joined by blue spires of lupins and violet-hued irises.

and those that are profiled in these pages were all photographed during the past two decades. They therefore represent a remarkably focused and detailed illustration of English country gardening in the twenty-first century. Many of them are long established, of course; but many others presented here were actually created only in the new millennium. I have grouped them into major thematic categories, and it was a ridiculously difficult task to whittle down the nine hundred or so gardens published during my eighteen years to just over sixty, for obvious reasons of space.

In her brilliantly philosophical masterpiece, *A Gentle Plea for Chaos*, Mirabel Osler declares, "There are many ways of starting a garden. Abstract ideas may originate in the mind, and are then meticulously transferred to paper ... Another impetus may come from a cherished longing to have one area of your own, where no one can constrain you and where no conformity compromises your imagination ... Yet others may be haunted by childhood memories of magic places of make-believe, of games, scents and secrets. Gardens may start from a bare piece of earth surrounding a newly-built house, or from the sheer necessity of hiding some hideous building, or maybe from a desire for self-protection from sea and tempests ... Whatever it is, once started a garden holds you in its thrall." The gardens presented here all possess barrowloads of magic, make-believe, scents, and, no doubt, secrets. They're the essence of English garden making, in all its astonishing variety, wit, and inspiration.

FOLLOWING PAGES Green shade for green thoughts: rich layers of planting in His Royal Highness Prince Charles's Scottish garden at Birkhall in Royal Deeside. Grass paths wind their way through dense plantings of hostas and ferns under the tree canopy.

1 TOPIARY

Snip, snip. Snip-snip-snip-snip … The gardener at work with hand shears, trimming pieces of topiary, is one of the more pleasant sounds related to work in the garden. Less so the powered hedge trimmer, however.

Topiary is presently very popular, and numerous contemporary designers are putting substantial, ready-made specimens into the gardens of their clients. There is no doubt it is expensive to buy topiary pieces "off the shelf" but, if time is of the essence, few things can give a garden such an instant feeling of maturity than craned-in substantial trees and large clipped specimens in hornbeam, beech, or yew.

Ready-made topiary is also standard stock at countless nurseries, in a range of shapes and variety of species that certainly were not offered thirty years ago. In our time, so much is readily available, and everything has sped up to such an extent that the instant garden is a viable option for those in a hurry. Yet this approach is by no means new. The absurdly appropriately named Herbert J. Cutbush of William Cutbush & Son, a nineteenth-century nursery owner trading ready-made topiary figures, had a specialty in native yew (*Taxus baccata*), a plant unequaled for its matte, dark evergreen presence and almost velvety surface when trimmed regularly over time. Cutbush's cut bushes were often tiered, like cake stands, and crowned with trained birds such as peacocks.

Much earlier than Cutbush, however, was the dizzyingly successful garden design and nursery business of George London and Henry Wise, whose Brompton Park nursery, operating from 1689 to 1714, supplied thousands of trees and topiaries for the instant gardens they designed for numerous great houses. Longleat, Burghley, Chatsworth, Grimsthorpe, and Wanstead, to name a few, benefited from their expertise.

One of the most admired gardens of that age was (and still is) Levens Hall in Cumbria. Set against the pale grey stone of an imposing Elizabethan house, its topiary dates back to the seventeenth century, when one Guillaume Beaumont laid out a formal garden there between 1689 and 1712. The fashion for landscape parks that swept through most of the country completely bypassed Levens, so what we see is an authentic old walled garden subdivided by hedges and peopled with abstract figures. Topiary can be very atmospheric

OPPOSITE Sympathetic to the old manor at Wyken Hall in Suffolk, the topiary display in the front garden was designed in the 1980s, inspired by the pattern of a Jekyll herb garden of interlocking rings at Knebworth House.

Ancient yew and box hedging at Bramdean House in Hampshire has turned into billowing cumulus clouds. Holm oak, *Quercus ilex*, has been fashioned into a tall and imposing colonnade progressing down the lawn at Arley Hall in Cheshire. Crisp yew cones and cubes of box are among the many topiary shapes at Hinton Ampner in Hampshire. Yew topiary in the formal garden below the house at Henbury Hall in Cheshire.

and romantic, and the Levens figures have developed remarkable shapes down the centuries. Almost as unusually, the garden beds around the topiaries are planted with some thirty thousand seasonal bedding plants each year, grown on-site in the garden's greenhouses. It all adds up to one of the most spectacular and entertaining historic gardens in the country.

English topiary frequently has elements of folk art and charm that have moved right away from the geometric designs of Tudor and Jacobean times and their rigidly formal French and Dutch influences. For some time, English topiarists have preferred free-form inventiveness in a way that others have sometimes found hard to fathom. That a garden as smart as Deene Park (page 37) boasts topiary teapots is clearly English in its symbolism; it is also a personal statement of wit and whimsy that says the garden is not only a place of beauty but also enjoyment. Likewise, a cottage front garden showing off to the world a steam locomotive lovingly carved for years out of privet, or a gigantic yew peacock perched above the cottage garden wall, are expressions of creativity that give delight to passersby.

Topiary is also now understood to have had a very early presence in the British Isles. The excavated remains of Fishbourne Roman Palace, near Chichester in West Sussex, reveal the largest Roman residential building discovered in Britain, dating from 75 AD, some thirty years after the Roman conquest. As part of the villa complex, a large, rectangular courtyard garden with shaped beds for hedging and trees and water supplies for fountains was discovered during archaeological explorations, which began in 1960.

That we know so much about how Roman gardens looked—and how imaginative was their topiary—is down to various contemporary references and the unearthed wall art of Pompeii, but especially the description by Pliny the Younger of the garden at his Tuscan villa. It had shady avenues, pleached and trained trees, and fantastic topiaries, including "diverse animals in box … [and] tonsile evergreens shaped into a variety of forms." Indeed, the very word *topiary* derives from the Roman "topiarius," the ornamental gardener whose responsibilities included training ivy and clipping the trees and bushes. You will find that topiary appears throughout this book in many forms and in gardens old and new.

LEFT Gently does it: the ancient topiary shapes at Levens Hall in Cumbria need to be clipped with hand shears to maintain their detailed contours.

ABOVE RIGHT A. E. Henson's 1926 photograph of Levens Hall and its topiary, revealing the maze of little beds worked in among the figures.

BELOW RIGHT She can't be making a phone call, as this is a vintage photograph! Remarkable topiary looms over a gateway to an old cottage garden.

DEENE PARK

Topiary teapots were added to a parterre created by David Hicks, a gifted landscape designer, though better known for his interiors

In 1572 Sir Edmund Brudenell wrote in his diary, "laid the foundations of my haul at Deene" an estate that his grandfather, lord chief justice in Henry VIII's reign, had bought in 1514. His enlargements to an earlier building are still at the core of the house today and a formal Tudor garden was surely laid out beside it. No trace of one remains, but a plan of 1604 shows an arrangement typical of the period, with a formal parterre, a viewing tower, and beyond, a rectangular pond.

Like the house, the gardens received further enhancements and alterations over the centuries and, occasionally, underwent more challenging times. The last was in the mid-twentieth century, when the house, already struggling after decades of lean times, was taken over by the War Office and occupied by troops during the Second World War.

Marian Brudenell (1934–2013), who came to Deene after the war with her husband, Edmund (1928–2014), wrote that "by 1945, the already dilapidated house was virtually derelict, the roof leaked, there was dry rot, no electricity nor heating and little plumbing—in short, it was exceedingly uncomfortable. The kitchen was so far away that my mother-in-law used to ride there through the house on a bicycle." It was Marian and Edmund who took on the enormous task of turning around the fortunes of both the house and garden, making Deene's restoration their life's work together, following their marriage in 1955. Marian was, she recalled, "a girl of 21 who knew nothing about gardens or gardening," but energy and determination clearly made up for any lack of experience or knowledge. She took on the job of restoring and enhancing the seventeen acres of ornamental gardens wrapped around the house.

West of the house, a four-acre, brick-walled kitchen garden dates from the early eighteenth century. Although the walled garden is no longer intensively gardened, its southernmost wall at some stage became the backing wall to the Long Border, a sun-trap but somewhat narrow. Marian engaged the famous mid-twentieth-century nurseryman and garden designer Jim Russell to advise. Russell doubled its depth, from a scant seven feet to fourteen feet and planted it with an assortment of roses and fragrant, white-blossomed *Philadelphus*, such as 'Virginal' and 'Belle Etoile'. The shrubs were underplanted with a mass of herbaceous perennials—"good doers," such as hardy geraniums, daylilies, irises, phlox, and verbascum. At the Long Border's midpoint, the Brudenells created an intimate area, enclosed by an ellipse of hornbeam hedge. This is the Four Seasons Garden, a calm area with statues of the seasons among plants in pale hues and a large planter as its focal point.

Since the early 1990s, the garden's main focus has been a splendid formal parterre, designed by David Hicks. Small topiary shapes rise out of its beds here and there, in spring surrounded by bulbs such as tulips and hyacinths,

Deene Park's formal parterre was designed by David Hicks in the early 1990s. Its box-edged beds are filled with lavender, irises, and hardy geraniums; the giant teapot topiaries (there is one in each of its four corners) were added later, celebrating Edmund Brudenell's enjoyment of a big cup of tea!

LEFT Here's looking at you, kid: a flock of horned Jacob sheep graze in the park, on the far side of the lake from the house. Just visible on the far left is the battlemented summerhouse built by the 7th Earl of Cardigan, who led the Charge of the Light Brigade.

ABOVE RIGHT Yew hedging forms a vista-stopper to a small formal topiary garden. Between the trees on the right, the 7th Earl's summerhouse can be glimpsed. Since these photographs taken by Val Corbett for *Country Life* a few years ago, Charlotte Brudenell has made some alterations and additions to the plantings and added new areas, such as a fragrant rose garden in pink shades east of the house, and a Golden Garden near the tearoom.

BELOW RIGHT An elevated view reveals the pattern of the parterre designed by David Hicks. Although the gardens were only made in the late twentieth century (with numerous tweaks and additions in recent years), the house dates back to Tudor times, and a plan of 1604 shows there had been a formal garden layout, later swept away.

ABOVE LEFT Seen in the low light of early morning, the hedged enclosures of the Hicks parterre feature a variety of herbaceous perennials sashaying through the beds. The standard (lollipop) trees are cockspur thorns. Below them are various cranesbill geraniums, seen with the sword-shaped leaves of irises and emerging flowers of lavender.

BELOW LEFT A magnificent stone planter in the Four Seasons garden, framed by an arched entrance through the surrounding hornbeam hedge. Because of its size, it contains numerous plants, including pelargoniums and the taller growing tree mallow, *Lavatera maritima*.

OPPOSITE LEFT An atmospheric shady walk beneath ancient gnarled yews on the far side of the canal, toward the upper lake. (Sometimes, a shady yew walk or tunnel of ancient trees, if in a straight line, can indicate the last remains of an old formal garden, completely grown out, of course.)

OPPOSITE RIGHT Autumn, one of the Four Seasons statues, originally from Gumley Park, holding grapes and a sheaf of corn. She is surrounded by discreetly "quiet" planting (foxgloves and a white-flowered shrubby potentilla, not yet in flower).

followed by summer's lavender, nepeta, irises, tradescantia, salvias, and geraniums, filling the beds with their soft colours. An inspired enhancement was the addition of topiary teapots in yew, placed on the four outer corners. They are not part of Hicks's original, disciplined scheme, but these charming bits of whimsy were shaped afterward, to celebrate Edmund Brudenell's renowned enjoyment of a cup of tea. They echo a teapot crowning a stone obelisk set on a hilly pasture north of the house, which was the Brudenells' celebratory millennium project.

The next generation has been in charge since 2013, with Robert and Charlotte Brudenell continuing to invest in the garden. "I am obsessed with the garden," says Charlotte, who has stepped up visitor access and planted new areas, including a Golden Garden near the Tea Rooms—"something bold and interesting for people to look at in the later season." East of the house is her newest addition, a re-creation of a formal seventeenth-century parterre, a fragrant garden of English shrub roses in shades radiating across the spectrum of pinks, from burgundy to ballet slipper, its layout inspired by a Jacobean ceiling in the house.

Together with their long-serving head gardener, Andrew Jones, the Brudenells are ensuring that the garden now "is better than it has ever been."

The topiary Chess Garden was replanted sometime around 1850. During the Second World War years and after, a devoted local gardener maintained the topiary, saving it from destruction.

HASELEY COURT

OXFORDSHIRE

The great twentieth-century tastemaker Nancy Lancaster designed a remarkable mid-century garden around a fine group of Victorian topiaries

In 1540 the antiquary John Leland noted the "fair mansion" at Little Haseley, with its splendid fair walks, topiary, orchards, and pools. Much the same could be said today.

The present mansion is early eighteenth century, built from the lovely pale stone characteristic of older houses and farmsteads hereabouts, and there is still a famous topiary garden (replanted about 1850). That the garden is as noteworthy nearly five hundred years after Leland's visit is due to the vision of the Anglophile American heiress Nancy Lancaster (1897–1994) and its continued development since 1994 by the present owners, Desmond and Fiona Heyward.

The Heywards first met Nancy Lancaster in 1968 when they bought the adjoining farm that had been part of the original estate. Fiona wrote later about how Nancy had invited them to lunch and showed them the garden. "We were enchanted with its beauty as well as the sense of drama everywhere. It certainly never crossed our minds that we might live there one day."

Having begun her life in America among the old-fashioned boxwood gardens of Virginia, the young Nancy Perkins was educated in France. There were visits to the châteaux of the Loire with her mother, where they stayed at Chenonceau. "There were flower borders, a boxwood maze, a potager, and an orchard. I loved the walled garden. I was about twelve when we stayed there, and it affected me," she recalled.

Married in 1917 but widowed within a year, Nancy enjoyed many famously creative years of house parties, hunting, and country house decoration (notably at Kelmarsh in Northamptonshire and Ditchley in Oxfordshire) during a twenty-seven-year marriage to Ronald Tree, which ended in 1947. And as Nancy Lancaster led a particular trend in interior decoration, so she did in gardens.

A taste for box-edged beds, cottage garden flowers, and old-fashioned roses (something that spread through countless country gardens in the later decades of the twentieth century) Nancy had absorbed way back, from early exposure to the gardens of Virginia and the Loire. It found expression in all her gardens. At Kelmarsh, a fan-shaped, box-edged rose garden she planted was "a spot where Nanny Weir could take the children for some sun on summer afternoons. I only used old roses, even though they were hard to find in England. I'd grown up with old roses in Virginia, and that's what I liked."

After a brief marriage to Lieutenant Colonel Claude Lancaster, Nancy bought the dilapidated but elegant Haseley Court for herself. Extensive renovations followed, then she turned her attention to the garden, with characteristic flair. Beside the long Queen Anne elevation facing southwest, Sir Geoffrey Jellicoe redesigned a formerly scruffy setting with smooth terraces of gravel and a central rectangular lawn, beyond which Nancy replanted a

LEFT An approach to the house. A succession of fins, or buttresses, ranged along the length of the path, creates a much greater feeling of progression and arrival than if the walk were just laid open.

BELOW At the central junction of the walled-and-hedged garden, where the two main paths cross, Nancy Lancaster had a large timber gazebo made, which it is said she painted in "Confederate Blue". The gardens of box and roses that she made were inspired by her memories of her childhood in the grand houses of Virginia. Her influence on English garden planting in the second half of the twentieth century was as profound as her interior styling.

FOLLOWING PAGES Further views of the Chess Garden; old roses, delphiniums, and foxgloves in the walled garden.

long double avenue, its original trees having been cut down in the war years. ("I found it awfully difficult with Nancy," confided Jellicoe, "because she was such a master in her own field.")

Around the next corner is the topiary Chess Garden, a series of large box figures, engagingly arranged. The terrace connects to an intimate, shady court with more whimsical topiaries, and a walk leads away to tree canopies underplanted with sheets of spring bulbs, beside a canal pond.

North of the house Nancy squared up two existing high walls using tunnels of hornbeam to form the other two sides, creating a bountiful four-square kitchen and flower garden. It is crossed by box-edged gravel paths and decorated with the roses and cottage garden flowers to which she was devoted. A laburnum tunnel was also planted, and sections were devoted to edible produce, a "cartwheel" of box, lawns, trained fruit, and, above all, an abundance of flowers.

Nancy's funds were running low in the 1970s and then Haseley Court caught fire. After repairing it, she moved into the Coach House close by and sold the main house while keeping control of the orangery, a cottage, and the walled garden, which were for her own use for life. The Heywards bought Haseley Court in 1982 and developed other parts of the gardens, until the walled garden became theirs in 1994, upon Nancy's death. Within Nancy's classic framework, Fiona Heyward has been very hands-on for twenty-five years, refining and refreshing the planting, while maintaining the old roses and traditional English garden look, aided and abetted by Bryn Davies, "our excellent head gardener, who is so knowledgeable about every aspect of the garden."

EURIDGE MANOR FARM

WILTSHIRE

Substantial, shapely yew trees are trimmed into numerous figures in a new garden that dips into design ideas from the past

The garden as a place of make-believe has a long tradition and, naturally, it comes in many forms. The Romans—whose extensive use of topiary is the earliest we know about (thanks chiefly to the writings of Pliny) were especially good at garden-as-theatre. Caligula had his floating palaces and gardens both at sea and on Lake Nemi, outside Rome. Emperor Hadrian inherited such vast imperial wealth that his "villa" near Tivoli—in reality, more of a "small town" of villas and gardens—was a veritable theme park, two millennia before the age of Disney, with representations of places he had admired in the eastern reaches of Rome's empire. A canal at Canopus in Egypt inspired Hadrian's own serene stretch of water at Tivoli, which he embellished with Egyptian and Athenian statues. Other areas of the villa complex brought to life the Stoa Poikile, haunt of Athenian philosophers, and the Vale of Tempe, a beautiful and mythologically symbolic gorge in northern Greece.

Gardens of the Italian Renaissance were, of course, full of theatrical high jinks—and topiary—as were many elsewhere in the courts of Europe. Ruins, real (if you were fortunate enough to have a despoiled Fountains Abbey to hand, as did John Aislabie) or custom-built, were de rigueur among eighteenth-century English landscape gardeners. In Queen Victoria's reign, James Bateman brought visions of Italy, China, Scotland, and Egypt to his Staffordshire acres at Biddulph (page 403) with much sculpting of yew hedges. So, it is engaging to see the tradition of high-budget fantasy garden-making continued in the likes of Euridge Manor Farm, on the windswept downlands of Wiltshire.

Fashion mogul John Robinson bought his house and its three-hundred-acre farm in 1980, but it was not until 2001 that he engaged the imaginative designers Julian and Isabel Bannerman to give his home a grand makeover particularly focused on medieval and Tudor themes featuring a great deal of topiary. Together, client and designers created a fantasy world of battlements and faux medieval monastic buildings added on to the old stone farmhouse, the lot wrapped around an open courtyard of tip-top turf, roses, and imposing topiary figures.

To create the backdrops, suitable material for the "medieval" structures was sought from salvage yards by Robinson as well as the designers, who have a great deal of experience in creating romantic stonework, from "church ruins" to fabulous rock-and-water gardens and grottoes.

In the courtyard, shrub roses (particularly the long-flowering, especially pretty 'Felicia') occupy the spaces between platoons of tall yew topiaries, heavily top-knotted and somewhat resembling chess pieces. The southeastern corner is filled with a Gothic-arched and battlemented gatehouse, its roof reached by a discreet spiral stair, for a bird's-eye view of gardens and rolling arable countryside.

Rising out of a complex formal pattern shaped in clipped box, the yew topiary figures began as cones, but later developed whimsical heads. The masonry is all new, forming part of the extended house, but designed in faux Gothic church style, with carved stone mullions.

ABOVE The gateway to the cloister garden and its topiary figures. Its walls are laden with rambling roses—'Albéric Barbier,' 'Paul's Himalayan Musk,' and 'Rambling Rector.' Where no roses can reach, patches of the little daisy *Erigeron karvinskianus*, and valerians (*Centranthus ruber*) in pink and white versions have been encouraged to settle themselves into crevices in the stonework.

North of the cloister garden is an elegantly fronted and furnished bathhouse with shell grotto, the roof of which supports a magnificent orangery, opening onto a spectacular Italianate terrace of formal-patterned box beds, fountains, and rows of orange trees in Tuscan terra-cotta pots. As this is a roof terrace, there is little soil, but you would hardly know it, for the generosity of its planting.

There is yet more visual drama to find, however, for the south end of the house is, perhaps, even more spectacular with its new wing, including a full-width "Elizabethan" loggia with master bedroom above. This elevation looks onto a spacious, stone-balustraded terrace, below which is a large, rectangular pool with thatched boathouse at the far end, accessed by a long flight of stone steps—a vision that might have impressed even Hadrian.

For much of the time, these gardens are a private paradise, but make-believe can be fun to share—and eye-wateringly expensive to maintain. Therefore, occasionally the orangery and grounds are hired out for weddings; surely such a place creates fabulous memories.

OPPOSITE A view in a different direction, looking over the cloister garden to the imposing, battlemented gateway, which is also part of the Bannermans' extensive overhaul of both the gardens and house. The elegant metal benches recessed into low hedging have a pleasing quality of lightness amid all the greenery.

Pure drama: three views of the water garden.

ABOVE Looking out from an upper room at the south end of the house, to a thatched oak "boathouse," with lovely views of the countryside beyond.

LEFT Even the ducks live in faux Tudor grandeur!

RIGHT A substantial new wing with an Elizabethan flair was recently added to the south side of the house, with a broad terrace beyond, which lies over the arcaded pool wall. The seventeenth-century theme was carried right down to the pool area with stone balustrading and carved obelisk fountains.

WARNELL HALL

CUMBRIA

Onion-shaped domes and clipped yew trees trained like perfume bottles are among the shapely features in this northern hillside garden

Ancient topiary has left its mark in the north of England, notably in Cumbria, home of the famous topiary garden at Levens Hall (page 31). It gives us quite a good idea of how gardens were laid out prior to the emergence and dominance of the English landscape park. Also in Cumbria, the extended house of Hutton-in-the-Forest, so atmospheric and castlelike, still has vestiges of its seventeenth-century formal garden and plenty of topiary, although much of the latter is believed to date from the Victorian revival for such things.

Quite near Hutton-in-the-Forest is a contrastingly new topiary garden, only made from scratch within the past three decades. Warnell Hall is a most attractive, sturdy manor house of the Tudor period built from the ancient pink sandstone that prevails in this part of the world. Tucked into its hillside and protected to some extent by trees, it welcomes the sun on the south (rear) side with an open apron of lawn, looking across a ha-ha (page 300) to the enormous, rugged Cumbrian landscape. Everywhere else is sectioned off with chunky but superbly straight drystone walls that look as solid as the house itself.

When the owners Nicholas and Kate Coulson bought the property it had already been well restored, but they wished to get involved with the garden and make it "theirs." With the rigorous approach of an academic, Kate informed herself by reading voraciously and exploring many gardens. There is no better way to develop an eye for what you like and, as importantly, what you do not. Kate also seized an opportunity to sign up for Plantsmanship and Garden Design courses at the English Gardening School in London to gain relevant knowledge. Having inherited from the previous owners "excellent bone structure"—a layout defined by hedges and topiary—she heavily edited the existing planting then added a pared-down range of colours, achieving the overall balance of structure and softness she was aiming for.

The neatest of walled kitchen gardens lies immediately east of the house. It is of a traditional four-square design with paths crossing through the middle and each bed crisply outlined in box hedging. Espalier apple trees cling to the sunniest walls. Little onion-shaped topiaries make their presence known around the central area. Their shape seems especially fitting for a kitchen garden, although their design was apparently inspired by the onion domes on John Nash's exotic Royal Pavilion in Brighton.

On the west side, attractive cobblestone paving is a feature of the small terrace tucked into the inverted L-shape made by the house. Its little parterre of four rectangular box-edged beds is a sun-trap for nurturing herby experiments, such as *Perovskia atriplicifolia* 'Taiga', a neater, dwarf form of Russian sage flowering in its first year from seed.

Topiary in the "front" garden, north of the house, consists of dark green "perfume bottles" in yew and mopheads of hawthorn. The strings are restraining the naturally upward inclination of some of the branches so that a rounded outline can be achieved. Little buns of *Hebe topiaria* form cushions around their bases.

A retaining wall advertises the start of the westward ascent and, from the terrace, the raised-up nature of the first border elevates its flowers to near eye level, increasing their impact. The punchy shots of scarlet 'Beauty of Livermere' poppies, vivid purple alliums, and 'Masterpiece' lupins are enriched by their various bright green and lime companions. Interestingly, Kate had recorded in her mind a visit to a Penelope Hobhouse garden on the windswept, treeless Isle of Oronsay, in the Hebrides. She noted how surprising it was that the saturated jewel-toned dahlias actually worked in that wild and barren place. (Confirmation of the rightness of this approach can also be seen at Durnamuck, page 355.)

It would be only natural to wonder how a border of this type can survive in this location where wind is a certainty and average rainfall is among the highest in Britain. The answer is that two professional gardeners keep everything tip-top, staking the border plants with woven twigs gathered from the nearby beech woods.

On the next level, a neat lawn rolls past, on one side, the box "onion domes" that back the bright lower border, and on the other, a softly coloured herbaceous and rose border. A soldier parade of Irish yew columns, interspersed with cascades of 'Ispahan' roses, forms the structural backdrop.

A long green walk of yew hedging and archways marks the top of the garden, but there is more topiary furnishing the north front of the house. Its lawns are populated with yew "perfume bottles" and mopheads of hawthorn, the latter rising out of little buns of *Hebe topiaria*. Nothing is left to chance; in this garden everything is thought about—the attention to detail is truly impressive.

ABOVE LEFT A small breakfast terrace on the east side looks across the path to the neat little kitchen garden.

LEFT A cut above: gardener Lyn Brunetti, who has much expertise in topiary, prunes yew on the Front Lawn using a bamboo framework as a guide.

OPPOSITE A framed view from the house, looking across the cobblestone courtyard with its four rectangular beds edged in box. Beyond it the dry-stone retaining wall signals the ascent of the garden up the hillside, with its view of the borders and onion-shaped box topiaries.

LEFT Looking northward along the top border, with its soldier line of Irish yews and abundant, soft-hued summer plantings of roses and nepeta. The splendid, rather Arts and Craftsy pavilion that terminates the view is also garlanded with roses on its southern piers.

BELOW LEFT Looking roughly south to north, across the end of the kitchen garden. The garden is full of thoughtful touches, such as its handsome gates, painted a donkey brown that blends with the stonework.

RIGHT Looking south, from the west end of the front garden, the various changes of level that occur on this hilly site really become apparent. Kate Coulson says she was lucky that the walls had already been installed or repaired by the previous owners, leaving her to concentrate on refining her ideas for the planting. The yew topiaries are being shaped to develop their individual characters.

ALLT-Y-BELA

MONMOUTHSHIRE

Trained pleached trees and plenty of topiary help to create characterful and sequestered spaces in designer Arne Maynard's own garden

Garden designer Arne Maynard had spent fifteen years living on the dead-flat fenland of Lincolnshire—and made a fine, formal garden there—before he and his partner, William Collinson, moved across the country in 2005 to the hills of Wales. Maynard recalls that, having grown up in rural Dorset, with its wood-clad hills and downland vistas, he felt a longing for higher ground and big trees again, after such a long time in a windswept, arable prairie.

They certainly got their hills at Allt-y-Bela, a property that they saw by accident, when looking through a copy of *Country Life* one day. "We fell in love with it instantly," Maynard recalls. The house, which is partly fifteenth century, part sixteenth, and part seventeenth, had been a derelict ruin when it was acquired by the Spitalfields Trust in London, a building conservation charity that rescues deserving old wrecks under threat of demolition. The trust spent four years painstakingly bringing the house back from the brink, after which it was offered on the open market.

Maynard recalls that gravel had been put down by the trust between the house and the lane, to provide access, but there was no garden whatsoever, just dense, impenetrable thickets of alder, blackthorn, and brambles, creeping all around and up the slopes of the hills. Although it seems to be in a remote location, the property would have been right next to a busy route in Tudor times, set beside a former drovers' road that once saw stockmen driving their livestock to market at Chepstow.

When they moved in, one of the first things Maynard did (after clearing the thorny jungles all around) was to flood the approach area with native bulbs, "because it gives the place a sense of history straight away," he says. Tens of thousands of wild daffodils and snowdrops were planted and rapidly established themselves in the damp ground. At the beginning, the house and its ancillary buildings were of a rather startling white, but the warm, orangey shade its walls now wear is much softer and more appealing, having a warmth about it that blends in magnificently with the greens of the garden and the landscape all around.

Maynard is very fond of topiary and uses it a lot in his garden designs; at Allt-y-Bela we see his gift for deployment of all manner of trimmed trees, all carefully placed to "ground the house in its landscape" and enhance the feeling of an old, informal country place that is looked after, but not too groomed or ornamental.

South of the house but facing it across the drive is the old granary (now Maynard's design studio), behind which a walled stream snakes by. This is something else that had to be created early on, to drain away winter rains that wash off the hills and previously had nowhere to go—with the consequence that house and granary were being routinely flooded through their ground

The courtyard in front of the house entrance was given greater definition by planting a screen of pleached crab apple trees *Malus* 'Evereste,' which follow their white spring blossoms with abundant golden fruits. Topiary is also crammed into this area, around a 'Cardinal de Richelieu' rose bearing deep crimson flowers briefly at midsummer.

OPPOSITE Copper beech was used to form the small spiral maze, which helps to visually screen off the rear garden from the entrance drive.

LEFT Topiaries are arranged in various configurations all around the house, except where the amphitheatre has been carved into the hillside.

floors. While relandscaping, Maynard created a turf-stepped amphitheatre, so that this part of the garden has become somewhere for occasional entertainment, such as open-air performances of Shakespeare, each summer.

Near the house, however, the grass is peopled with topiary, in various rounded shapes and sizes. "I wanted the topiary to come out of the grass, and there's nothing in pairs; it's very informal," says Maynard. As well as dark green yew, and little buns of box, many of the topiary figures are of beech, which has a lovely freshness to its new foliage each spring and a glorious autumn display. Topiaries also populate a small courtyard serving the doors to the house, where a row of pleached, white-blossomed 'Evereste' crabapple trees link arms and provide a subtle screen between house and drive. A small, double-spiral maze, planted west of the house to mark the beginning of the garden proper, is actually in copper beech, another of Maynard's signature plants, whose deep plum foliage turns into mutable copper and green hues with the arrival of autumn.

Where the land rises again to the north of the house, prodigious quantities of soil were dug out to prevent the hillside, which previously came up to the door, from draining its largesse of rainwater into the house. Having solved that second source of floodwater, informal and uneven lattice patterns of box hedging were planted behind the house, along with more topiary figures, so that they seem to cushion the peachy orange elevations in a protective embrace. The unusual near-white rambler rose 'Astra Desmond' is one of Maynard's favourites and is pinned to a lattice framework, so that it tumbles its masses of shapely little stars around the window frames in due season.

Moving away from the garden, the rising land becomes wildflower meadow, with choice non-natives stitched in too: *Iris reticulata*, for example; light blue grape hyacinth 'Valerie Finnis'; and elegant crocuses such as 'Snow Bunting' and 'Cream Beauty'.

And uphill northeast, but not far from the house, is the loveliest small kitchen garden, enclosed with hazel wattle fencing and with fruit trees trained into arches and stepovers. It is all highly productive and organic, with the details, flourishes, and blended-in floral abundance that make the idea of grow-your-own extra interesting and appealing.

The handsome tower house of Allt-y-Bela (the first of its kind to be built in Wales, says Maynard) is most fortunate to have been paired with such sympathetic owners, for they are prepared to create and maintain a garden that absolutely complements it in every way.

LEFT The kitchen garden has a very rustic, "deep in the countryside" feel, which is almost medieval, with its arrangement of squared-up raised beds and enclosure of rustic wattle fencing. The last blooms of the cutting garden are visible, dahlias and cosmos. Vegetables grown are things you can't easily buy. "We're almost self-sufficient in what I call 'delicatessen vegetables,'" says Maynard. A central path is spanned by pears trained over hazel arches.

ABOVE RIGHT Watch the birdie! Maynard's cat Hudson among the pumpkins.

BELOW RIGHT The henhouse on wheels, which can easily be moved to different parts of the garden as required, for the free-ranging hens.

2 GOD'S ACRES

England's and Europe's monastery gardens inherited the earlier plan of the Roman *villa rustica*, the agricultural estate that included orchards of fruit and nut trees, a vineyard, and a vegetable garden. Monasteries usually had a cloister garth (descended from the Roman peristyle) and fish ponds, but a dedicated area for the cultivation of healing herbs was also important. Huxley reminds us that, "Just as lords, barons and kings shut themselves up within walls, so did the religious communities, the monasteries not so much seeking protection from attack as imposing seclusion upon themselves. Within the monastery walls, the whole community was frequently entirely self-supporting."

When Brother Cadfael (Ellis Peters's fictional twelfth-century Benedictine monk who solves murders) brews up an herbal remedy, we learn he is drawing upon knowledge he picked up during travels in the Holy Land. Indeed, all through the post-Roman era, monastic communities, being linked with Continental Europe and beyond, were the keepers of herbal and horticultural knowledge. Their physic gardens were of special importance, with medicinal herbs grown in a series of small rectangular beds, often raised to about knee-height; this orderly arrangement made cultivation easier, but it also prevented susceptible plants from becoming waterlogged. As keepers of the widest range of species known at the time, and with the knowledge of their medicinal uses, the monastic orders were key to the continuation of a gardening tradition between the fall of the Roman Empire and gradually more settled times after the Norman Conquest.

In the garden profiles of this chapter, we see an interesting but often overlooked area of English horticulture: the gardens attached to several of the great Norman cathedrals. In "the time of Cadfael" these enormous feats of architectural design were just built, or still under construction. Originally set out as cultivated lands serving their communities, cathedral grounds, where they still exist, are these days more fragmented but are sometimes given over to public enjoyment and often used for charitable fund-raising.

In the case of Burford Priory (page 71), the photographs illustrate the refreshed Edwardian gardens as they were until 2008, when the priory was sold. Brother Anthony contacted me at *Country Life* some months before

OPPOSITE A perfect composition: the great cathedral of Wells in Somerset, reflected in the waters of one of the actual freshwater wells, from which the city got its name. The serpentine path around the well pool enables visitors to enjoy one of the richly planted areas that adjoin the further horticultural wonders of the Bishop's Garden.

All creatures great and small: a mallard puts her best foot forward, leading her ducklings to the waters surrounding the gardens of the Bishop's Palace at Wells. Serenity above, paddling madly below: a swan leads her brood of downy cygnets along the waters of the moat around the Bishop's Palace gardens. The ecclesiastical pecking order at Canterbury Cathedral Precincts: free-ranging hens in the dean's garden.

the sale, in the hope that we could record the garden as it had been for its monastic community, which of course we were happy to do.

A particularly interesting reinvention of "God's Acres" is to be found at Lambeth, London, where the Garden Museum makes use of the church of Saint Mary-at-Lambeth. Substantially rebuilt in the 1850s, it was deconsecrated in 1972 and scheduled for demolition. It has truly ancient origins, however—the first church on the site having been built before the Norman Conquest and attached to the religious community established by the Archbishops of Canterbury. In 1976, by extraordinary good fortune, the derelict churchyard was explored by history enthusiasts John and Rosemary Nicholson, who discovered there the elaborate tomb of two seventeenth-century royal gardeners and plant explorers, John Tradescant the Elder (ca.1570–1638), the first great gardener and plant hunter in British history, and his son, John Tradescant the Younger (1608–1662), whose own botanical garden, full of plants collected overseas, had been close by. Through their indefatigable efforts the Nicholsons saw off the imminent demolition, planned to make way for a coach park for Waterloo Station. Instead, they created a charitable trust in 1977 to establish and fund what was for many years known as "The Museum of Garden History," housed in the former church.

Since those early years, the Garden Museum, as it's now known, has gone from strength to strength, particularly since 2006 under the energetic directorship of Christopher Woodward. Its contemporary and airy interior houses interesting displays from horticulture down the ages and a lively year-round series of exhibitions and friends events, supported by an award-winning café, and new courtyard gardens by Dan Pearson and Christopher Bradley-Hole. Interestingly, during renovations in 2016, workers uncovered a vault containing thirty coffins, including those of five Archbishops of Canterbury; one of them was for Richard Bancroft (1544–1610), who oversaw the production of the King James Bible. Indeed, it's fortunate that this remarkably historic and thriving piece of old London was saved.

The grassy cemeteries surrounding old country churches are beyond the scope of this book, but it is interesting to see that many of them are now treasured as nature reserves, with unmowed areas managed for wildflowers and sometimes the addition of purpose-made homes for bats and hives for honeybees.

BURFORD PRIORY

OXFORDSHIRE

The substantial grounds of an old priory were documented and photographed by Country Life *before the property was sold and its gardens altered*

Most of the hordes of visitors who come to the pretty Cotswolds town of Burford are unaware of its ancient priory, though its expansive acres lie just behind the High Street, with woodlands and meadows rolling down to the meandering Windrush river.

Until recently, the priory was home to a small Benedictine Anglican community of monks and nuns, although it has had a history of fluctuating fortunes. As long ago as the thirteenth century there was a religious house on the present site and a hospital dedicated to Saint John, which cared for passing travellers as well as the locally poor and sick. It enjoyed some modest prosperity in its early years but that was not to last and, with the Dissolution of the Monasteries, the "late Hospital of St John the Evangelist in Burford" was granted by Henry VIII to one Edward Harman, his barber surgeon, in 1543. It stayed in secular hands for more than four hundred years, until it was bought by a community of sisters in 1947, with the Benedictine Brothers arriving in 1987.

Little is known about the medieval buildings, although some Gothic arches survive; a large, E-shaped Elizabethan country house followed, and a chapel was added to one side in the mid-seventeenth century. The house was reduced in size some two hundred years ago, but it lay dormant and unoccupied for most of the nineteenth century, a period when the house fell into steep decline. Its rescue only occurred in 1908, when the energetic Colonel Fenwick Bulmer de Sales La Terriere and his wife spent three years making substantial repairs and renovations. The colonel's time is also when the gardens were laid out, to early twentieth-century taste, their design and planting apparently having fallen largely upon the shoulders of Mrs. de Sales La Terriere.

There are far more famous Edwardian Cotswolds gardens nearby: Lawrence Johnston's Hidcote at Chipping Campden, begun in 1907; Abbotswood, at Stow-on-the-Wold, redesigned by Edwin Lutyens in 1901; the Biddulph family's Rodmarton Manor near Tetbury, commissioned to Ernest Barnsley in 1909; and Charles Wade's Snowshill Manor near Broadway, transformed from 1920 in the Arts and Crafts manner. These are sophisticated, architecturally strong gardens whose reputations have withstood the test of time, but many others in the region are more modest, homespun efforts. The garden at Burford Priory was one of the latter, utilizing stone quarried within the grounds for its sheltering and retaining walls and embracing the Edwardian fashion for topiary.

The garden has been substantially altered in recent times, since the Anglican community sold it in 2008, so these photographs have special value as a record of the twentieth-century garden as it had been, and not as it is now.

Until the community left the priory, it fell upon Brother Anthony to mastermind management of the grounds. Most striking were the huge topiary

A view across the gardens of Burford Priory, as they were before the property was sold and its Anglican community moved out in 2008. Although it had been a priory in medieval times, it was in secular hands for four hundred years until it returned to housing a religious community in 1947. The gardens and topiaries are Edwardian, having been restored in 1908 by its then-new owners.

figures spanning the width of the lawn, progressing two-by-two in their neatly clipped tiers, immediately above the first low retaining wall. The tiered "cake stand" shape was evidently popular a hundred years ago, for such things can be seen in countless old photographs in the *Country Life* archive. At that time, the aptly named nursery of Messrs. Cutbush, topiary specialists, regularly advertised ready-made yew specimens in the magazine.

Beyond the yews, the community laid out a turf maze on a substantial stretch of lawn, marking it out with a piece of string and a mower. To follow its route, one would walk for more than a third of a mile. Traditional turf mazes, or labyrinths, were created all over the British Isles in medieval times, although their patterns and symbolism are very much older, and many myths prevail. Those laid out beside religious establishments were thought to be connected with contemplation or penitence, but equally, many more were temporary structures with more prosaic or entertainment value. Followed correctly, the pattern could guide its walker for some 650 yards;

beyond it a wildflower meadow was established by the community, with seed from local plants.

In an old orchard on high ground, most of the apple trees date from the Edwardian period. Brother Anthony was particularly enthusiastic about a quince tree, whose prolific fruiting could produce as many as fifty jars of quince jelly in a good season. A substantial walled garden provided the community with plenty of fresh produce, but an even greater surprise lies beyond it: a twelve-acre wood, full of snowdrops in winter, followed by colonies of the wild *Tulipa sylvestris* in spring, before the leafy canopies of the trees close over.

When the property was sold, its owners engaged garden designer Mary Keen to modify the gardens to suit their family use. Although the grounds have been stylishly upgraded and a few areas modified, the turf maze has been maintained and the walled kitchen garden flourishes, along with some beautiful border plantings.

LEFT In an upper part of the garden, the brothers laid out a turf maze on a large stretch of lawn, marking it out with a cane, a piece of string, and a lawnmower. Traditional turf mazes, or labyrinths, have an intriguing history; many had medieval origins although their patterns and symbolism are very much older.

OPPOSITE The scene looks timeless, with the old priory half-concealed by the branches of trees in burgeoning summer growth. Most of its foxgloves are over, but the border is still bright with poppies and lupins. A grass path seems very suitable for the location and its atmosphere.

NORWICH CATHEDRAL, THE BISHOP'S GARDEN
NORFOLK

Ancient walls and historic buildings enclose a peaceful four-acre garden with a diverse range of plants and habitats that support wild creatures

In the heart of the city of Norwich, its Anglican cathedral lies within a shapely meander of the River Wensum. Begun in 1096, the cathedral took some fifty years to build and its spire, still dominates the city skyline; it's also an uplifting focal point seen to advantage from within the western and southern sections of the cathedral cloister. As is usual in such places, the cloister galleries enclose today nothing more interesting than a great big square of lawn, but the turf at Norwich has been dignified with a labyrinth maze of a traditional circular design. Created in 2002 to commemorate the Queen's Golden Jubilee, it's an alluring feature that reliably draws in visitors to walk its contemplative switchback paths to find the one way to the endpoint.

Some four acres of gardens lie to the north of the cathedral, lending peacefulness and wildlife habitat to the heart of the city. They're graced by ancient walls, historic buildings contributed by early bishops, mighty trees, and, above all, much ongoing horticultural activity. These grounds, known as the Bishop's Garden, have been cultivated for nearly a thousand years; although some of the walls date back six hundred years or more, the gardens are further partitioned and sheltered by big old yew hedges planted in the 1850s.

If you take the area as being roughly square, then divide it crisscross into four sections in the customary way, it's easy to separate the garden into convenient, evenly sized sections serving different purposes and moods. And

LEFT A view along the double borders toward Bishop Reynolds's Chapel on the left and Bishop Salmon's Porch, glimpsed through the trees on the right. The borders tend to fairly "soft" shades in the first half of the season—pinks, blues, and whites—with "hotter" reds and oranges taking over later.

RIGHT A section of the formal rose parterre, with the Bishop's Chapel as a splendid backdrop beyond the ornamental ironwork and fountain.

LEFT The cathedral looms above the ancient flint-and-brick garden wall, laden with roses. The border contains a mixture of "good doers," including many roses but also hostas and some tree ferns.

RIGHT Looking down from Bishop Salmon's Porch at the cushioned undulations of the Victorian yew hedging. In the distance on the left, one of the sixteenth-century arched recesses in the garden's west-facing flint wall. In the distance on the right, the tower of Saint Helen's Church in Bishopsgate.

BELOW A gallery of special plants. Very different from the usual garden buddleias: the white-throated, crimson flowers of *Buddleja colvilei* 'Kewensis.' *Sinocalycanthus raulstonii* 'Hartlage Wine' is a medium-sized deciduous shrub, a cross between an American species and a Chinese one, which was fairly recently introduced by the J.C. Raulston Arboretum of North Carolina. *Indigofera howellii* (syn. *subverticillata*), a small- to medium-sized shrub with delicate pinnate foliage and racemes of pink flowers, which start to appear in June and go on appearing until autumn.

OPPOSITE In an open area of the large walled garden, the ancient idea of a turf labyrinth has a contemporary twist, as it is a "wildflower labyrinth." At its heart is an old survivor from kitchen garden days, a very rare Uvedale's Saint Germain pear tree. The variety is believed to date from the 1690s; its pears are large and heavy, but the juice is sour.

since the plot has a long stretch of west-facing wall on its boundary, many unusual and half-hardy shrubs and trees manage not only to survive but thrive.

The northwest is occupied mainly by buildings and service areas, but the southwest section, by the cathedral, is a large square of lawn that serves numerous public functions and also gives enticing views of the more intensively gardened areas beyond.

The southeastern portion, walled on two sides, shelters long mixed borders margined by straight gravel paths. Its central area, long since decommissioned from producing food, is home to a time-saving wildflower labyrinth with winding paths mowed into an irregular pattern. In between, native wildflowers rise out of the long grass: vetches and cowslips, oxeye daisies and terrestrial orchids. The labyrinth's heart is marked by a splendid old pear tree, identified as 'Uvedale's Saint Germain'. This very old variety is capable of producing large golden but somewhat hard pears, well suited to stewing.

West of the wildflower labyrinth and separated from it by lengths of yew hedge is a crisp rose parterre, symmetrically divided into triangular beds by low box hedging. Planted with monochromatic blocks of hybrid tea and floribunda roses, it includes a bed devoted to the Norwich Cathedral's eponymous rose, a versatile soft-yellow hybrid tea bred by the late Peter Beales, renowned rosarian and expert on old and species roses.

A fine double herbaceous border runs west to east, marking the garden's central path. As well as displaying a variety of summer stalwarts, it has a special role as trial and display area for the local branch of the Delphinium Society, nurturing around fifty different cultivars.

The northeast section is a hive of productivity, with a three-bed rotation of organically raised crops, a greenhouse, and a soft-fruit cage. The high walls, facing west and south, protect a collection of unusual half-hardy species that thrive in the sheltered conditions and light soil. Not the least remarkable thing about the Bishop's Garden is its diverse range of plants and high standard of maintenance. Simon Gaches has been the driving force in upgrading all areas and developing new ones. Just one part-time assistant and a small team of volunteers help him maintain this locally valuable resource that in 2018 raised £27,000 for local charities via its schedule of summer open days.

HEREFORD CATHEDRAL

HEREFORDSHIRE

A collection of varied gardens is arranged around the cathedral and leads down to the peacefully flowing waters of the River Wye

From the top of the crenellated central tower at Hereford Cathedral, there are, of course, great panoramic views of the city, but also, closer to hand, bird's-eye views of the cathedral's own variety of gardens and cloister garth, beyond which are the lovely tree-margined meanders of the River Wye.

Most of the gardens lie south of the twelfth-century cathedral, on ground sloping gently down to the river. The lion's share, not unnaturally, is devoted to the Bishop's Garden, which garden writer Tim Longville nicely described as "a sort of history through plants," since it records the plants and planting styles fashionable during the episcopates of the most horticulturally interested bishops of the last two centuries. Covering some 2.4 acres, it has a large stretch of lawn across the upper area for guest events but ranged through the Bishop's Garden are many fine trees and, along the palace wall, a vibrant run of red hydrangeas. Some relandscaping for Bishop Musgrave (bishop of Hereford, 1837–47) in 1841 included the planting of cedars and pines, considered fashionably exotic at that time. Some 130 years later, Bishop Eastaugh (1973–90) brought in some more exotic trees in the 1970s, but Bishop Oliver's (1990–2003) interests reflected a more natural style with a penchant for native species. Tucked around the corner at the bottom of the Bishop's Garden is a meticulously maintained kitchen and cutting garden of board-edged beds. (Beside it used to be the original walled garden, now converted to tennis courts, used by the Cathedral School.)

LEFT   The arresting view across the River Wye to the pinnacled tower of Hereford Cathedral. In front of it is the Bishop's Palace, with its broad lawns, immense cedar tree, and gardens reaching down to the river.

RIGHT   One side of the College garden. The yellow rose in the foreground is 'Golden Wedding'; behind it the deep pink rose is 'Vanity,' part of the Pemberton rose collection. The old timber-framed building on the left was originally the Vaga Inn, serving those engaged in commercial traffic on the river in bygone days.

Single hollyhocks brighten the dark stone of the cloister garth.

The handsome gravel walk that runs from one side to the other of the Bishop's garden. The mighty cedars with their muscular limbs were planted in the 1840s by Bishop Thomas Musgrave (later Archbishop of York).

The Dean's Garden also reaches down to the river, but is more enclosed and richly planted, presumably by successive deans, with a range of flowering trees and shrubs, a rose arch, and shrubby herbs that tumble over a small rocky bank. A high stone wall provides partial separation from the Bishop's Garden from where, appropriately enough, the far-reaching rose 'Rambling Rector' cascades down, bearing extravagant clusters of fragrant white blossoms.

Several other gardens are ranged around the buildings of the Close, all of them maintained by a team of enthusiastic volunteers. Of these, the College Garden has ancient origins, going back to at least pre-Reformation times, when the vicars choral lived in the college built for them in 1472. It would have been chiefly cultivated to feed the community but today is entirely ornamental. Its theme focuses largely on plants associated with Anglican clergy, such as the hybrid perpetual roses bred by the Rev. Joseph Pemberton. They include famously excellent cultivars, such as 'Penelope,' 'Cornelia,' 'Buff Beauty,' and the less well-known, tall-growing 'Vanity,' with open flowers of crimson to deep pink. Dahlias named for various bishops (such as 'Llandaff,' 'Canterbury,' 'York,' and 'Oxford') feature too, as well as Shirley poppies bred around 1900 by Rev. William Wilks (1843–1923) and his eponymous apple tree. The volunteers also tend the newest area of all, the Lady Arbour Cloister Garden. This stylish, substantial courtyard adjoining the cathedral was recently designed by Robert Myers Associates and features subtle herbaceous and shrub plantings themed in blues, yellows, whites, and greys, ranged around its central lawns.

An unusual enfilade view in the Lady Arbour Cloister Garden, an area reworked recently by Robert Myers. The garden's pared-down design of lawns and paving contains plants in a restricted palette, with plenty of *Hydrangea arborescens* 'Annabelle' (shown here) and lady's mantle, *Alchemilla mollis*.

The rampart walk that partially margins the island containing the Bishop's Palace and its extensive gardens. The high wall gives a series of contained, elevated views outward to surrounding countryside beyond the moat and inward, over sections of the gardens. Its southernmost point has a bastion, which has views of Glastonbury Tor.

THE BISHOP'S PALACE GARDENS, WELLS

SOMERSET

Ancient walls and a moat surround what must be one of the oldest continuously cultivated gardens in the country

Wells is exactly "what it says on the tin"—a place with wells. Three important ones rise in the heart of the small attractive city, two of them within the grounds of the Bishop's Palace and cathedral. In Roman times a small community developed by the waters and a minster church was founded in 704 AD, under the Anglo-Saxon kings. Building of the great cathedral followed from 1175 onward, under the Normans, with the Bishop's Palace being the home of the bishops of Bath and Wells for some eight hundred years.

A medieval deer park originally surrounded the palace and development of the gardens was piecemeal, but sometimes intensive, according to the interest (or not) of the bishops down the centuries. Its area is considerable: some fourteen acres, which these days are nearly always open by day, only closing when private functions are taking place.

Owing to the springs that bubble up, bringing water from the limestone caverns of the nearby Mendip Hills, the palace and part of its gardens occupy a moated island—a great feature itself. Within it are several linked areas, all enjoying some sort of alluring backdrop, whether of medieval masonry or an eye-catching view of the cathedral.

Around the palace and associated buildings, the present layout of big lawns and contrastingly floral areas is largely inherited from George Henry Law (1761–1845), bishop of Bath and Wells from 1824 until his death. As a keen gardener with an eye for the then fashionable Picturesque aesthetic, Law had just the right location in which to develop a garden. He was able to make use of a decaying building that had been the thirteenth-century Great Hall built by Bishop Burnell (a powerful man, longtime adviser and Chancellor of the Exchequer to King Edward I). In lean times after the Reformation, the lead of its roof had to be stripped off and sold. Bishop Law "ruined it" a bit more by removing two of its elevations to get the right effect for his garden and created new "ruined" walls elsewhere in the garden to continue the theme.

Law and his Victorian successors planted specimen trees into the lawns, a number of which still thrive, including an imposing black walnut, copper beech, Indian bean, and *Ginkgo biloba*. The tree-planting tradition reignited in 1977 when Bishop Bickersteth planted a small arboretum beyond the moat for the Queen's Silver Jubilee, helped by his friend Sir Harold Hillier.

The gardens enjoyed further uplift with the appointment of Peter Price (bishop from 2002 to 2013), a keen gardener, who took on in 2004 a new and energetic head gardener, James Cross. Their joint aim was to create an expanded and more interesting garden that would respect the historic setting, while engaging and drawing in the visiting public. So, over recent years, many new plants have settled in, some highlighting the Victorian love of foliage

plants and exotic flowers with, for example, bananas, dahlias, *Tetrapanax papyrifer*, ginger plant, and yucca.

The wells, with their luxuriant plantings of moisture-loving perennials, are reached via a wooden bridge over the moat. Alongside the biggest pool, a border created by designer Mary Keen in 2003 has been enhanced to extend its season; it leads toward the gardens' newest creation: the Garden of Reflection, opened in 2013. Here, eighty-five silver birch trees rise out of spring bulbs, followed by wildflowers in the long grass, the naturalistic vision to be viewed and contemplated from a forty-foot curved stone seat. Beyond it is the Community Garden, a supremely popular educational space for people to learn new skills, growing flowers and edibles for sale and for display in the palace. Heritage Lottery funding was required to extend and improve visitor facilities; there's no doubt it has been money well spent.

ABOVE The warm, sheltered Terrace Bed in front of the old apple store. Since these photographs were taken for a *Country Life* article, much of the planting has been refreshed. The sylvan views across the fringes of the city are unchanging and appealing.

OPPOSITE The waterfall is produced by opening the sluice controlling the level of water between the different sections of the moat.

OPPOSITE The "hot" border, fairly early in the season, when it isn't looking its hottest! The yellow flowers are *Phlomis russeliana*, the blue, *Nepeta sibirica*, and the red rose is 'National Trust.' For the later season, banana plants and dahlias are now a regular feature. The dahlias include a selection of 'Bishop' cultivars.

RIGHT Part of the parterre in the East Garden, near the hot border. This is the most formal of the surviving parts of the garden, dating from the mid-nineteenth century, with its original urn as a focal point.

CANTERBURY CATHEDRAL PRECINCTS

Free-ranging chickens have the run of a small wildflower meadow and a number of lovely gardens are associated with the clerical residences

Occupying one of the easternmost locations in the south of England, Canterbury is an ancient city with UNESCO World Heritage Site status, lively with both tourists and students year-round. The first archbishop of Canterbury was Augustine, who had been the prior of a monastery in Rome, but was sent on a mission by the pope (Gregory the Great) to Æthelbert's kingdom of Kent, in the year 596. He came to convert the pagan Anglo-Saxons following the retreat of the Romans. Æthelbert, king of Kent, was quickly converted (he had already married a Christian princess), and Augustine made his power base at Canterbury.

The seat of the archbishop of Canterbury (leader of the Church of England and symbolic head of the worldwide Anglican Communion), the cathedral was founded in 597 but rebuilt soon after the Conquest and its Gothic grandeur is due to further rebuilding in the twelfth century. Famously the location of the gory murder of Archbishop Thomas Becket, in 1170, and with renown for its part in the signing of the Magna Carta, the cathedral is extraordinarily important in English history.

Naturally, it is surrounded by supportive administrative and residential buildings, most of them very old and known collectively as the Precincts. A number of the residences have nice little gardens attached (and one or two boast quite decent-sized ones). They include the gardens of the dean, the archdeacon, the canon treasurer, the canon librarian, and the canon pastor.

Free-ranging chickens cluck about in a small wildflower meadow that is part of the dean's garden, underlining the essentially Christian message

LEFT The flint-and-brick walls of the deanery shelter its garden, enabling palm trees and banana plants to thrive. The curved path margins a big lawn, around which are laid out further small garden areas in variety, including a kitchen garden and wild meadow.

RIGHT The free-ranging hens enjoy foraging among oxeye daisies in the small wildflower meadow in the deanery garden.

Roses galore among the old walls. The precincts have numerous garden spaces, large and small, many of them sheltered by ancient walls, even, in one or two areas, parts of the massive Roman city wall.

that there's a place for all God's creatures, great and small. Interestingly, Dean Robert Willis, who is very involved in his garden, has planted on one side a thicket of young trees that protect his chickens and guinea fowl from peregrine falcons that live in the heights of the cathedral tower. Herbaceous and exotic plants fill the border of the deanery's main garden. A kitchen and cutting garden lies to one side; an orchard lies beyond, and a small stream of pumped water enlivens a shady area of primulas and other bog plants. The front garden of the deanery is dignified by a box-hedged rose garden, many of them David Austin roses. Among them is 'Brother Cadfael', a lovely mid-pink rose named after Ellis Peters's fictional twelfth-century monk, who brews herbal remedies and solves murder mysteries.

The canon librarian's and canon pastor's gardens are more intimate and enclosed but with nice views. The archdeaconry has standard roses and wonderful hostas; the home of the canon treasurer has a fine old copper beech tree and a huge border alongside a section of the old Roman wall. Appropriately, there's also a medicinal herb garden in the Precincts, linked to the cathedral's copy of Gerard's *Herbal* of 1597.

ABOVE LEFT The golden rose 'Graham Thomas,' potentially a bit of a climber if given suitable support but never rampant.

ABOVE RIGHT Assorted pots on the terrace by the deanery back door, with lilies and peonies.

3 THE FORMAL GARDEN

From the second half of the eighteenth century, an "English garden" was widely understood to consist of rolling green acres of lawn, dotted with trees, with an essentially "natural" presentation. So by the nineteenth century, France had its creators of *le jardin a l'anglaise*; Germany its *Englischer Landschaftsgarten*; in Spain it translated as *el jardín inglés*; and in Portugal, *jardim inglês*, all of them based on the "informality" of the landscaped park (page 129). Prior to the eighteenth century, however, an English person's garden was likely to be as "formal" as any in continental Europe. But what is a "formal garden"?

Typically, formal design shows "unnatural" signs of control: straight lines, geometry, containment. A formal garden is frequently designed to be symmetrical and may have an intricate pattern, such as a maze (page 72), parterre, or "knot" (a pattern of interwoven low hedges, perhaps in box and santolina, page 118). Topiary, being ultra-controlled vegetation shaped with shears, often features in formal gardens, although it also often appears in informal ones, so topiary itself is not necessarily a hallmark of formality.

If we consider, from a purely practical point of view, how garden design developed over many centuries, we see that, at some stage, people perceived that a tidy arrangement of beds made for growing useful things—such as edibles and herbs—is much easier to maintain if the beds are not too wide. When the beds are rectangular and orderly, you might fit in several within the space available, and have practical paths running between each, to access them. If the crops are sowed in straight lines, it is very much easier to tend them—water, weed, and harvest—and to plant new things without disturbing others nearby. So the standard style for a garden's design was, for many centuries, "formal," both for edibles and ornamental plants. (By that measure, formal is still the layout of choice in kitchen gardens [page 241], with their orderly rows of produce.)

Numerous illustrations of European gardens from late medieval times and well into the Renaissance show variations on the formal themes described above. Planting beds were often raised to somewhere between ankle – and knee-height, and edged with fencing, such as woven willow, or with planks, perhaps ornamented with metal lattice and vividly painted. Roof tiles and

OPPOSITE Wimpole Hall in Cambridgeshire: the Victorian parterre was restored in 1996, following the discovery of an outline of its original pattern. The flower beds were recut into the turf and are filled with blocks of vivid bedding plants through the summer.

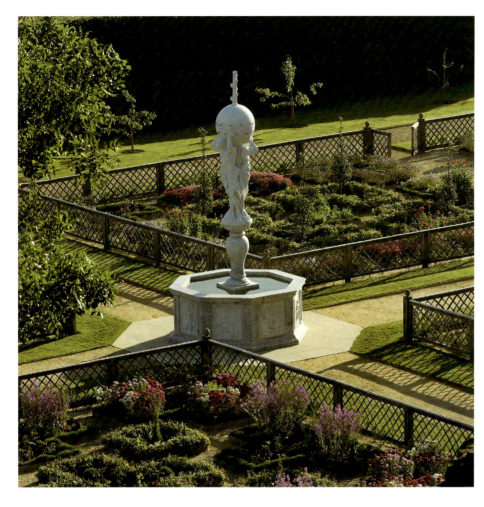

cobblestones were also put into service, but less appealing to most modern eyes would be animal jawbones. (John Parkinson, botanist and herbalist to King Charles I, thought this decoration "too gross and base." But who knows? Perhaps there were practical gains, via the slow release of phosphorus and calcium into the soil.)

The garden of a Tudor nobleman, enclosed by walls or hedges and criss-crossed by central paths, has its origins in earlier gardens of monasteries and their Roman and Persian antecedents. Parkinson noted in 1629, "the four square form is the most usually accepted for all, and doth best agree to any man's dwelling, being behind the house, all the back windows opening into it." As ornament became more important, the popularity of patterns that mimicked embroidery designs increased. The *parterre de broderie* developed in France in the late sixteenth century and was taken up for a while in English Renaissance gardens. (A formal revival, in the mid-nineteenth century, saw *parterres de broderie* return, the best exponent being W. A. Nesfield (pages 14, 97), whose magnificent swirly patterns were infilled in the traditional way, with coloured gravel.) When the seventeenth-century formal garden became a place to show off flowers and ornamental patterns, edibles were still grown, but elsewhere, in any garden of note. William Lawson's *A New Orchard and Garden* and *The Country Housewife's Garden*, both published in 1618, advises "it is meet that we have two gardens, a garden for flowers and a kitchen garden."

The flourishing landscaping business of George London and Henry Wise occurred at the apex of the age of grand formal gardens in England, in the second half of the seventeenth century and earliest decades of the eighteenth. They were by far the most important garden makers of their age. London and Wise were primarily nurserymen but their Brompton Park Nursery, which covered a hundred acres (in what is now the museum quarter of South Kensington in London) held stock of everything the ambitious garden owner could want. There were fruit trees in great variety—seventy-two different pears alone, and thirty-five different plums, for example; topiary shapes were ready-made; and thousands of trees were used in each client's park for creating avenues and plantations. London and Wise worked for everyone who

was anyone, designing and creating vast ambitious gardens of symmetrical patterns, parterres, excessive amounts of geometric topiary, plus canals, fountains, and avenues. The fabulous garden at Versailles, for King Louis XIV of France, was a template they knew well enough to adapt in various ways for their English clients. The London and Wise gardens, however, were eye-wateringly expensive to maintain and, within two generations, along came Capability Brown in the 1750s and swept them all away (page 129), with their owners' blessings.

Formal gardens made a reappearance, however, in the first half of the nineteenth century. "Old English" styles—those formal, symmetrical patterns and knot gardens that were ubiquitous prior to the eighteenth-century age of the landscape park—became popular again, being deemed correct and "honest," as in uncontrived. Brent Elliott observes in *Victorian Gardens*, during the first half of the nineteenth century, "The recovery of the English past entailed the abandonment of classical styles … and the exploration of styles which could be regarded as native."

In the late nineteenth and early twentieth centuries, Arts and Crafts gardens (page 301) were formal and frequently symmetrical in their design, but with a freer and livelier approach to planting than earlier Victorian gardens prescribed. From the First World War years onward through much of the twentieth century, formal gardens fell out of style as labour became scarce, and more naturalistic approaches with shrubs and ground covering plants took their place. A revival occurred again in the 1980s and '90s, when there was a surge of interest in historical gardens and serious restorations (page 399).

The gardens in this section show varied interpretations of the formal garden style, with all of these examples having been created in recent times. Among them, an interpretation of the late-seventeenth-century Anglo-Dutch style of William and Mary, at Hilborough House, has been exquisitely executed with plenty of topiary and precise symmetry. At Barnsley House, Rosemary Verey's formal geometric designs become subtly submerged by the lush exuberance of her planting, but strict formality, perhaps surprisingly, underpins it all.

HILBOROUGH HOUSE

NORFOLK

Extreme formality that recalls Anglo-Dutch gardens of three centuries past complements a recently built house in the Dutch style

Connections between the Netherlands and England's easternmost counties have existed for many centuries through trade and the exchange of knowledge; the influence of Dutch immigrants can be seen in various aspects of Norfolk life and architecture. Attractive Dutch gabled roofs can be seen across the county on houses, shop fronts, public buildings, and some churches. The Dutch influence is also apparent in numerous aristocratic and gentry houses created in centuries past. Hilborough House, however, is entirely new, having been designed by the classical architect Francis Johnson (a late commission, executed just before his death in 1995) in an early eighteenth-century Anglo-Dutch style. And such a building, of course, does require the right sort of setting.

So, while the flint-and-brick house was being built, designer Arne Maynard was engaged to create a suitable garden that could match and complement Johnson's magnificent mansion. The long front of the house faces directly to the north, where the entrance court lies. To the south, a magnificent garden in the Anglo-Dutch style fashionable towards the close of the seventeenth century, highly formal in its geometry and symmetry, rolls away in a sun-drenched sweep of crisp lawns, clipped trees (holm oaks), and complicated scrolls and flourishes in box and yew. This is a world apart from Arne Maynard's more domestic, English vernacular creations at Allt-y-Bela (page 61) and South Wood Farm (page 179). Further intricate garden areas occupy either side of the south lawn, but first consider what lies north of the house.

LEFT Wondrous swirls of low box hedging contrast with a squared-up plinth of box, around an "obelisk" of clipped copper beech. The formal trees are holm oak. The crisp design recalls formal gardens of the seventeenth century.

RIGHT The north front of the house, seen from the sunken north parterre of geometric hedges and topiary.

The splendid view of the house from the
end of the south garden, with its golden
yew and box swirls around the central
fountain. The garden, although new,
like the house, immediately suggests
seventeenth-century Dutch formality.

Another view of the formal garden north of the gravel courtyard at the front entrance. In the distance is a seat beneath an elegant arch. The stone urn in the foreground sits amid a "tabletop" of bronze-leaved beech, square-cut with admirable precision.

A farmhouse was demolished to make way for the new house; its derelict farmyard, opposite the front entrance on the north side, has been turned into a square, very formal parterre garden of precision-clipped geometric beds with corners marked by topiary cones and spirals. This virtuoso seventeenth-century-inspired composition is enclosed by a stilt hedge of pleached beech, under which are further hedges of yew, with planted terra-cotta pots placed at regular intervals.

Returning to the south garden and its unimpeachable lawn, splendidly terminated by a fountain jet of water rising out of a huge, shallow bowl, further gardens beckon to right and left. These maintain the symmetry by being formal rose gardens that exactly mirror each other, each side containing a hundred or so old shrub roses, all with pink, purple, or white flowers and, of course, many releasing exquisite scent in due season. They include beloved old gems such as cerise 'Belle de Crécy,' velvety deep-ruby 'Tuscany Superb,' and purply crimson 'William Lobb.' The supporting cast of underplanting continues the colour themes via geraniums, alliums, lavender, and salvias.

There is still more beyond, with the symmetry and mirroring applied to an orchard on each side and small mazes—one square, the other circular—both in purple beech. A rectangular area east of the house pulls ahead, though, with one last flourish all its own: a double herbaceous border is planted for the late season with dependable long-flowerers such as violet blue Geranium 'Brookside,' monardas, Michaelmas daisies, and the tall, purple-flowered daisy, *Vernonia arkansana*.

Much of the Hilborough gardeners' time must be spent with shears and hedge trimmers in hand, but the results are spectacular, and undeniably pitch-perfect with the Dutch-style house.

ABOVE To one side of the rose garden, near the house, the view leads down a succession of broad arches, each one garlanded with 'Madame Alfred Carriere' roses.

RIGHT For the rose garden, Arne Maynard planted shrub roses galore in shades of pink, deepening to burgundy. The ancient and deeply fragrant shrub rose 'Ispahan' flowers abundantly in the foreground, alongside *Geranium psilostemon*. Just a handful of the hundred or more shrub roses on each side of the rose garden, all in character-istic shades of purple and pink, set off by white.

HERTERTON HOUSE

NORTHUMBERLAND

An old-world atmosphere is contained within the shapely and vibrant gardens of a restored farmhouse in the far north of England

There is a sort of irony that Capability Brown, the master of big, open landscapes, who swept away so many enclosed formal and intimate gardens, was born and grew up just a stone's throw from the symmetrically ordered garden at Herterton House.

Frank and Marjorie Lawley, who live at Herterton, came here in 1975, a couple of young artists who took a lease on a ruined, sixteenth-century former farmhouse and its outbuildings from the National Trust. Over several years they rebuilt the stone house and ancillary buildings, which had been in a derelict state, after which they began to make a suitable garden around it.

From the lane, the front garden announces itself as somewhere interesting, having neat, squared-up beds edged with trim box hedging and a variety of topiary shapes, some of the taller ones in yew now making splendidly tiered cottage garden specimens. (It looks out over a typically rolling Northumberland landscape of green pastures, a stream, and trees, which uncannily resembles one of Capability Brown's own creations, so you can see immediately how the eighteenth-century master's home ground was a source of inspiration.)

The house, an inverted L-shape, looks into the main garden from two sides, but you are likely to encounter first the physic garden, on the other (east) side of the house. Its simple symmetrical design focuses on a dense, clipped dome of silver pear, 'Pendula,' around which are beds edged with

LEFT Since the Lawleys settled into the sixteenth-century former farmhouse deep in the Northumberland countryside more than forty years ago, they have developed a sequence of hedge-enclosed gardens of varied character, but always with the integrity of an underlying pattern.

RIGHT A riot of herbaceous flowers invigorates one of the garden "rooms" at midsummer.

ABOVE Frank Lawley gets busy with his shears, shaping the varied topiaries in the front garden.

RIGHT Viewed from an upstairs window in the house, the remarkable tapestry of the Lawleys' central garden is plain to see, with its structural topiaries and hedges all carefully balanced to create a satisfying picture, leading the eye to the pastures beyond.

miniature London Pride and white thrift. Recalling physic gardens of the Renaissance period, the beds are filled out with pot herbs, medicines, dye plants, some poisonous species, and also scented strewing herbs such as meadowsweet.

The main event is in a long, somewhat narrow plot rolling away northward from the L-shape of the house in a series of formal, symmetrical arrangements crossed with narrow paths. But the underlying formality becomes lost through the growing season by the abundance of very carefully chosen herbaceous plants. Marjorie Lawley has for long been in charge of the floral colour scheme, which runs from pale pinks, cool yellows, and whites near the house into stronger blues and oranges toward the middle, developing into rich reds and purples at the further end. These colours are planned to represent the passing of a summer's day with the soft light of dawn closest to the house, followed by the heat and clarity of midday, and the richness of a summer sunset beyond. Although the ground patterns in the gardens are inspired by Tudor designs, Lawley's inspirations as a colourist are modern, having come from her studies of the artists Piet Mondrian and Paul Klee. Many of the flowering plants are old-fashioned cottage garden stalwarts, including unusual variants of native wildflowers. Margery Fish at East Lambrook in Somerset was an early influence, and the Lawleys acquired plants from her in the 1960s. Such plants include special forms of Welsh poppy, hawkweed, old-fashioned pansies, campions, buttercups, and daisies. Being seven hundred feet up and as far north as they are, the season is short, but Marjorie Lawley wants it to be intensely colourful.

A central vista runs through the garden to the farmyard's old boundary wall, terminating at a pitched-roofed, double-height gazebo looking from one side into the garden and from the other side out to the sheep pastures. The Lawleys built it some twenty years ago and from its upper floor you can get a bird's-eye view of the Fancy Garden, a crisp parterre of low, geometrically arranged box hedging, which looks as neat and fresh when dusted with snow as it does in its simple green beauty at any other time of year.

OPPOSITE Northumberland can be a cold county at the best of times and doubly so in winter; nevertheless, a light dusting of snow lends the garden a magical quality, the little gateway looking welcoming and inviting further exploration.

ABOVE RIGHT A view back to the house, where a snowfall has made the topiary shapes indistinctive.

RIGHT Even a very ordinary back door can be made elegant with some creatively shaped creepers grown around it.

BARNSLEY HOUSE

GLOUCESTERSHIRE

Very formal geometric patterns underpin the exuberantly planted gardens created in the second half of the twentieth century by designer Rosemary Verey

In the early 1950s, as a young woman setting up home in Barnsley House in rural Gloucestershire, Rosemary Verey initially focused on making her garden a pleasant place for the children to play. As they moved away to boarding school, however, David Verey encouraged his clever and energetic wife to take greater interest in developing the garden.

Rosemary learned a most useful tip from a highly admired garden designer of the day, Percy Cane: "that you should always make the longest possible distance into your most important vista and give it an interesting focal point."

This was achieved by Verey at Barnsley House by extending an existing path between pleached lime trees, planted by her husband, to lead into a tunnel of laburnum and wisteria, terminated by a sundial at the garden's southwestern perimeter. The famous view along the laburnum/wisteria tunnel has launched a thousand calendars and magazine covers worldwide and need not be repeated here; instead, consider it another way—overleaf, for example. Ravishing, sumptuous, and explosive—if only for a short period in late spring.

One of the most interesting things about the garden at Barnsley House is that, on plan, it is intensely formal, with straight lines and underlying symmetrical patterns—a number of which were directly inspired by designs from seventeenth-century books Verey had in her library. Yet her approach to planting ensured that nearly all of the disciplined geometric patterns she laid out were substantially disguised by the exuberance of the flowers for much of the year, lifting the whole composition in to three dimensions instead of the flat geometric two prescribed in her books.

"When this house was built in 1697," wrote Verey, in *Making of a Garden*, "formal gardens were still the fashion in England, so historically it was appropriate to give the garden a basic formal design."

Percy Cane, by the way, was not engaged to redesign the Vereys' garden, but Rosemary admitted that a visit from him, procured by her husband, was enough to spur her into action in the very early days, "as I wished the garden to be our design and not someone else's." Its form therefore developed through the 1960s to a point where, in 1970, she opened Barnsley House to the public for the first time, for a National Garden Scheme charity day and also wrote the first of many articles for *Country Life*.

With the publication of some timely books from 1980 through to the mid-'90s, certain set-piece garden views that are an art director's and calendar publisher's dream, and with invitations to create high-end gardens for a select list of clients in England and the United States, Verey's own garden became internationally famous. She was generous with advice on how to garden

"When this house was built in 1697, formal gardens were still the fashion in England, so it was historically appropriate to give the garden a basic formal design," wrote Rosemary Verey, in *Making of a Garden* (1995). On plan, the pattern of the potager shows its strict, geometric, symmetrical layout, less evident when the growing season is underway.

PREVIOUS PAGES Looking across the famous Laburnum Walk, rather than along it, gives it a different, very painterly effect. Purple alliums (*A. aflatunense*) and occasional yellow dots of *Doronicum* were an inspired choice to match the canary yellow laburnum tresses.

well and a famously strict taskmaster with her garden staff. She took copious notes; importantly, she recorded errors not to be repeated as well as the many successes. When you're exploring a garden, "always remember to turn around and look the other way," she advised, to get a different perspective.

In its heyday, more than 25,000 pilgrims annually visited the 3.5-acre garden. They admired exuberant beds burgeoning with a nonstop show of annual and perennial flowers through spring and summer. The garden's style could appear quite laissez-faire, but it actually was very time-consuming, to maintain abundant, fresh-looking flowers within a crisp, formal framework. A wealth of evergreen shrubs and early bulbs continued the show through each winter.

When Barnsley House came up for sale in 2002, a year or so after Rosemary Verey's death, naturally there was much talk about what might happen to the garden. These days the elegant seventeenth-century stone house is a smart boutique hotel, and its present owners have kept faith with Verey's imprint to a remarkable degree.

ABOVE A view from the parterre beds to the Yew Walk. Again, the underlying plan is very formal indeed, but Verey's planting, especially in its maturity, blurs the geometry, making the garden softer and more appealing. The tree is *Cornus controversa* 'Variegata.'

Verey based her famous potager kitchen garden on a design in William Lawson's *The Country Housewife's Garden* (published 1618). "His advice was never to have your beds more than five feet wide so the 'weeder women' need not tread on them," she wrote, when the garden was new. "We have found this very good counsel." With the needs of a hotel restaurant requiring more than an intimate potager could produce, a larger kitchen garden has been established on a former paddock close by. There, in a bed of brassicas, you might find 'Black Tuscan' kale, 'Purple Sprouting' broccoli, and 'Romanesco' cauliflower; the salad beds are particularly beautiful, with an array of colourful lettuces. The permanent herb bed is a traditional assembly of shrubby sage, rosemary, marjoram, and floaty fennel.

The gardeners don't expect guests to rush to inspect the range of compost heaps, impressive as they are. But if you take an interest, they will tell you with pride that the horse manure spread on the soil is sourced locally, from famous racing stables just up the lane. Yes, high standards have been maintained at Barnsley House, even down to the muck on the flower beds.

ABOVE Another view of the potager, less neat and tidy than in Verey's day, with a fashionable look of relaxed abundance, with self-sowed poppies and granny's bonnets, and foamy thalictrum among the broad beans and lettuces.

THE LASKETT

A succession of garden "rooms" and theatrical spaces define the formal gardens made by the noted historian Sir Roy Strong and his late wife

In 1973 the historian and museum curator Sir Roy Strong and his wife, television and theatre set designer Dr. Julia Trevelyan Oman, bought a small 1830s villa, attached to which was a four-acre triangle of rough pasture. It was to be a peaceful escape from the pressures of their busy London lives, but the desire to make a garden there soon gripped them. It became a joint passion and, since the earliest days, the development of its designs, collections of plants, and the ideas of its creative owners have been fully recorded in a series of beautifully bound albums, as well as Sir Roy's extensive essays, articles, and books devoted to the same subject. With the benefit of frequent photography by Julia and others, it is surely by now the most well-documented garden in the country.

Its beginnings coincided with the start of kindled curiosity among gardening and historical fraternities, as to how the early formal gardens that were made all over this country might have looked. The Garden History Society, a scholarly group dedicated to the study and preservation of historic gardens, was formed in 1966 and Sir Roy, an expert on the art of the Tudor period, published a timely book, *The Renaissance Garden in England* in 1979, in which he pointed out the difficulties of trying to know more about England's old formal gardens, for so many were swept away in the eighteenth century. "Bridgeman, Capability Brown, and Repton, and their imitators from 1720 onwards were responsible for the mass destruction, on a scale unmatched in any other European country, of the old formal gardens in the Renaissance, Mannerist, Baroque and Rococo styles. There is no English equivalent to

LEFT The house entrance with its knot garden: green and golden heather form the intertwining "ropes" or hedges, of the two square knot designs. The oval plaques on the house walls commemorate Julia Trevelyan Oman and Sir Roy Strong. *Pax Intrantibus* is inscribed above the door: "peace to those who enter."

RIGHT The whimsical pleasures of topiary are found throughout the garden.

the Villa d'Este at Tivoli or to the Palace at Hellbrunn outside Salzburg," he wrote.

The Strongs decided to make their own formal garden inspired by the vistas, hierarchies, enclosed spaces, and eye-catching ornaments that typified gardens of the Renaissance period. Their garden therefore has a particular route that takes you through a sequence of classically symmetrical spaces of varying size, shape, and mood. It is also an autobiographical garden, which celebrates a number of the key moments in the lives and careers of its creators, with commemorative statuary, for example.

Sir Roy's scholarly understanding of Renaissance garden design and how palatial themes could be scaled down to suit a smaller space ensured that this garden was created with wit and whimsy, including the making of plenty of topiary, one of his primary horticultural interests. Julia's contribution was certainly grounded in a knowledgeable appreciation of plants, and she assembled important collections of, among other things, varieties of quince, crab apple, Herefordshire apples, lilies, and snowdrops. Her own sharply developed and professional eye for creating spaces and set pieces should not be sidelined, however; a walk in the garden with the Strongs rapidly revealed her own interest in its spatial arrangements and theatricality.

Very many evergreens were planted in the early years and, after his wife died in 2003, Sir Roy decided to make radical changes, cutting down trees and hedges, which, by then, overshadowed the garden with too much shade and gloom. Having written earlier books about the garden they made together, his poignant book, *Remaking a Garden: The Laskett Transformed* (2014), describes the literal "bringing-in" of new light, air, and energy. He wrote, for *Country Life*, in 2005: "Never cease to be brave, I say, even if you are about to enter your seventieth year. I'm tired of emails from elderly friends always downsizing and disappearing into retirement homes or sheltered housing. My instincts are to do exactly the opposite and go out in a blaze of madness. So what's in it for the garden? It solves the problem of the junipers, for one. They will go and so will the hedge in front of the house ... A new path will be made so that the visitor's first experience of the garden will be as a frame to a classical house ... It is exciting that, thirty years on, innovation is still possible. The worst thing that could happen to The Laskett garden is for it to atrophy."

Atrophy it won't, for in 2015 Sir Roy bequeathed the garden to the gardening charity, Perennial, with a generous endowment to ensure its maintenance as well as a provision for this fascinating and touching garden to continue to be open to visitors.

OPPOSITE The orchard, begun at the end of 1974, was Oman's province; she gathered a small collection of historic apple varieties, especially ones of local provenance. The orchard performs in at least three seasons: blossoms of the fruit trees are joined by swaths of spring bulbs, followed in summer by wildflowers and roses. Autumn of course brings the russet and golden hues of the fruits themselves.

RIGHT A westward view from the house into the fountain court, and the topiary garden beyond it. The shapes were chosen to recall those common in gardens of the Arts and Crafts movement.

OUSDEN HOUSE

SUFFOLK

Symmetry achieved by yew hedging, some of which is ingeniously designed, shelters the garden but focuses the eye on lovely western views

The village sign for Ousden is an attractive piece of folk art, showing an ancient church in the background while the arresting foreground is taken up with a swooping owl above scampering rabbits—or are they hares? The owl points to the origin of the village's name, believe to be derived from "the valley of the owls." Its old church of Saint Peter is especially admired for being an unspoiled example of a small place of worship built soon after the Norman invasion and is therefore some nine hundred years old.

For centuries the "big house" hereabouts was Ousden Hall. Indeed, old photographs show that it was a very big house but, like so many mansions of earlier centuries, it was requisitioned by the War Office during the Second World War. There being no apparent use for it afterward, the house was demolished in 1955. Its stable block, granary, and laundry were, however, left standing and have since been converted into a handsome and substantial home, dating from the 1730s.

Alastair and Lavinia Robinson saw the half-converted building for sale in 1993 and were immediately drawn to the idea of finishing off its refurbishment and making a garden in the surrounding land. The "potential" house was a fine building in itself and its elevated location, with spectacular rural views, was a prime opportunity to make something special. One feature that did remain from the hall was a redbrick clock tower, standing apart, but ripe for inclusion as a focal point in the garden-to-be.

Wide-open views, handsome buildings, a clean slate—potentially daunting, but there were also challenges posed by the hilly ground, and expertise was required. The Robinsons called in the celebrated landscape architect Arabella Lennox-Boyd to make sense of it all and the results speak for themselves. Levelling out unappealing gradients near the house and on the west side enabled a sensible approach from the road and an opportunity to make a formal garden, taking in the distant vistas and often spectacular sunset.

Three linked spaces lead away from the house: a wide lawn, flanked by short but deep herbaceous borders progresses into a more enclosed rose garden, beyond which is a much more open lawn, ending with a curved ha-ha that takes the view on into the countryside. These three well-proportioned areas are enclosed by hedges in yew and beech, which are not merely decorative; they also provide welcome wind shelter.

Continuing the theme of the east-west focus, another linear garden lies just to the south, with a straight turf walk leading alongside the house, through various smaller garden incidents and beyond again, to the pastures at the western end. This is a preamble to the garden's most spectacular feature: a "crinkle-crankle" corridor in crisp yew hedging, which again runs parallel to the preceding areas, along the east-west axis.

The dramatic crinkle-crankle hedge in yew reaches out westward to the far-reaching views of Suffolk countryside. Crinkle-crankle—said to be an Old English term for zigzag—was a certain type of serpentine wall in some old kitchen gardens, developed to assist fruit trees in ripening.

LEFT When the big house, Ousden Hall, was demolished, its clock tower was left standing. Today it makes a great feature within the garden.

RIGHT The main vista from the house progresses in three stages. A wide lawn is flanked by short but deep herbaceous borders, then you get to the hedge-enclosed rose garden, beyond which is a much more open lawn ending with a curved ha-ha.

ABOVE LEFT The long cross vista from the lawn beyond the rose garden looks across another large lawn known as the summerhouse lawn and one to the distant focal point of a single large urn.

ABOVE RIGHT White foxgloves and blue irises in the rose garden.

Crinkle-crankle (also known as crinkum-crankum) is an interesting expression, said to be an Old English term for zigzag; whatever its origins, it's a term chiefly used for a certain type of serpentine wall. Suffolk is especially rich in crinkle-crankle walls, which were built by the Dutch communities who arrived in large numbers in the seventeenth and eighteenth centuries. When a crinkle-crankle wall was built on an east-west axis, it not only enjoyed extra square yardage of sun exposure, for training and ripening fruit; it could be economical, as the wall was usually built just one brick thick without fear of collapse, the alternating concave and convex curves giving it stability and resistance to lateral forces.

So far, so formal. But when the Robinsons were able to acquire more land, it was time to take the garden in a different direction philosophically, as well as literally. The Spring Wood and the Moat Garden are striking for their contrasting informality and plantsmanship; Alastair Robinson is very keen and hands-on. Since the early days, everything has evolved exponentially. A number of new areas created by the Robinsons take full advantage of the extra ground they acquired, and numerous refinements have enhanced the earlier plantings. As these pictures show, the garden does both formal and informal in a spectacular and stylish manner.

OPPOSITE Remarkable lushness of growth and intensity of the flowering in the damp, sheltered depths of the Moat Garden. Yellow trollius, orange, white, and red candelabra primulas, *Iris sibirica* in both blue and white forms, and hostas and *Hemerocallis* are among its herbaceous riches.

4 OVERVIEW: THE PARK

For most people, an image of a park is likely to be somewhere with pleasant grass and trees, an invitation to recreation or respite. A public park is a shared amenity valued by its community and, in cities, a green lung amid the humdrum and the high-rise. Think of rural English landscape parks, such as those by Capability Brown, and the image of grass and trees will be somewhat more bucolic, supplemented with a pleasing stretch of lake flooding the lower ground and the spreading arms of cedar trees hinting at things brought from foreign shores.

A park originally meant something much more than recreation, however, and indeed, parks were the superyachts of the 1700s. Many of the greatest were created by the rich and powerful merchants and aristocrats who aligned themselves politically with Whig interests from the late seventeenth century. It took serious money to build a truly splendid house, but very deep pockets were required to put an appropriately smart garden and park around it—and then maintain it.

The earliest parks were deer parks, which began popping up across the countryside soon after 1066 since hunting was a popular pastime of Norman noblemen. For people of high rank, they were top-drawer expressions of power and prestige, with venison regarded as a very high status meat. Some 3,000 parks are thought to have been created by the year 1300. Parks differed from royal hunting forests and chases since a park was always enclosed, usually within a "pale." This structure was created by digging a deep ditch with the earth banked up along one side. A palisade of cleft-oak stakes was then run along the top of the bank. Once deer were within the pale (the design enabled them to leap in), they couldn't get out again, because of the ditch. Although most parks were not very large, at seventy-five to two hundred acres, some were enormous. An exceptionally large deer park in the Ashdown Forest in Sussex extended over some 14,000-plus acres; at one stage it belonged to John of Gaunt, Duke of Lancaster (1340–1399), who possessed dozens more elsewhere.

Many parks also contained grazing sheep or cattle, and some had fish-ponds; often there were valuable trees for timber, so it wasn't necessarily only about the deer.

OPPOSITE From 1755 onward, at Burghley House in Lincolnshire, Capability Brown designed the parkland and gardens and also several buildings. It is thought to have been his longest commission and Brown later recalled his work there as "25 years of Pleasure." This view, across the lake to what is known as the "gothic summerhouse" of the late 1760s, shows its lacy parapet and pinnacles brilliantly against the darkness of the cedars.

Later, in more peaceful and prosperous times, people found other things to be interested in and numerous early parks were converted into farmland or, if adjacent to a house, gardens. Under the Stuarts, elaborate gardens were laid out around houses but, adopting a Continental approach, you could indicate the vastness of your landholding by sending long, straight avenues through it, reaching to the distant horizon. Among the aristocracy and richest of the merchant classes, having an extensive park with strategically planted blocks of forestry was a useful way of distancing yourself from the workaday aspects of agriculture, peasant life, and, of course, towns.

By no means were all eighteenth-century parks created as bosky bling, however. The opposing Tory side included great numbers of local gentry who were closely involved with a working countryside and not distanced from it. If the farming squire wanted avenues, he could proudly run them through his fields. Joseph Addison (1672–1719) suggested, "Why may not a whole Estate be thrown into a kind of Garden, by frequent Plantations, that may turn as much to the Profitt as the Pleasure of the Owner?" In this spirit, the "wilderness" in the park of a lesser property might be planted with orchard trees instead of a curated collection of decorative ones.

A more consciously artistic version of this is seen in the niche interest known as *ferme ornée*, codified in 1718 by the master gardener and author Stephen Switzer. Both productive and ornamental, the *ferme ornée* aligned itself with the romantic movement, undoing the corsetry of straight-line gardening, in favour of serpentine walks, flowing water, grottoes, and framed views of attractive buildings, within a hardworking environment. Famous examples were Philip Southcote's Wooburn Farm in Surrey and William Shenstone's The Leasowes in Herefordshire.

Another kind of park developed at Stourhead in Wiltshire, created by banker Henry Hoare in the 1740s and '50s. Purely ornamental, it takes a circuit around a lake, its sequence of temples, buildings, and grotto recalling episodes of Greek mythology. Painshill (page 427), begun in 1738, also leads the visitor through a fantastic, exotic lakeside journey, uphill and down dale, via assorted eye-catching sights and a spectacular grotto.

Places such as these contained references to the classical world and were therefore written about by the intellectual essayists of their day. Ever since, art historians have focused on a still-repeated myth: that eighteenth-century landowners were all interested in poetry, painting, and philosophy, transmitting to their acreage scenes from the paintings of Nicolas Poussin, Claude Lorrain, and Salvator Rosa. Though true for some, they were very much the minority. Landscape historians Anthea Taigel and Tom Williamson redress the balance: "In reality, most gentlemen were predominantly concerned with planting things and killing things. Their diaries and memoranda books show them busy with their home farms, with brewing, with the establishment of plantations, with hunting, with the management of fishponds and dovehouses—and with the care of their gardens. We see them buying plants and seeds from the growing network of provincial nurseries, exchanging cuttings with their neighbours, pruning fruit trees and planting vegetables."

But what about the Grand Tour, routinely a young milord's gap-year journey through the great cities of Europe, seeing the finest art and architecture in the company of his tutor? "The truth is that most of these young men went abroad not to improve themselves but to live it up with fellow

Ugbrooke Park in Devon: classic Capability Brown landscaping in the 1870s included moving a road deemed unsightly, removing a double avenue of an earlier period, creating lakes by damming the Ug Brook, and planting new trees among existing ones; his included English oak, holm oak, turkey oak, and Spanish chestnut.

playboys—carousing, wenching and networking," says Charles Quest-Ritson. "Most returned home with confused memories, and a firm conviction that their own country was vastly superior to any other they had seen."

The eighteenth century saw an unprecedented economic boom in England, driven by empire, mercantilism, manufacturing, and agricultural improvements. Lancelot 'Capability' Brown (1716–1783) appeared, mid-century, with his own ideas of the new direction an English park should take. He knew the backstory; in his twenty-fifth year he had been taken on as head gardener at the baroque park of Stowe, where William Kent was consultant garden architect. Within ten years Brown was ready to spread his wings and set out on his own, having built up his reputation in the meantime, through giving advice to the friends of his employer, Lord Cobham.

Brown was energetic and personable, a quick learner and a successful busi-nessman. He was also a skilled water engineer and accomplished architect.

Notwithstanding the attractiveness of Brown's trademark curvy grassland, sinuous lakes, natural-looking copses, and stretches of woodland, the genius of his parks and their unstoppable popularity is down to their dual-purpose nature, providing the landowner with both income and sport. Income was brought in via grazing livestock, which also usefully kept the grass short. They looked decorative in the park without getting too near the house, owing to the ubiquitous ha-ha (pages 299–301). The copses facilitated a rapidly increasing interest in foxhunting, while woodland plantations provided forestry timber.

Brown's landscaped parks were masterpieces, but not without cost to others. Vast acreages of non-private land were seized by landowners from

At Endsleigh Cottage in Devon (now the stylish Hotel Endsleigh), there is one of the best restored Humphry Repton landscapes, with a lawned terrace and several garden buildings. This view (from 1961) shows the rustic verandah of the house by Jeffry Wyatville, its knobbly floor made from sheep's knuckles.

Fallow deer in the eighteenth-century landscape park at Dalemain in Cumbria. Deer parks were made all over the country after 1066, as the Norman occupiers were keen deer hunters. Parks went through several phases of development over subsequent centuries.

the common people and brought into their private estates. Numerous entire villages were relocated, the originals perhaps disappearing under a new lake. Some 250 parks are associated with Brown; many survive and in their maturity we can appreciate his long-term vision (see Blenheim, pages 142–3, 145).

For the next generation, Humphry Repton (1752–1818) achieved stature as "the man who restored flowers to English gardens," sometimes following in Brown's footsteps. Famous for his Red Books, showing "before" and "after" views of the parks he proposed to improve, his talent was to suggest makeovers that brought people and their plants back into the picture. Some of his best work was at Endsleigh Cottage, Sheringham Hall, Attingham Park, and Woburn Abbey.

Nodding bluebells, flowering in April and May, often signify ancient woodland in parks. They occur all over England and are numerous in the southeast. The English bluebell *Hyacinthoides non-scripta* is a quite dark, violet blue and very dainty. It's important they don't mix with garden Spanish bluebells, which are stouter, upright, and paler, since the two cross-pollinate easily; mixed colours ruin the authentic experience of a bluebell wood.

5 WATER'S MANY MOODS

The Romans who came to Britain used their knowledge of piped water and fountain-making in the gardens they made during their four centuries of occupation. Indeed, the word *fountain* itself is derived from the Latin "fons," referring either to a natural spring or artificially channelled and spurting water. Fountains go back even further, though, to the early Bronze Age in Greece and also the Indus Valley, providing people with fresh water from springs or aqueducts, the manipulation of water being fundamental across world civilizations and especially eloquently celebrated in hot and dry climates.

With the spread of Christianity in the British Isles, medieval monks chose with great care the places to site their abbeys. Frequently they settled for glorious locations beside running water, which provided obvious usefulness, but also spiritual refreshment. Water can be enchanting and mood-enhancing, stimulating or contemplative. At Fountains Abbey in North Yorkshire—ruined, of course, in the time of Henry VIII—one of England's largest Cistercian monasteries was set up beside the lively, splashy waters of the River Skell (that name itself derived from the Viking word *skjallr*, "resounding").

That most articulate of twentieth-century garden designers, Russell Page, commented: "If water is a necessity for the cultivation of plants it has other and less easily described functions. 'White' water, breaking waves, waterfalls, cascades and fountain jets are known to produce negative ions, which 'clear the air' and make people feel well." At Fountains Abbey, Page observed, "the sick-bay was built over a weir on the river which flows under the buildings. Running water has special properties easily perceptible if you choose to examine your impressions of, say a duck-pond on a village green compared with a fast-flowing stream in a narrow valley." Working as much as he did in France and Italy, Page was used to designing with water; his rill and pools at La Mortella, on the island of Ischia, Italy, reveal his talent for creating joy out of simplicity.

In the Derbyshire Dales, Chatsworth House (pages 8–11) sits beside the Derwent river, where it has exploited the advantages of its geography for half a millennium. The garden's remarkable feats of hydraulic engineering, dating

OPPOSITE Still waters run deep— or appear to do so. "The black water" at Westwell Manor in Oxfordshire is a large formal pool filling an area previously occupied by a tennis court. Created by the noted garden designer, the late Anthea Gibson, it is only three feet deep but a harmless black pond dye (which prevents algae and improves reflections) makes it seem as deep as the Mariana Trench.

Good hydrations. A characterful fountain spurts forth at Sezincote in Gloucestershire. An attractive natural stream garden at Dallam Tower in Cumbria, where the banks are brightened with Japanese candelabra primulas and ferns. Fountains in a disciplined framework of stone-edged pools and box "boxes" in the gardens at Badminton House in Gloucestershire, designed by François Goffinet. With a surface like glass, the recently restored Cow Pond in Windsor Great Park in Berkshire, where water-lilies flourish.

from the late seventeenth century onward, have produced some of the most exciting and splendid water features, both animated and serene, to be seen in Britain. To ensure an adequate supply of water to its gravity-fed system, three lakes were dug on the hill above the house, with channels and pipes carrying their precious cargo to the gardens. To watch the water, newly switched on at the top of the cascade, find its way, step-by-step, down the hillside, gathering momentum and volume with each passing minute, is a thrilling buildup to the spectacle of the cascade in full, noisy flow. Designed by Grillet, a French hydraulics engineer who had worked on elaborate waterworks for Louis XIV of France, it was two years in construction and completed in 1696.

In the same year, the Celia Fiennes (1662–1741), one of the first women to travel through much of England at a time when the idea of travel for its own sake was still novel, wrote a long description of Chatsworth's formal gardens, its walks, statues, varied waterworks, and new Willow Tree Fountain, only installed the year before. "All of a sudden by turning a sluce it raines from each leafe and from the branches lik a shower, it being made of brass and pipes to each leafe but in appearance is exactly like any Willow." The Willow Tree Fountain has been remade twice since Fiennes passed through on horseback and is still capable of soaking the inquisitive visitor, in the manner of Renaissance Italy's *giochi d'acqua*, the water jokes that probably caused more mirth in their owners than their unsuspecting visitors.

Chatsworth's Emperor Fountain, focal point of the magnificent, much older Canal Pond, was created in just six months in 1843–4, despite it necessitating the creation of an eight-acre lake and feeder streams, hand-dug out of the hills to supply enough gravity pressure. Capable of spouting a magnificent plume of water some 296 feet, it is usually run on partial power these days for water conservation but is still very impressive at half its potential height.

The gardens that follow in this section all celebrate water in very different but alluring ways, from Capability Brown's great lake at Blenheim to the stepped cascade at Alnwick, via an Edwardian Japanese water garden in Wiltshire and conservation streams in Dorset.

A classic view of the magnificent Capability Brown landscape park at Blenheim Palace in Oxfordshire. The palatial house by Vanbrugh sits on the highest point. A very complex (and expensive) early-eighteenth-century formal garden by Henry Wise was swept away by Brown in the 1760s. Flooding most of the structure of a colossal bridge, he made it make sense, by straddling a huge stretch of water instead of the former piddling little channel.

BLENHEIM PALACE

OXFORDSHIRE

The great sweeps of water, created by Capability Brown, surrounding the palace were supplemented with formal water parterres in the early twentieth century

Throughout 2016 England celebrated the 300th anniversary of Lancelot 'Capability' Brown (1716–83), the most famous and influential gardener the nation has produced. His fluid landscape style transformed the look of large areas of England and, indeed, became widely adopted overseas, particularly among the elite of Europe, as *Jardin a l'anglaise, der englische Garten,* and *il giardino all'inglese.*

Today Brown's work can be fully appreciated, with his grandest masterpiece in its maturity. Yet the huge park began as something else entirely, when it was laid out for John Churchill, the first Duke of Marlborough. During Queen Anne's brief reign (1702–7), she had given the 2,000-plus-acre Woodstock estate (formerly a royal deer park) to Churchill in recognition of his stellar military career; the estate's new name reflected his victory at the Battle of Blenheim in 1704. The public purse was shaken up to fund, at least in part, the creation of the stately house and its grounds, a "welcome home" for the nation's war hero.

While Vanbrugh was engaged in creating a monumental palace of honey-coloured stone on the crest of a low hill, a suitably grand and complex garden was being laid out all around it by the leading royal gardener of the moment, Henry Wise (1653–1738).

Wise was in partnership with George London at the famous Brompton Park Nursery (long since buried under the buildings and infrastructure of London's South Kensington district). Together, they were not only the go-to design duo of their day, in demand by everyone who was anyone, but their hundred-acre nursery was the greatest supplier of plants in the land.

At Blenheim, a complex formal garden of symmetrical, intricate parterres formed an apron rolling away from the south front of the house. Set upon a huge terrace enclosed by a hexagonal stone wall, the corner of each wall was marked by a curved bastion to look out over further crisp landscaping in the formal French style. Here were complex geometric patterns of avenues and rides extending over half a mile, the paths, or allées, slicing through tightly packed coppices of trees, like knives carving up portions of cake.

Despite the eye-watering costs attached to the formal gardens' creation and maintenance, only the kitchen garden was destined to survive longer than a half century. The 4th Duke, who inherited it at age nineteen, in 1758, was still in his early twenties when he engaged Brown in 1763 to sweep away Wise's patterns and parterres. And why not? They belonged to another age, a different aesthetic sensibility, and were undoubtedly suffering from being prohibitively expensive to maintain.

Brown's scheme (itself, by no means cheap) replaced the formal areas with a huge sweep of grass. Around it he altered the contours of the ground to accommodate spacious copses of trees that would frame desirable views.

Woodlands were planted to fill out distant horizons with billowing
greenery where shelter or screening was required. His choice of trees was
paramount to achieve the very English look; most were native hardwood
species: oak, elm, beech, sycamore, ash, planted in clusters or as single
specimens. Cedar of Lebanon, an exotic conifer, was a fashionable novelty;
several planted in conversation together were deployed here and there to
enhance or draw the eye to a particular view.

Brown's genius saw that by tweaking the landscape so as to bring the
lakes together, flooding most of the bridge's structure, a great sweep of
water could be achieved, and the bridge given dignity and purpose. Indeed,
in 1767, Lord Cadogan of Caversham Park wrote to Brown following a
visit to Blenheim, "The water is, by much, the finest artificial thing I ever
saw; when I say that, I include the banks and the advantageous manner in
which you have set it off … "

Brown did much more work at Blenheim, including redesigning the
north entrance, building ha-has to keep out the grazing sheep, fashioning
new drives, creating an impressive Grand Cascade with splashy water
foaming over the rocks, and designing little buildings within the park.

Landscapes never stay still, however, and in the summer of 1833, John
Claudius Loudon, the leading horticulturist of his day, was unimpressed
by his visit to Blenheim, commenting on "the present ruinous state of this
princely demesne … " under the "profligate" 5th Duke's tenure, and lean
times continued through Queen Victoria's reign. Nevertheless, something
of the style of André Le Nôtre was reintroduced to Blenheim by Charles
Spencer-Churchill (1871–1934), the 9th Duke and husband of the American
railroad heiress, Consuelo Vanderbilt. In the early twentieth century,
Consuelo's magnificent dowry enabled the formerly impoverished duke to
carry out much-needed restorative work in the house and around the park.
He also engaged Achille Duchêne, the fashionable French garden designer
of the Belle Epoque, to remake formal gardens close to the house.

Duchêne created a symmetrical Italianate parterre, tucked up against
the eastern end of the palace. Its formal beds of swirly patterns in box
frame a centrepiece made by the society sculptor and creator of flamboyant
fountains, Thomas Waldo Story. On the west side, Duchêne was engaged
from 1925 to create a magnificent water parterre, several years in the
making, and laid out across two large terraces that stepped down toward
the Great Lake.

The genius of the place continues to rest with Brown, however, and
a great deal of his work survives at Blenheim, 250 years after he made
it. Many trees are now ancient and characterful and if his "Harry Potter
cedar" draws thousands of extra visitors each year, it also immerses them in
the master landscaper's greatest work.

HEALE HOUSE

WILTSHIRE

Existing streams along the edge of the property were put to use in the early twentieth century to create a water garden with a Japanese theme

A number of rivers drain the waters that seep through the high chalk plateau of Salisbury Plain and one of these is known as the Salisbury (or Hampshire) Avon, for it takes a north-south, zigzag route of exaggerated meanders, through Wiltshire's cathedral city and on into Hampshire, eventually feeding into Christchurch Harbour and the sea. More or less midway between the enigmatic prehistoric monument of Stonehenge and the city of Salisbury, the Avon skirts around Heale House, a handsome brick-and-stone mansion, and its splendid eight acres of gardens.

The architect Detmar Blow was engaged by the owner, Louis Greville, to enlarge and remodel an older house in the early years of the twentieth century and, at around the same time, Harold Peto, then in the prime of his garden-designing career, drew up plans for the gardens. (Louis Greville was no doubt familiar with Peto's extensive work for his brother, Lord Warwick, at Easton Lodge in Essex.)

With its squared-up terraces of stone and lawn, aligned on the elevations of the house, and disciplined views along prescribed vistas, the garden is a model of its Arts and Crafts period and of Peto's mastery of spaces, with areas margined by stone balustrades and vistas terminated by curved stone seating, backed by crisp, high hedges. Peto is not credited with designing the delightful water garden on the southern boundary, however, which appears to predate his involvement. It's understood that this was the creation of Louis Greville himself, inspired by a diplomatic career that had seen him spend a

LEFT The Japanese water garden, complete with thatched teahouse. Although Harold Peto worked elsewhere in the gardens, the water garden was made by Heale's owner, Louis Greville, whose diplomatic career took him to Japan. He brought in skilled craftsmen from there to make it exactly right.

RIGHT Follow my leader: lambs investigate a stone bridge over the shallows.

number of years serving the Foreign Office in Japan. Greville's masterstroke was to make use of what was naturally to hand: the water meadows that had been a feature of agricultural life in this part of the world for centuries.

Networks of channels were long ago cut into the land, in order to flood riverside pastures with the water that sprung out of the base of the chalk hills. This had the effect of warming the ground and starting the meadow grass early into growth each spring, giving the farmer a few weeks' advantage to fatten up his livestock on fresh pasture, ahead of those on higher, drier ground.

Importing skilled craftsmen from Japan to create the water garden with its tea-house and Nikko bridge, Greville used the immediately available trout-stream waters to create something tranquil, contemplative, culturally interesting, and, perhaps, a celebratory feature to commemorate his career.

The water garden continues to be a triumph, extended along its banks with lush plantings of all the traditionally favoured waterside perennials, such as *Gunnera*, lysichiton, rodgersias, *Epimediums*, ferns, and primulas.

In 1941 Heale House passed to Greville's nephew, David Rasch, whose wife, Lady Anne, did a great deal to develop and enhance the gardens over a period of some forty years. It still remains in the Rasch family, the property having passed to Guy Rasch and his wife, Frances, in the 1990s. This latest generation has also taken on the gardens with gusto, adding to the plantings, increasing the impact of the vistas with new trees, and enhancing the garden's romantic atmosphere in its sheltered, broad valley, protected by the surrounding hills and tall trees.

OPPOSITE The gardens at Heale House are extensive and varied. Harold Peto sorted out the terraces near the house and the Rasch family has been very active, developing the gardens for many years.

RIGHT The red Nikko bridge, as seen from the interior of the thatched teahouse.

ABOVE Another area with a Japanese aesthetic is a bog garden where damp-loving iris species and primulas flourish. The stone lanterns date from the time of Louis Greville.

RIGHT Another view of the red bridge, positively laden with tresses of wisteria. The trout stream waters are shallow, but reliably flow with clean, clear water.

STANBRIDGE MILL

DORSET

The fragile habitats of Dorset's freshwater streams are being cared for in an interesting garden that is arranged around an old mill

England's chalk rivers and streams are famous around the world, not least for their fly-fishing opportunities, in idyllic landscapes. They occur only in very specific locations, having filtered through the chalk hills, producing water that is very pure and clear, but rich in minerals and fairly even in temperature, year-round.

It is good habitat for aquatic plants and many invertebrates. Fish species such as brown trout, bullhead, and brook lamprey love to breed in the gravelly riverbeds but they have for long had to share their waters with the activities of people. Of the two hundred chalk rivers known globally, 85 percent of them are found in southern and eastern England. Yet they face many challenges—in the past from busy mills, but these days chiefly from unsustainable use by water companies and agricultural chemicals leaching into the waters. These exceedingly fragile habitats require constant monitoring and conservation, not just for the streams but their associated landscapes of floodplain and grazing marsh.

In 1992, the Australian newspaperman James Fairfax (1933–2017) acquired fifty-five acres of land on both sides of the River Allen, a lovely choice for his English country home. It came with its own network of "working water"—Stanbridge Mill, its headrace, tailrace, spill pool, and associated channels that had been created to power earlier mills. He engaged the interior designer John Stefanidis to refurbish the millhouse and landscape architect Arabella Lennox-Boyd to design new gardens around the house, a project on which the two worked together for several years and during which Stefanidis designed several small buildings within the gardens.

Lennox-Boyd's design takes the carriage drive in a sweeping arc through a wildflower meadow (grazed periodically by Dorset Horn sheep), to meet an avenue of black walnut (*Juglans nigra*), followed by a stretch of common walnut (*Juglans regia*)—trees that thrive in soil where the water table can get high at times. Around the extended millhouse are formal but not overdone gardens, where the essence of the place is more important than extreme horticulture. The mill's southwest-facing front is festooned with wisterias, below which the tailrace of water bubbles out, to flow away under tresses of weeping willow. It's a scene that would have moved Monet to paint a series of canvases. Behind the house, a pretty terrace looks out onto a lawn with a surprising turfed mount. It raised the curiosity of Fairfax's guests over the years, as to whether it might be an Iron Age burial mound? A bunker? An anthill or icehouse?

East of the house where the land rises, a progression of straight hedges cut across, starting low with box, then yew, then beech, flanking a flight of steps that lead to an open lawn framed by a double row of pleached lime trees with clear trunks. This walled rectangle, at one time a kitchen garden,

A scene to move a modern-day Monet to paint a series of canvases, perhaps? The mill and the tailrace, seen between the tresses of a weeping willow tree. The lush plants in damp soil at the waterside includes hostas, *Rodgersia*, and yellow flag iris, *Iris pseudacorus*.

OPPOSITE Among foxgloves and roses, a winding path leads out to cross a nice oak bridge over the headrace and then eventually to the water meadows.

gives a glimpse of the enclosed swimming pool garden. From it, one route leads through a succession of rose-and-wisteria-draped arches out and down a long vista to the countryside, beyond a ha-ha. The most easterly enclosure conceals a working kitchen garden, with central glasshouse. The gardens take up some ten acres, but the other forty-five or so are devoted to conserving the water meadows and streams as a private nature reserve. The landscaping is elegant and respectful. As popular comedian Kenny Everett used to say, "It's all in the *best possible* taste!"

ABOVE The hard landscaping around the house features interesting changes of surfaces, with plentiful use of bricks and flints. Repetitions of plants such as box, catmint, and alliums have a calming effect.

LEFT Beside the huge leaves of *Gunnera manicata*, an inviting seat under the willow tree offers all sorts of opportunities to pause and look—in any direction.

ABOVE RIGHT Just passing the time of day. A sight to inspire relaxation.

BELOW RIGHT Toward the far end of the water meadows and subtly located among the willows, a simple thatched summerhouse designed by John Stefanidis.

THE ALNWICK GARDEN

NORTHUMBERLAND

Clever uses of fountains and rills can be found throughout the new gardens created by the Duchess of Northumberland for public enjoyment

The small market town of Alnwick lies amid the gently rolling hills of Northumberland, near the Scottish border. The castle that frowns over it is skirted to the north by the winding River Aln, which, although not a wide river, was important strategically since at least Roman times. The imposing Norman castle, begun in the 1090s (described as "very strong" in the twelfth century) is the second largest inhabited castle in England (only trumped by the royal residence at Windsor). It has witnessed numerous battles and sieges, but the crowds queueing to get inside Alnwick's castle in recent years have often come to explore the battlemented fortress used as "Hogwarts School" in the early Harry Potter films.

Home since the 1300s to the Percys, the Duke of Northumberland's family, it was Hugh Percy, a patron of the arts (who had married into the family and taken on the name and titles), who engaged Capability Brown, a fellow Northumbrian, to relandscape the adjoining parkland, from about 1760 to the 1780s. Brown, with engineer James Brindley, refashioned the river into the landscape and made a series of cascades to slow down the water's flow, giving it a more serene appearance. One contemporary commentator observed, "At the foot of the hill is the Aln, which scarcely appears to flow, or even yield a murmur, except where it turns over two cascades; and on the opposite side of the river is a large pasture-ground, beautified with clumps and single trees most tastefully disposed." The serenity of the water as it moved slowly through an artistically "natural" landscape was one of the most admired features of the grounds. Fast-forward to the twenty-first century and water again has a prominent role, but this time within an area known as the Alnwick Garden.

Some three hundred yards southeast of the castle, the twelve-acre, eighteenth-century walled garden had been, in its day, a hive of horticultural productivity, raising food and ornamental flowers under the care of a huge team of gardeners. It reached its zenith in the time of Algernon, the 4th Duke, who invested in the grounds and engaged W. A. Nesfield to create an ornamental attraction of symmetrical formal beds, decorated by patterns of low hedges, gravels, and seasonal plants raised in the range of glasshouses. As is the universal story for such places, it became obsolete in the twentieth century, especially after the effects of two world wars, eventually becoming an outcast area, closed off from 1950 and partially used for raising crops of Christmas trees.

In the mid-1990s, the present Duchess of Northumberland came up with an audacious scheme for the old walled garden and its surroundings, launching an ambitious plan for a new garden, designed by Belgian father-and-son design team Jacques and Peter Wirtz. Its main feature was a staircase

LEFT AND FOLLOWING PAGES
You can almost hear the splashy noises of the water: the formal cascade and fountains, designed by Jacques and Peter Wirtz. The staircase of water descends the hill of the former walled kitchen garden. An iceberg of a water feature: to get such quantities of water jetting and tumbling down a hill requires an enormous amount of earth-works and engineering hidden beneath the surface.

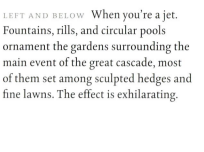

of water descending the walled garden's hillside, flanked by curvaceous hornbeam tunnels, with adjacent formal flower gardens. The nine million pounds raised to build this early phase of the garden might have seemed a big expenditure at the time, but this is an iceberg of a water feature: to get quantities of water jetting and tumbling down a hill requires an enormous amount of earthworks, infrastructure, and engineering, all hidden beneath its calm stone surface.

Two decades from the start, numerous additional areas have matured and include a Serpent Garden with stylish water features in variety by fountain maestro William Pye; a rose garden of some three thousand plants, displayed with a supporting cast of herbaceous perennials; and a vast treehouse that serves as a restaurant. The Ornamental Garden is an immense formal area of hedge-defined beds for mixtures of flowers, fruits, and vegetables among pools and rills of water. The Cherry Orchard is a spring spectacle, with 350 'Tai-Haku' cherry-blossom trees in rows, sweeping down a grassy bank. Educational features include a Poison Garden, illustrating plant toxicity; Roots and Shoots is an area for schoolchildren to learn to grow their own food, while the Elderberries, a project for seniors, is a venue designed to combat loneliness and help local people affected by dementia.

The duchess's efforts have been vindicated. The Alnwick Garden, a charitable trust, is a triumphant success on multiple levels. With some 500,000-plus visitors annually, it's one of the biggest garden attractions in the country and a key employer and investor in the community. The place which, close to a millennium ago, was a dour military fortress of the Norman conquerors lording it over the people of Northumbria, is now part of the region's beating heart of regeneration and opportunity.

Total immersion: a plunge pool is somewhat surprisingly positioned near the public entrance to the gardens (which are now opened by the National Trust), jazzing up a rather low-key entrance experience, with bright herbaceous perennials and pale stonework.

WOOLBEDING HOUSE

WEST SUSSEX

Water appears in various ways here, from swimming pools near the house to distant streams and ponds presided over by a river god

The River Rother of West Sussex makes a picturesque and lazy journey from west to east through the rolling arable lands and fertile meadows of several great estates. Along the way, its great meanders help shape and drain the ancient place of Woolbeding, a hamlet down a quiet lane near the attractive town of Midhurst.

Woolbeding House has had many owners, but in the mid-1950s, when it came to the National Trust in lieu of death duties (but without the sort of endowment funding routinely expected today), its farmland was of primary interest to the trust; the house was let. In 1973, however, Simon Sainsbury (1930–2006), collector, philanthropist, and scion of the famous grocery dynasty, took over the lease and, with his life partner, Stewart Grimshaw, set about meticulously restoring the fine Georgian house and making a garden to complement it.

First sight of the garden is actually (and generously) open for all to see from the road, for a straight drive from the wrought-iron gates to the house leads past a pair of magnificent mixed borders, each one margined by a broad carpet of turf. This area west of the house was the first to be tackled by Sainsbury and Grimshaw, who called on the advice of the fashionable designer of the day, the Anglophile American landscape architect Lanning Roper. Famed for his love of tasteful pastels, particularly combinations of white, pink, and grey, Roper focused on the white flowers and silver foliage that look so good in English gardens in the freshness of May and June. Roper's design was later modified, however, with added flower colours— principally blues, mauves, and lemon hues—injecting floral interest over a much longer season. *Buddleia*, agapanthus, and salvias in variety, *Campanula lactiflora*, *Solidago*, *Hebe*, *Potentilla*, and tall lemon hollyhocks all reinforce the vision of summer abundance. With your back to the house, looking down the drive, between the borders, the vista majestically continues across the lane, sweeping up through an eighteenth-century avenue of oak and beech.

An old garden lay immediately south of the entrance borders, partially enclosed with high walls. It lent itself to being carved up into several rectangular enclosures, separated by high yew hedges. Against the west wall, Lanning Roper designed a formal herb garden with paths of stone and herringbone-pattern brickwork, a sundial, and box topiaries; around and between them billow the aromatic herbs and annual flowers that concentrate the attentions of native wild bees and honeybees. Another compartment, crisscrossed with herringbone paths, features colour-themed beds edged in knee-high box, with the central focus on a carved Italian wellhead.

In a longer rectangle the architect Philip Jebb created a brick dining gazebo and a structure doubling as both an orangery and pool house, aligned on a swimming pool, the enclosure made more formal and decorative by

ornaments including a pair of urns; keyhole openings in the yew lead to the adjoining "rooms." Another compartment has as its focus a replica fountain of Neptune and dolphins, while the kitchen garden is a small, formal potager with obelisks supporting climbing beans and sweet peas towering over a changing cast of vegetables and salads.

Explored now, in the second decade of the twenty-first century, we see how well this garden illustrates late twentieth-century English country garden taste in "formal revival" mode, inspired by the manner of a prewar, high-maintenance Hidcote or Sissinghurst, its large spaces carved up into numerous garden "rooms," each of different character and planting. In the last decades of the twentieth century, the nation rediscovered its garden history, and began once again to enjoy formality and the craft of gardening after three postwar decades of "ground-cover," lower-maintenance designs, and preoccupations with shrubs.

Yet this is a garden with many more moods and surprises, away from the formal enclosures. Broad lawns and grassy banks with beautiful trees lead away from the house and down toward the river. Bulbs and wildflowers erupt through the long grass in spring and early summer and a particular feature is the pair of gigantic Oriental plane trees that have layered their lowest branches over a huge area, creating dapple-skinned, arthritic serpents writhing through the cow parsley.

Around the turn of the millennium the design duo Julian and Isabel Bannerman began working on a theatrical water garden at the lowest area, found at the end of a walk across sheep pastures. Its big rockwork, follies, and waterfalls are accessed via a "Gothic ruin" folly. Hidden among the ferns, a water god leans on an overturned urn spilling "springwater" down some steps and elsewhere a thatched, rustic hut with pebble mosaic floor and twiggy walls suggests late eighteenth-century Picturesque tastes. More recently, the Bannermans have created another, more modern use of water, back at the garden's public entrance, where zesty perennial planting in rich reds, violet, and orange surrounds a blue plunge pool beside the old farm buildings.

One last and unforgettable water feature, however, is installed in the main garden near the house. When an ailing cedar of Lebanon was condemned in 2008 Grimshaw commissioned the fountain designer William Pye to commemorate the venerable cedar with a striking new work where its trunk had stood. The result is Cedra, a huge polished steel vessel shaped just like the sort of champagne coupe popular in the 1960s. When Cedra is switched on, water spills evenly over the brim, coating the shiny exterior in an interesting way; when switched off, its mirror finish ensures fascinating, distorted views (including upside-down ones) of the garden, casting yet another light on this interesting, energetic, and still evolving garden.

PREVIOUS PAGES The first area to be tackled by Simon Sainsbury and Stewart Grimshaw was the straight drive, with potential for nice planting on either side. The broad grass margins set off mixed borders planted for a long season of interest.

LEFT Walls and hedges screen off the different rectangular pieces of the gardens in a very Arts and Crafts sort of way. One screened-off area is devoted to the swimming pool, dignified by paired classical urns.

OPPOSITE Aspects of a rather charming, make-believe water garden in a dell, some distance away from the main gardens.

OPPOSITE, CLOCKWISE A Gothic summerhouse perched above tumbling waters. A fine river-god, dressed in oyster shells. A pretty chinoiserie bridge, giving access across the water to a circuit.

6 COTTAGE GARDENS

The original cottage garden was a place of utility and necessity. Detail about the earliest cottage gardens is difficult to come by, but it is possible to gather enough threads of information from the medieval writings of, for example, Geoffrey Chaucer, in his rustic *Canterbury Tales*, and William Langland's *Piers Plowman*, both dating from the 1380s.

The cottage garden of their time was an enclosed space devoted to vegetables, herbs, probably some livestock, and perhaps a few decorative flowers. In those early examples the plants were chiefly native species useful for their medicinal properties, aromatic strewing herbs, and edibles. When we get to the time of Queen Elizabeth I, we learn from Shakespeare's poetry and plays much more about the flowers enjoyed by people in Tudor England. Shakespeare's contemporary John Gerard writes a great deal about the properties and medicinal qualities (sometimes accurate, sometimes not) of a wide range of plants in his famous *Herball*, of 1597.

Thomas Tusser's *A Hundred Good Points of Husbandry* (1557) offers more detail about the cottage garden looked after by the typical farmer's wife. It was a place to grow edible herbs and salad plants, as well as orchard fruits and some decorative flowers for the house. Preserving summer's bounty for the lean winter months was an important aspect.

The last three decades of the sixteenth century and early part of the seventeenth saw increased population and also the start of land enclosures that led to dire consequences for many among the peasant classes, who had relied on an open-field system to raise their own food and found it taken away from them. Some enlightened landowners, however, ensured that there was quality cottage housing built for those who worked for them. When the formal, geometric gardens of England's finer houses made away for landscape parks during the eighteenth century, cottage gardens sometimes became a valuable repository for all manner of rare and unusual plants that could no longer find a place in the opened-up landscapes of rolling grass and clumps of trees. (The walled kitchen gardens, hidden in out of sight, also took in many flowers deemed unsuitable for the newly fashionable landscape parks).

English cottages vary in style from region to region depending upon the nature of the soil and the underlying rock. The most enduring of them

OPPOSITE There are certain things one can well expect to see in a cottage garden, whether real or imitated. Roses framing the door make a good start; a muddle of relaxed and cheerful planting, too. In this case, cranesbill geraniums are joined by daylilies, red valerian, and cotton lavender.

171

have been built with bricks, brick-and-timber, or stone, depending on local materials to hand. Many more, however, were built from far less durable materials and have simply vanished. Cottages built in areas of limestone and chalk frequently have gardens displaying topiary in box and yew, these plant species naturally occurring on calcareous soils. Box and yew continue to be popular, although there have been grim times recently for box, which has been subject to major attack from diseases and the recently arrived invasive boxwood moth. Hopefully, these problems are now largely controllable, within the confines of a garden, albeit with vigilance, for box has unique desirable qualities, not entirely matched by the alternatives on offer.

Typically, as utility buildings, cottages have been erected beside the main village street or on their own lane, with a no-nonsense straight path leading up to the door. The cottage garden is always an enclosed space (though it might be shared with its neighbour), whether bounded by a rudimentary fence, hedging, or a wall. Topiary often forms part of its evergreen structure and climbing plants such as honeysuckle or a rose might well frame the entrance to garden or house, both prettily and fragrantly. Floral stalwarts are many, but may well include foxgloves, hollyhocks, primroses, columbines, lady's smock, sweet peas, marigolds (*Calendula officinalis*), tulips, wallflowers, and larkspur.

The Picturesque aesthetic of the mid-eighteenth-century onward saw people among the aristocracy and gentry building rustic cottages for their own entertainment. A fine example of this can still be seen in Queen Charlotte's cottage, located in a woodland area of the Royal Botanic Gardens, Kew. The eighteenth-century brick-and-timber house with its quaint thatched roof enabled the royal family then resident at Kew to refresh themselves and rest during their walks through the park and its bluebell wood. Numerous other examples of the cottage orné still exist in the parks of grand houses across the country.

For many families of the increasingly prosperous nineteenth century middle class, a "cottage" in the country, albeit quite a substantial one, was the ideal weekend and holiday retreat. E. M. Forster's novel *Howards End* (1910) weaves its story around the people involved with one such house. On the other hand, the paintings of Helen Allingham (1848–1926) portrayed real cottages and front gardens—their thatched roofs were often tumbledown and most likely leaked, but the bitter pill of hard workers' lives was sugared by the inclusion of relaxed and sociable inhabitants, their children, doves, geese, and whatnot. Illustrations of this type were a huge hit, though, and enhanced the notion, however mistaken, of a rural idyll, free from the cares of modern life.

A book by Sir Lawrence Weaver, *Cottages: Their Planning, Design and Materials*, was first published by *Country Life* in 1913, just prior to the First World War. In a third edition, published in 1926, gentrification of the cottage appears to be complete. Weaver notes that the war "has not destroyed but rather increased interest in the cottage which, while small and comparatively inexpensive, is built in a holiday atmosphere, provided with a garage and set in the midst of a comparatively large garden for people who want a country retreat, although the high cost of building may well postpone or modify many such projects." The book is full of examples of how to build a small and economical cottage for your staff, or a larger one with beautifully laid out garden, for your own enjoyment and leisure. A chapter devoted to designs for an "Eight-roomed Holiday Cottage" includes admirable plans for their surrounding gardens that include an orchard, kitchen garden, lawn-tennis court, rose garden, flower garden, front garden, bowling green, and pergola walk.

It's important to remember, though, that a cottage garden need not be attached to a cottage, whether with two rooms or eight. The English cottage garden style of laissez-faire planting and informal design was long ago taken up by the owners of much grander houses. The most influential examples can still be seen in the National Trust properties of Sissinghurst Castle in Kent and Hidcote Manor in Gloucestershire. Their creators made influential, enclosed cottage gardens within the framework of more splendidly architectural layouts, covering many acres.

From its adoption by influential advocates such as William Robinson and Gertrude Jekyll in the last quarter of the nineteenth century onward right up to today, the English cottage garden style is still widely adopted to surround houses both old and new, in the country or in town. The abundance and artlessness might appear to be unplanned, but successful combinations of herbaceous plants, herbs, edibles, shrubs, and perhaps some topiary usually require some thought and planning and, indeed, commitment to their regular maintenance.

OPPOSITE, CLOCKWISE Cottage garden charmers. *Astrantia major* 'Roma' at South Wood Farm. Rosy hollyhocks at Upton Grey. A tumble of roses and violas, with some *Sisyrinchium striatum*, at Shandy Hall. Striped tulips 'Carnaval de Nice,' at Shepherd House in Inveresk.

LEFT In the early years of *Country Life*, Gertrude Jekyll encouraged the magazine to celebrate the honest toil of real cottage dwellers, especially because they saved and propagated a wealth of plants that could disappear.

RIGHT Village scenes were made more picturesque with carefully placed yokels. These people, in 1910, are too smart to be yokels, but might represent the new ideal of the cottage retreat, away from the smoke and smog of the cities.

FOLLOWING PAGES A section of the cottage garden at Pettifers in Oxfordshire. Gina Price's village home is her canvas for experimental planting, often in a carefree, cottage style, but with considered plantsmanship.

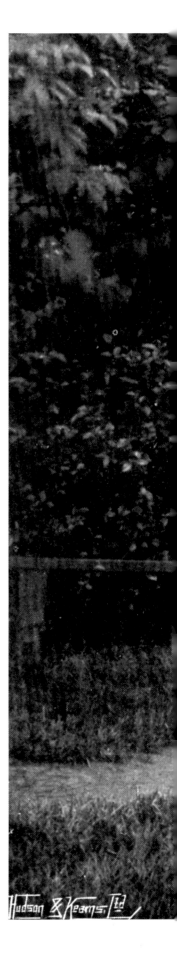

SOUTH WOOD FARM

DEVON

Despite its appearance of relaxed abundance, the garden surrounding an old thatched farmhouse is intensively cultivated and cared for

Well hidden away down rural Devonshire lanes, the garden at South Wood Farm is very much at the smart end of cottage garden style, yet it fits seamlessly into its deeply rural surroundings, cradling the farmhouse. The house, with its stone mullioned windows, thatched roof, and neat chimney stacks will be many people's dream idea of a country home. It is also very ancient, being a cross-passage house of the late 1400s, which was extended a century later, dignified with a handsome porch in the mid-seventeenth century, and then became for centuries a simple tenanted and largely untouched farmhouse and remained a working dairy farm until the early 1990s.

Its present owner, Clive Potter, acquired the property in 2005. He is personally very involved in the garden's ongoing development and, with his gardener, Will Smithson, collaborates on new planting ideas and expanding the cultivated areas with further projects.

An academic whose specialty is plant biosecurity and tree health, Potter decided early on to call in garden designer Arne Maynard to give guidance on setting out a coherent design. Maynard recalls that there had already been a charming and uncomplicated garden but "no celebration of the front of the house." This was changed by moving the vehicular point of arrival away from the house; the car parking area was relocated behind a fine old barn, and a new approach, via a cobbled footpath, leads through a handsome wooden gate into the formal garden. This walled area is a crisp design of straight paths, neat lawns, some topiary trees, and cubes of yew, all carefully placed to

LEFT Outside the wall of the front courtyard garden, ancient espaliered perry pear trees frame the gateway. The grass is filled with fritillaries, cowslips, and oxlips in spring, followed by summer's oxeye daisies.

RIGHT Through the gateway, the front garden unfolds with its lavender-edged lawns and pivotal clipped bay tree. The path and bay tree have an anchoring and balancing effect, though they are not aligned with the entrance.

create a balanced composition, with the central east/west path aligned on a smart gate in the east wall and a parallel walk aligned on the offset handsome front porch. Planted beds on the perimeter are designed to give interest in each season, within the harmonious colour range of pinks, lilacs, and purples that are magnificently set off by the backing of pale, taupe-grey stone.

Another beautifully crafted wooden gate designed by Maynard pierces the north wall, giving access to the orchard via a serpentine path winding its way between lovely native wildflowers springing out of the pasture turf. Maynard's own description of the garden (in *The Gardens of Arne Maynard*) perfectly articulates the level of craftsmanship that has so completely married this garden to its house: "We used the pattern of the banister spindles inside the house as a model for the lattice in the top half of the gate, so the carpenter who built the house has a direct hand in the new gates that lead around the garden today." Planting has been equally well thought through: "I wanted the garden to be like a beautiful piece of embroidery around the house, but one that very carefully unravelled and became simpler and more agricultural as it flowed out and met the landscape," he recalls.

The orchard north of the house is a squared-up arrangement, three rows of three, plum, gage, and damson trees, each tree set into a cube of green beech and benches in the orchard enable beautiful views back to the house. Another old wall separates the orchard from the kitchen garden. Here are formal raised beds made of oak providing productivity and prettiness in equal measure. Much use is made of step-over apple and pear trees; these useful dwarf trees, of single low espaliers, make harvesting easy and ensure that light is still able to reach the other crops in the formally laid out beds. And, as this garden is also about pattern as well as productivity, four tiny knot gardens have been created in miniature box hedging, seasonally infilled with airy annual flowers.

This kitchen garden confirms the good sense in taking an old-fashioned approach. Smithson runs it on organic principles, with a crop rotation, no digging, and regular mulching. Staking is with homemade supports from hazel trees growing elsewhere in the garden. Head south back to the house from the kitchen garden to a small courtyard that, although it is on the west side, is shaded by trees and therefore invigorated with pots of ferns, agapanthus, and white annual flowers.

Those are the formal areas of garden, beyond which lie the informal areas that blend into the countryside: the hazel copse, a large and informal orchard of old local fruit varieties, and, across the drive, extensive wildflower meadows. This remarkable collaboration between owner, gardener, and designer provides many lessons in how to achieve harmony and chic cottage garden style through spatial awareness, craftsmanship, and respect for the environment as a whole.

LEFT Still in the front courtyard: the roses left and right of the gate are 'Felicite Parmentier.' A yew topiary bulks up the corner.

OPPOSITE Oak-edged raised beds in the kitchen and cutting garden, with a knot-garden arrangement down the left-hand side. Knee-high, step-over apples edge some of the beds, a good way of growing some apples without taking up any room.

LEFT The formal nature of the front courtyard is plain to see from an upstairs window. Around the foot of the bay tree is a low-growing thyme, *Thymus serpyllum* 'Magic Carpet.' By late June the alliums are over, but their globular seed heads are sculptural; white foxgloves and roses take over and the lavenders have yet to start their flowering.

RIGHT Rich burgundy 'Masterpiece' lupins, alliums 'Mount Everest,' 'Purple Sensation,' and *A. aflatunense*, with thalictrums and roses.

COTTAGE ROW

DORSET

The classic children's book The Secret Garden, *by Frances Hodgson Burnett, inspired the creation of this partially walled, small country garden*

In rural Dorset, Cottage Row consists of three adjoining cottages, turned into a single homey-but-spacious dwelling in the twentieth century and further enhanced in this century by its present owners, Michael and Carolyn Pawson. They took it on as a place to enjoy peaceful retirement, but Carolyn was already a gardener of long experience, having personally created and tended a four-acre garden of complex borders, choice shrubs, and trees at Windsor for nearly two decades.

Moving to the Dorset cottage was a different challenge altogether—much more manageable, at half an acre, but in a windier location, and with very different soil: alkaline (chalks and flints) instead of Windsor's heavy, sticky clay. The chalky earth at Cottage Row didn't present a problem, since Carolyn chose to develop interests in calcareous plants that would thrive. But it is potentially hungry ground, and therefore regularly enriched with cow dung.

The garden slopes gently southward away from the house and its best views are in the area known as the Formal Garden, beside the lane that gives access to the property. From the lane, a wooden gate in a high brick wall leads directly into the garden. "I'd read *The Secret Garden* as a child and the idea of going through an old wooden door and finding something special inside was what I wanted to create," Carolyn recalls.

In order to fulfil that vision, an old privet hedge that had formed the boundary along the lane was dug out. In its place, the Pawsons built a high wall of mellow bricks, which blend in with the old brickwork of the house. On the wall's lane side, annual and biennial flowers such as corn cockle, nigella,

LEFT From the central part of the garden, looking back to the new wall built alongside the lane. The idea of having a gateway into a "secret garden" had been somewhere in Carolyn Pawson's mind, probably since she read Frances Hodgson Burnett's famous story of *The Secret Garden*.

RIGHT A relaxed place to sit, looking southward onto the main garden.

PREVIOUS PAGES The main border, with magenta wands of *Gladiolus byzantinus*, blue *Iris sibirica*, white astrantias, seed heads of alliums, and the emerging coppery foliage of a purple *Cotinus coggygria*.

poppies, and hollyhocks flourish in a semi-wild way. A soft pink rose, 'The Garland,' tumbles over its top, while inside the garden, the wall backs a luscious border that includes *Rosa complicata*, the moss rose 'William Lobb,' magenta spires of *Gladiolus byzantinus*, blue *Iris sibirica*, a purple-leaved *Cotinus* grown for colour contrast, sprinklings of alliums, and various hardy geraniums.

Single-flowered *Rosa glauca* has blue grey leaves that tone well with the wall, and the border is also home to some of Carolyn's speciality: her very large collection of clematis species and cultivars. Alongside the bottom edge of the lawn, a long pergola is draped in white Japanese wisteria, 'Adelaide d'Orleans' roses, and the clematises 'Perle d'Azur,' 'Prince Charles,' and 'Comtesse de Bouchaud,' taking over for the summer, providing flowery shade over a York stone path.

Westward, another path is aligned on the kitchen windows, with borders alongside and openings through a backing yew hedge. These lead to a small kitchen garden (Michael's domain) and "the grandchildren's garden" with a croquet/football lawn but plenty of interest in the plantings that surround it. On one side, a tall *Robinia* tree is garlanded with a beautiful pink rose, 'Dentelle de Malines,' and also the very high-reaching rambler rose, 'Bobbie James.' From there, another path leads northward, up a series of broad, shallow steps that terminate in a small water feature and a seat for relaxation. It's hard to imagine that Carolyn ever relaxes, though, for her garden is full of horticultural treasures, including many more clematis.

The clematis plants are everywhere: adorning walls and a pergola, weaving into trees and shrubs and clambering over arches. There seem to be too many to count, but one of them has pride of place above all others. *Clematis* 'Jewel of Merk' was specially created and named for Carolyn and was a surprise landmark birthday gift from her husband. Such things are not done in a trice. The plant was three years in development and Michael drove to Leiden in Holland just before Carolyn's birthday to collect her plants. He is, she says, "the most romantic man on the planet!"

ABOVE, LEFT TO RIGHT A gallery of Clematis, with amethyst 'Comtesse de Bouchard'; ruby 'Madame Julia Correvon'; dainty pink *C. texensis* 'Princess Diana'; violet 'Jewel of Merk,' also listed as 'Happy Birthday.'

OPPOSITE The south-facing terrace surrounds an old well, outside the kitchen window. *Erigeron karvinskianus* seeds itself into cracks between the paving stones.

The garden at Greyhounds is long and slim, widening from about halfway up; many gardens in the town are of odd shapes, as cottages were tucked in here and there down the centuries. As Greyhounds was formerly an inn, its garden area used to be stabling for horses. The garden now flourishes.

GREYHOUNDS

OXFORDSHIRE

Stepped and sloping ground elevate this elongated cottage garden in a rural market town, giving a series of views over its richly planted beds

A row of secret gardens—long, thin, and with higgledy-piggledy boundaries—creeps up the hill behind closely packed stone houses lining the south side of Sheep Street in Burford. One of them enjoys local renown for having been attached to the editorial office of *The Countryman* magazine for a substantial part of the twentieth century, although in 1999 it returned to being a private house.

When Rosemary Verey was invited to write about it for *The Countryman*'s Spring 1986 edition, she first marched the reader up to the orchard at the far end of the garden, also its highest point, in order to turn around and look northward over the rooftops and across the Windrush Valley to the hilly pastures beyond. "The view will take your breath away, for every day there is a subtle difference in the light, the clouds, the direction of the sun's rays ... the spire of the church, the stone roofs of the snugly built houses, distant fields and the long skyline help to make time stand still ... "

The remarkable views and timeless Cotswolds cottage atmosphere are still as Verey would have known them, but the quantity and variety of plants at Greyhounds has been vastly extended, thanks to the green-fingered ministrations of Christopher Moore who, divides his time between work commitments in Ireland and Cotswold life in Burford.

Originally the building now known as Greyhounds was a wool merchant's house, probably built in the late fifteenth century. At some stage it became the Greyhound Inn, a hostelry on what used to be a drovers' road linking Gloucester with Oxford and London, along which shepherds drove their flocks of sheep to market. It remained an inn after 1805, which is when the ancient timber house was refaced in stone. Moore dates the creation of a proper garden behind the premises to the years following 1908, when one Elizabeth Percival, sister of the local rector, bought the property for £700.

Percival seems to have extended the garden area by acquiring adjacent pieces of ground. She graded the sloping land, creating terraces and low retaining walls on the area where horses had been stabled previously. Greyhounds, as it later came to be called, remained a *maison de maître* in various ownerships until 1946, when it became the publishing home of *The Countryman* magazine for half a century, with an open door to the garden for any passerby curious enough to step in through the large arched passageway.

Since 1999 Moore and his partner, antique dealer (and Burford native) Michael Taubenheim, have painstakingly restored and stylishly furnished the house, revealing its layers of history without compromising on modern comforts. The garden has also burgeoned, not least through Moore's passion for a completely different genre: the historic houses and gardens of Ireland.

Abutting the rear of the house is a sun-trap terrace, paved with local stone a century ago, and now furnished with comfy loungers and iron chairs.

Terra-cotta pots filled with box and bay tree topiaries and assorted hostas are carefully arranged, and the walls on three sides are decorously smothered by a huge *Magnolia grandiflora*, grapevines, and an ancient wisteria. Salvaged things, such as old signs and decorative ironwork, also find a home here.

A few steps lead on into the garden, past a tiny box parterre where choice ferns are cultivated. Suddenly, all the restraint and greenery garlanding the house give way to the first in a series of exuberant borders, jam-packed in true cottage garden style with memories, cuttings, things swapped and given away, things sown and things—such as the very beautiful hollyhocks—that have lingered here for decades.

This is also where a small cottage comes into the frame, straddling the boundary between this garden and that of the house next door. "It was cottage for a gardener whose labours were shared by the two houses," says Moore. "Apparently, Duncan Grant and Vanessa Bell rented it and used it as a studio in the early 1930s." In summer it is almost hidden by a huge espalier pear, an abundance of hollyhocks, salvias, meadow rues, poppies, steely blue *Eryngiums*, and the "seriously wonderful" but unaccountably neglected (in English gardens) *Lactuca plumieri*. The latter is an ornamental lettuce bearing bright blue dandelion flowers similar to those of common chicory.

A stone footpath climbs the steady slope, leading between a narrow bed margining the foot of the east wall and the abundance of deep, open borders on the west side, around an old croquet lawn.

Many plants are from celebrated old Irish gardens, now passed on from their original ownership. They come from places such as Beech Park (where plantsman David Shackleton cultivated some ten thousand species and cultivars in the two-acre walled garden of his estate at Clonsilla in the years after the war) and Primrose Hill, the Dublin home of Robin Hall, another member of Ireland's gardening cognoscenti. The rose 'Lady Hillingdon,' and "huge old corms of *Cyclamen hederifolium*" came from Woodville, the now demolished home of the twentieth-century Irish painters Eva and Letitia Hamilton.

Beyond the smooth croquet lawn is a small orchard of large old apple trees, a very large walnut, and a mulberry, the last two almost certainly dating from plantings made a century ago by Elizabeth Percival, though the apples could be older.

Reaching the top lawn, from where Rosemary Verey had so much enjoyed a lookout over Burford's ancient roof tiles, the borders are set back close to high, dry-stone walls and in the very top southwest corner is an elegant reading room designed by Christopher Moore containing a fireplace and Georgian furniture, with a window looking down the garden to the village rooftops and upward sweep of the valley.

PREVIOUS PAGES A view looking back down from near the top end of the garden. It takes in the quaint and wonky rooftops of the town's old houses, overlooking the Windrush valley. The croquet lawn is edged with topiary buns of box and elegant garden seats.

OPPOSITE One of the garden borders, containing phlox, geraniums, euphorbia, and backed by topiary figures of yew, about to be trimmed.

RIGHT The borders are crammed with Christopher Moore's plants. In front of an old espalier pear against the wall, *Crambe cordifolia* has done its bit; hollyhocks and lilies are yet to come, while egg-yolk-hued *Inula magnifica* rises behind amethyst campanulas.

GWAENYNOG

DENBIGHSHIRE

The garden that belonged to author Beatrix Potter's uncle was the original home of Mr. McGregor, featured in her Tale of the Flopsy Bunnies

Set in gently rolling countryside just southwest of Denbigh, Gwaenynog in North Wales originated as a late medieval house of the prominent Myddelton family who became increasingly powerful in North Wales in Tudor times, acquiring a number of important estates. David Myddelton was receiver-general (a chief financial officer) for North Wales under the kings Edward IV and Richard III and it's believed his son, Roger, built Gwaenynog's timber-framed, Tudor hall house. Later in the sixteenth century it was extended it into an H-plan and, in the mid-eighteenth century, there was further enhancement in the time of Colonel John Myddelton, who redecorated the interior with rococo plasterwork, marble chimneypieces, and other refinements suitable for hosting VIP guests, such as Thomas Pennant, the noted antiquary and traveller, and Samuel Johnson, the famous man of letters. When the Burton family (who still live there) acquired Gwaenynog, in about 1870, they also made alterations, covering the timber-framed house in limestone on the garden side, while adding some of the Gothic flourishes that were then the height of fashion in Victorian architecture.

All of this is of special interest because Frederick Burton of Gwaenynog was the uncle of Beatrix Potter, who naturally spent a number of holidays there. We know that the much-loved creator of Peter Rabbit used the gardens of Gwaenynog as background scenery in *The Tale of the Flopsy Bunnies*, for a number of views that appear in the children's story are still there today. The potting shed in the walled garden, for example, with its Gothic window in the upper floor, became Mr. McGregor's house. Views down the box-edged path, along which Mr. McGregor trudged, and another, across a broad lawn, remain pretty much as they were.

Always keenly observant of her surroundings, Beatrix Potter noted the house's layers of architectural interest, once describing it as, "Very odd, a date on the back premises 1571, the front black and white, and the more modern garden-front, stone. Two large rooms, dining-room and music-room 1776, the most modern. Upstairs all up and down and uneven, low beams and long passages, some very fine chimney-pieces, and one room panelled." She made sketches of the interesting interiors, but, as always, it was the outdoors that had greatest appeal. "The garden is very large," she confided in her private journal, which was written in code, to confound any prying eyes. "Two-thirds surrounded by a red-brick wall with many apricots, and an inner circle of old grey apple trees on wooden espaliers. It is very productive but not tidy, the prettiest kind of garden, where bright old-fashioned flowers grow amongst the currant bushes." It inspired the way she planted her famous Hilltop garden in the Lake District, when she moved there as a successful author.

Foxgloves, delphiniums, lupins in various shades, and pale pink to white astrantias all form a jolly jumble in a cutting bed in the walled garden. As the house belonged to Beatrix Potter's uncle, she visited from time to time and established the garden in her mind as Mr. McGregor's.

LEFT The cabbage patch, which would have been a beloved haunt of Beatrix Potter's naughty fictional rabbits. The walled garden was the setting for *The Tale of the Flopsy Bunnies*, first published by Frederick Warne in 1909.

ABOVE RIGHT Flowers for cutting but also ornamenting the walled garden, including lupins, lady's mantle (*Alchemilla mollis*), red valerian, and a deep violet campanula.

BELOW RIGHT The Gwaenynog potting shed, with its unmistakable outline and Gothic window, which served as the model for Mr. McGregor's house in *The Tale of the Flopsy Bunnies*.

Another description of it appears in "Llewellyn's Well," an unfinished, later book. "In summer there were white and damask roses and the smell of thyme and musk. In spring there were green gooseberries and throstles [song thrushes], and the flowers they call ceninen [daffodils]. And leeks and cabbages also grew in that garden ... and between long straight grass alleys, and apple-trained espaliers, there were beds of strawberries and mint and sage. And great holly trees and a thicket of nuts; it was a great big garden."

During the twentieth century, much of the garden disappeared and was grassed over for lower maintenance and pony paddocks. The walls, the potting shed, and some old apple trees remained, however, and since the 1980s, substantial restoration has been done, with reference to old family photographs and, of course, Potter's drawings and paintings. The return of its old-fashioned plants completes the picture of an old walled garden, much as the artist knew it.

ABOVE LEFT An illustration by Beatrix Potter, drawn up from sketches she made within the walled garden at Gwaenynog. Here, in *The Tale of The Flopsy Bunnies*, the Bunnies watch Mr. McGregor go into "his house" in the far distance, (the actual building is shown bottom right, on page 199).

ABOVE CENTER The entrance to the stone-built potting shed at Gwaenynog, which served as "Mr. McGregor's house" in *The Tale of the Flopsy Bunnies*.

ABOVE RIGHT Structures supporting tree fruit and climbers within the walled garden, as sketched from life by Beatrix Potter. Note the traditional box-edged beds lining the paths. In this illustration, the "flopsy bunnies" are scampering home.

RIGHT Brightening up the potting shed interior: a more recent sketch (not by Potter), based upon the scene shown in the top left illustration.

OPPOSITE A lead model rabbit lurks among the foliage and flowers of lady's mantle, *Alchemilla mollis*.

LOWDER MILL

WEST SUSSEX

Rare-breed ducks take to the water and vibrant dahlias fill out the cutting beds in this joyful cottage garden laid out beside an old water mill

Across the country throughout the year—but chiefly in summer—temporary bright yellow arrows and posters at the roadside point to a suggested direction of travel, along with the tempting words, "Garden Open Today." This is the livery of the National Garden Scheme, a charity founded in 1927 that gives access on prearranged days to more than 3,500 exceptional private gardens in England and Wales (Scotland has its own similar scheme, separately run). The generosity of garden owners and volunteers has enabled the NGS to raise more than £55 million for nursing and health charities so far (particularly those involved with hospices and cancer nursing), achieving a record donation of £3.1 million for 2018. Many gardens in this book are part of the scheme including the charming Lowder Mill on the River Wey.

Meandering northward through the "Gertrude Jekyll country" of west Surrey, the Wey eventually adds its fresh waters to the Thames. Lowder Mill's owners, John and Anne Denning, bought their house and mill in 2002 and were interested to discover that water extraction (though not necessarily milling) has occurred there since at least 1367. From the seventeenth century, the Wey's banks were peppered with many mills producing a variety of goods such as flour, corn, animal feed, paper, cloth, leather, and gunpowder.

The Dennings painstakingly renovated the eighteenth-century house and derelict mill (although none of its machinery remains). They also restored the millpond, now much enjoyed by various rare-breed ducks. Of their six acres, three are woodland, about one acre is water, and the remaining two acres are plant-rich gardens in continuous development and refinement.

Garden designer Bunny Guinness was called in early on; she was a good choice, providing a sympathetic approach to the farmhouse vernacular surroundings, where trained apple trees cling to the house walls. In *Country Life,* Steven Desmond's description of the courtyard between the house and mill perfectly captured it: "filled with an organised riot of select bricolage. Pots of every description are grouped in a distinctly rococo way ... a skilful ordering of objects ... a happy blend of prettiness and elegance, with neither quite gaining the upper hand."

On rising ground above the entrance court, a simple cross path divides four large, box-edged beds that in summer are crammed with assorted dahlias, while sweet peas clamber over hazel frames. Their free-form jumble of colours certainly suits the overall cottage garden ambience. Follow a straight path westward to the highly productive kitchen garden, where raised beds are neatly contained with boards. Iron arches over the pathway are festooned with dangling broad beans, giving keyhole views back to the pretty house. Anne Denning propagates everything, so there are keepsake plants to buy on the days the garden is open to the public.

Near the source of the River Wey, Lowder Mill and its house close by were painstakingly restored by the owners, who then turned to making the gardens. Four box-edged beds on rising ground are crammed with jolly summer flowers such as these assorted dahlias, zinnias, and sweet peas growing on hazel frames.

ABOVE LEFT A quacking good idea: assorted rare breed ducks make their way across the garden to the header pool that for long fed the working mill.

BELOW LEFT Is it time for tea? Daisy the fox terrier sits patiently among the hostas and ferns.

RIGHT Damp ground is awash with pale blue *Iris sibirica*. The old mill building, which was painstakingly restored by the Dennings. It has not been used as a mill for a long time, but on days the garden is open, teas are served from it, in a quaint assortment of cups and saucers.

7 PLANT COLLECTIONS AND COLLECTORS

The actress Elizabeth Taylor famously collected diamonds. Another Elizabeth, the Tudor Queen, had a passion for pearls. Elvis Presley collected statues of Joan of Arc; countless numbers of people collect statues of Elvis. If I had the garage space and an acquisitive nature, I'd be tempted to collect not Ferraris, but Fiat 500s—the modern ones that come in such an array of lovely colours; I've never seen an unappealing one. Psychologists say that all collectors are seeking pleasure when they search for and find something new to add to their existing cache, owing to psychological reinforcers that feed into a primitive pleasure centre in the brain (the *nucleus accumbens*, since you asked).

Although most collections consist of passive objects, botanical accumulations of living plants go back into earliest known history, from the Sumerians and Egyptians to the ancient Greeks and Chinese. Those very early collections were for necessity rather than pleasure, being medicinal and perhaps for ritual or magical purposes. Chrysanthemums in China were grown as a flowering herb some 1,500 years BC, but the tradition of cultivating different ornamental varieties began in the fourth century AD. Tree peonies, herbaceous peonies, apricots, hollyhocks, and waterlilies followed, and later, camellias.

Given sufficient rolling acres of slightly acidic ground I could be tempted to align with the Chinese and have a crush on camellias. No land is required, however, for today's most fashionable collectors' plant: *Galanthus*, the snowdrop. This little bulb's cult status had been building, reasonably quietly, for well over a century before it became worthy of the national news. But in February 2012, a single bulb of *Galanthus woronowii* 'Elizabeth Harrison,' with unique yellow markings, sold on eBay for £725. More than thirty online bidders were in the end outbid by Thompson & Morgan, the mail order seed company based in Suffolk. (That eBay record has since been trumped, however, by a cultivar named Golden Fleece, bred by nurseryman Joe Sharman and ten years in the making; it achieved £1,390 for a single bulb in 2015.)

It's easy to see why so many people are in thrall to snowdrops. Individually, they are very small, so anyone with the tiniest pocket of outdoor space can amass a significant collection in scores of little pots of the tiny bulbs, each one containing something a little different from the next and, to the galanthophile

OPPOSITE Delectable collectibles: psychologists say that all collectors are seeking pleasure when they search for and find something new to add to their existing cache; snowdrops are among the plants that fire up a collecting instinct in many gardeners. At least they are small and easy to accommodate. This double-flowered beauty is *Galanthus* 'Hyppolyta.'

Diminutive treasures, the appeal of snowdrops is that so many variables have occurred, in such a small plant.

The inner markings resemble a somewhat gloomy countenance, leading to this snowdrop being called *Galanthus elwesii* 'Grumpy.'

The long outer petals in this one inspired someone to name this *Galanthus nivalis* variety 'Walrus.'

People go mad for the yellow ovary and inner petal markings of 'Galanthus Primrose Warburg.'

A perfect poppet, *Galanthus plicatus* 'Tomoko.'

(as snowdrop fanciers are called), desirable. You can spend not very much money on the more common ones, or part with quite a lot of cash and go for the rarities. Snowdrop fancying is a convivial occupation involving luncheons, galas, and teas, albeit confined to the coldest and darkest part of year, January and February being their season. Traditions of snowdrop collecting are particularly strong in the Cotswolds (which has many areas of ground that suit them admirably), and also Scotland, both regions boasting a long history of collecting, though plenty of wonderful snowdrop gardens exist elsewhere.

Despite the great sheets of snowdrops that inhabit numerous woodlands with heavy, damp ground, *Galanthus* species hail from southern and eastern Europe, Asia Minor, and the Levant. The common, spreading snowdrop arrived here mysteriously, advises botanist Mark Griffiths: "Perhaps sometime early in the Renaissance. It was already becoming naturalized by the seventeenth century when John Gerard tentatively recorded the vernacular name by which we still know it. It muddled along largely unnoticed for nearly two hundred years. Then, towards the nineteenth century, just when one might have expected its monochrome modesty to be eclipsed by an empire's worth of exotica, we fell in love with it."

Snowdrops never reached the feverish feeding frenzy that accompanied tulipomania, the speculative trade in tulip bulbs in seventeenth-century Holland, which both made and lost fortunes. Tulips were, however, the first of the "florist" flowers to be bred according to a strict code regulating size, form, and colouring, followed in the late eighteenth century by auricula and polyanthus, carnation, pink, hyacinth, anemone, and ranunculus, grown by artisans, who raised their blooms expressly for winning prizes on the show bench.

Other tales of English plant obsessions are profiled in the gardens that follow. Suffice to say, though, the subject of plant collecting past and present is so vast that it deserves several volumes on its own account. And will the striking Elizabeth Harrison snowdrop, so famously acquired by Thompson & Morgan in 2012, be distributed through the nursery trade soon? Unfortunately, it was despatched to Holland for "bulking up"—i.e., propagating—and has never been seen again.

ABOVE Snowdrops make lovely winter displays around the feet of trees, as at Painswick Rococo Garden in Gloucestershire.

RIGHT Part of the snowdrop collection at Worcester College in Oxford.

LEONARDSLEE

WEST SUSSEX

The rhododendrons and azaleas collected by Leonardslee's nineteenth- and twentieth century owners create dazzling displays through the spring months

Saint Leonard's Forest in Sussex is one of the ancient woodlands of England. Having soil too sour to be cultivated, it was left intact in the Middle Ages when substantial acreages elsewhere were cut down to make way for crops. Only in the sixteenth and seventeenth centuries did its mighty trees get felled, when great tracts of the locality were turned rapidly into an industrial landscape; it became the hub of iron-smelting, making cannon for colonial and overseas campaigns. Although the woods have regrown in recent centuries, the region is still peppered with reminders of its industrial past; in particular, there are many "hammer ponds" that held the water that once powered furnace bellows and the hammers used to crush ore-rich stone.

This industrial legacy is put to spectacular use at Leonardslee, a tranquil two-hundred-acre garden largely set on the slopes of a valley. It was planted throughout the nineteenth century and into the early decades of the twentieth, when shiploads of exciting new plants were arriving from far-flung expeditions. Its hammer ponds are now a series of reflective mirrors for two-hundred-year-old plantations of exotic trees, supplemented with brilliant displays of spring blooms.

Several families contributed to the garden's early development. In 1803, the Aldridge family, who owned most of Saint Leonard's Forest, sold a thousand acres of it to one Charles George Beauclerk, who built a house and walled kitchen garden on the crest of the hill. It's a great location for such a venture: the hilltop enjoys magnificent views along the valley and across to the distant hills of the South Downs. Beauclerk extended his landholding and also began planting the valley with ornamental trees and shrubs, in particular, an "American garden," very much a novelty in his time, containing magnolias, rhododendrons, azaleas, and other flowering shrubs "of great height, growth and beauty."

The estate came up for sale again in 1852 and was bought by landowner-businessman W. Egerton Hubbard, who demolished the earlier house and replaced it with a much grander Italianate mansion. He also gave the property the name of Leonardslee (i.e., Leonard's valley), and maintained the high standards of the gardens.

Close by, Robert Loder, also a rich landowner with substantial estates in several countries, was creating a garden of similar type at the High Beeches, near Handcross. He later became high sheriff of Sussex and was made a baronet, conferring him with the hereditary title "Sir." Through business and social connections, the Loders and Hubbards were almost certainly already intertwined, and Robert Loder's eldest son, Edmund (1849–1920) married Marion Hubbard of Leonardslee in 1878 (and his younger brother, Gerald, later acquired the Wakehurst Place estate, also in the vicinity). So began the

Numerous little paths lead up, down, and around the rhododendron woodlands that cover the valley sides. The season for viewing the flowering of the rhododendrons is chiefly April, May, and June, although the walks and ponds are lovely at any time, and autumn boasts lots of vivid fall foliage.

PREVIOUS PAGES A gallery of views of the extraordinary Leonardslee gardens.
LEFT A woodland walk through bluebells.
MIDDLE Within the Rock Garden, among its bright azaleas.
TOP RIGHT One of the great rhododendron 'Loderi' hybrids, bred in the garden
BOTTOM RIGHT Another dazzling walk, with pale pink rhododendron 'Loderi Venus' at the end of the visible path.

development of a multibranch dynasty of plant-collecting, exchange, and no doubt a certain amount of rivalry among these three great woodland gardens being made by relatives on the sandstone hillsides of mid-Sussex.

In its heyday, Leonardslee was noted for its collections of, among other things, camellias, rhododendrons, alpines, and bamboos, all of which had peer group approval among connoisseurs. But there were also extensive orchards with 120 varieties of apples and pears and, under glass, 100 varieties of carnation.

Leonardslee stayed in the Loder family throughout the twentieth century, although nine hundred of its acres were sold in lean times after the First World War. For many years it was opened as a visitor attraction, but eventually it was sold to an overseas buyer in 2010 and thereafter closed to the public.

But these are exciting times for the garden. In 2017, South African–based entrepreneur Penny Streeter bought the (by now) two-hundred-acre Leonardslee estate and has invested heavily in restoring the gardens, which had been neglected in recent times. Dredging the silted-up ponds, reopening glades and paths that had become lost in undergrowth, and creating state-of-the-art visitor facilities have been expedited with speed and vision. There's also a young vineyard on the bare hilltop. It's a family business, with Streeter's energetic son, Adam, at the helm.

Leonardslee was—and is again—a place worthy of pilgrimage during spring, its peak season. Early spring is dominated by towering magnolias and the huge collection of camellias. As the season progresses, we see the main season of plant hunters' rhododendrons, and the vividly blooming azaleas. The latter coincide with the flowering of a homegrown range of 'Loderi hybrid' rhododendrons—towering shrubs weighed down with trusses of huge, ice-cream-coloured blooms wafting dolly-mixture scents along the winding valley paths. Other months have their highlights, but there is no lovelier time to get lost on the woodland and lakeside paths than May. In summer there's a soft green-ness to the valley and lovely shaded walks, while autumn is again spectacular, due to the number of species whose fall tints are reflected in the lakes.

It's interesting to note that *Country Life* magazine featured the garden in one of its first editions, in 1897. Then, the article's chief interest was a menagerie of exotic animals. "In this paradise … the new animals which have made their home in this old country wander at large," the author observed. "None but interesting and beautiful creatures have been introduced … they all produce young regularly, a great part of the stock have been born and bred in the park." Sir Edmund Loder's private free-range zoo included wallabies (whose younger generations are still a feature of the gardens), plus, for many years, beavers, Algerian moufflon, emus, Patagonian hares, antelope, axis deer, Persian gazelles, bush turkeys, barasingha, capybaras, kangaroos, and kookaburras.

Only the wallabies' younger generations are still resident. A much more recent attraction, added by Robin Loder in 1998, is a fascinating one-twelfth scale model country house garden. Devised by model maker Helen Holland, the exhibition was added to yearly. It now fills a barn, displaying a pint-sized country estate and its local market town, complete with shops from butcher's to haberdasher's, the display brought to life with numerous automata. "It's somewhere people can go and enjoy when it rains," Loder once said. Well, rain or shine, this garden is both welcoming and fascinating.

OPPOSITE Spring wonder: a gallery of details in the gardens at Leonardslee. Since this set of photographs was taken, the gardens were bought by South African-based entrepreneur Penny Streeter in 2017. She has invested heavily in the gardens, restoring the neglected paths, dredging the sequence of silted-up ponds, and creating state-of-the-art visitor facilities. Leonardslee is back on the map, the glorious Technicolor of the woodland occurring chiefly April to June, inclusive.

One of the loveliest places to visit in West London in springtime is the Royal Botanic Gardens at Kew in Richmond. Spring bulbs carpet the ground and the bluebells in the arboretum run an inky-violet-blue carpet through the woodland. The collection of blossoming Japanese cherries is a wondrous sight, especially with trees like this *Prunus* 'Shirofugen,' among the daffodils.

ROYAL BOTANIC GARDENS, KEW

GREATER LONDON

The world-famous botanical gardens contain very many specialist collections of plants, both within the glasshouses and in over three hundred acres of the park

On the western reaches of London, in a glorious riverside setting, the Royal Botanic Gardens at Kew hardly need introduction. The premier seat of learning for all things horticultural and botanical is also an enormously popular visitor attraction, on the to – do list of millions of visitors from all over the world. Kew therefore continually revises and adds to the enjoyment of its three hundred acres with refreshed areas of planting and spectacular installations, such as the Hive, an enormous mesh frame you can walk into and experience "being in a beehive"—listening in on live bee activity—the whole structure set into a wildflower meadow. The Treetop Walkway is exactly as described—a raised walk through the treetops to gain aerial views over the gardens and magnificent historic glasshouses.

That these wonderful gardens have survived so close to the capital is due to the area having been favoured for various royal residences in times past. "Kew Gardens" embraces an area that was originally two royal estates. King James I had a hunting lodge in a nearby area known as the Old Deer Park, and in the late seventeenth century William III had a house and park with a formal garden by George London, reaching down to the river. Down the centuries and up to modern times, numerous great names have been associated with the grounds, which were enhanced early on by the interest of Princess Augusta (1719–1772) and, especially, Queen Charlotte (1744–1818), who was an amateur botanist and collector of trees. Some gifted people have brought permanent features to the grounds—Victorian architect Decimus Burton's Temperate House and Palm House (both recently restored) and Sir William Chambers's Great Pagoda (also just restored) are among the great historical landmarks, while temporary delight is refreshed almost yearly, with treats such as Dale Chihuly's wondrous glass installations of 2019.

Kew's vast web of links across the world goes back to the earliest days of plant exploration, which now embraces the crucial work of plant conservation. (The Millennium Seed Bank, housed at Kew's satellite "country garden" at Wakehurst Place in West Sussex, is a global resource of frozen living seed, preserving wild species, especially those at risk of extinction.) Its international reach is also celebrated in the gardens, of course, not least through its living plant collections displayed within the gardens and glasshouses, and features such as its atmospheric Japanese landscape. Sheets of crocuses lighting up the lawns see off the end of winter and the cherry blossom collection, depicted here, is one of the highlights of spring in the arboretum area, along with Queen Charlotte's Cottage, set among bluebell woods, a fleeting glory for just three to four weeks each year.

LEFT "Come down to Kew in Blossom Time ..." Reaching for the sky, *Prunus* 'Matsumae-beni-tamanishiki.'

OPPOSITE, CLOCKWISE More of Kew's cherry blossom collection. *Clockwise, from top left*: Pink in bud, opening to frilly white, *Prunus* 'Matsumae-beni-tamanishiki.' Soft, baby-pink *Prunus* 'Oshokun.' Simply white, *Prunus* 'Taki-nioi.' Changeable, rose-tinged *Prunus* 'Matsumae-shizuka.'

FOLLOWING PAGES The architectural wonders of Kew.

LEFT The Great Pagoda, one of several Chinese buildings by Sir William Chambers, was completed in 1762 for Princess Augusta. Following major restoration, it reopened in 2019. Now visitors can climb its stairs to see the spectacular views.

RIGHT The Temperate House, reopened in 2018 after detailed restoration, is the world's largest Victorian glasshouse. Built in 1860–63 from a design by Decimus Burton (also creator of Kew's great Palm House), it houses some fifteen hundred plant species, including some of the rarest and most threatened.

BRAMDEAN HOUSE

HAMPSHIRE

As well as its carefully chosen palette of herbaceous plants for its famous twin borders, there are collections of sweet peas and nerines in great variety

In the western reaches of the South Downs, Bramdean is an ancient village in a shallow valley, with a Norman church and pretty houses strung like beads on the busy-ish road linking Winchester and Petersfield. All around, the gentle arcs of the chalk hills are patchworked with arable fields, while close by, at Cheriton, emerge the source springs of the famous Itchen trout stream. The region is loved by many for its seemingly timeless and unchanging appearance, its great trees, and its vernacular buildings, but such resonance has only been achieved through strenuous local efforts to keep it so against innumerable pressures of the modern age.

Bramdean House, built about 1740 in mellow, rosy brick, sits near the road, although it's easy to miss, being effectively screened by a huge cumulus cloud of closely clipped box and yew. Glimpsed through the fine wrought iron of its tall gates, the Georgian house echoes the appealing longevity of its surroundings. Its gardens are of equally high quality, strongly linear in design and marching purposefully northeastward, straight up the hill behind the house. Sheltered by massive broadleaf trees and the high old walls that create squared-off enclosures, the flower gardens offer an intense, heady experience of graded colours and scent, underpinned by the meticulous care and formidable plantsmanship of the present owners, Hady and Victoria Wakefield.

Victoria Wakefield is accustomed to guiding her horticulturally inclined visitors through the front door and straight on to the back of the house, all the better to experience the unexpected wallop of being plunged almost headlong into a pair of vast herbaceous borders that mirror each other, plant for plant, all planned with precision. Getting the plant heights and colours to work harmoniously together is much harder than it sounds, and only achieved by a painstaking process undertaken by Victoria and her head gardener early in the year. They each take a border and mark it out in three-metre sections with string. Then follows a comparing of notes, volleyed out to each other across the central grass path, as to what was successful and what was not, what should be moved around or substituted for something new, or just something more reliable. The "mirrors" must remain intact, though their contents will be refreshed from year to year.

After spring, with its lemon zesty highlights of euphorbias and bulbs, the key border colours of early summer are multiple blues and yellows, shot through with violent magenta (from *Geranium psilostemon*), plummy pink, and white *Dictamnus albus* cultivars and highlights from herbaceous clematis and sweet peas, grown on hazel twiggery. The blues are strong in the spires of delphiniums, softer in the mounds of catmint—there are several here but the garden's own *Nepeta* 'Bramdean,' upstanding and with dark stems, is especially good; violet tints emerge with the flowering of *Salvia* 'Mainacht'

LEFT A treasured collection of classic herbaceous border plants at Bramdean House, displayed in the traditional way. It is probably unsurpassed anywhere today for the plantsmanship and precision involved in preparation. Via a painstaking process of measuring out, the borders are planted to be mirror images of each other. In this view, from the higher ground by the kitchen garden, the borders appear to roll all the way to the lovely Georgian house itself.

FOLLOWING PAGES The view in the other direction, from the house up to the walled kitchen garden and its own collections of sweet peas and nerines.

and *Clematis* × *diversifolia* 'Hendersonii.' The yellows range from pale lemons in *Thalictrum flavum* ssp. *glaucum* (repeated rhythmically through the beds, along with foamy *Thalictrum* 'Elin'), to bright sulphur in border achilleas and dark egg-yolk *Inulas*. The borders are unusual in having no backing of wall or tall hedge behind them and resist the punishing forces of a west wind largely because so many plants are carefully corseted with staking and pea sticks.

A lawn to the west of the herbaceous borders is skirted by a perimeter bed of choice shrubs and perennials and the broader lawn on the opposite side is a former Victorian "Ladies Walk," now a lawn for croquet.

Victoria Wakefield, a former trustee of the Royal Botanic Gardens, Kew and a long-serving judge on Royal Horticultural Society plant committees, is the driving force in the garden and "very hands-on," ably aided by two full-time gardeners. It was her parents who bought Bramdean House in 1944 and moved in at the close of the Second World War. Victoria therefore grew up at Bramdean and has spent almost all of her life there, which has no doubt contributed to its feeling of continuity. Having a ready-designed garden, largely remade by her mother within the framework of the old walls, has allowed her to concentrate on the detail of its plants and there are several substantial collections at Bramdean, notably in species and cultivars of Nerine bulbs from South Africa, old-fashioned border carnations, and Victoria's favourites, the sweet peas.

OPPOSITE The borders in closer detail: the shades of early summer are multiple blues and yellows, sharpened up with magenta (from *Geranium psilostemon*) and also plummy-pink and white from *Dictamnus albus* cultivars. The blues are strong in the spires of delphiniums, softer in the mounds of catmint, which include the garden's own *Nepeta* 'Bramdean.' Yellows are provided by thalictrums, such as 'Elin' and *Thalictrum flavum* ssp. *glaucum*, flat-topped flowers of achilleas and dark egg-yolk inulas.

ABOVE RIGHT *Clematis* × *durandii* works well in borders. It does need some support, but as an herbaceous clematis, it only grows to some three to six feet.

BELOW RIGHT This remarkable hedge, resembling a great rolling cloud, is very old and protects the house from the road beyond. Although it takes very many years to get this sort of effect, something quite characterful (although smaller!) can be achieved within five to ten years by growing a hedge with plants of varying size and trimming them carefully to avoid making the effect too uniform.

BRICKWALL COTTAGES

One thing led to another for the garden's owner, who now has the National Collection of Geum cultivars which ornament spring and early summer

Gardening can be solitary, or it can be a very clubby activity. A specialist interest can easily lead to joining up with others devoted to a particular plant group or species (see snowdrop collectors, page 208). There are societies for amateur enthusiasts of all manner of special interests, such as the Alpine Garden Society, the Hardy Plant Society, and the Cottage Garden Society; societies for cacti, clematis, conifers, carnations, and carnivorous plants; heathers, hebes, and herbs; pelargoniums, pansies, primulas, and much else besides. Some are international, such as the European Boxwood and Topiary Society and Mediterranean Plants & Gardens, which is a different club from the Mediterranean Garden Society.

There is also a wonderful specialist society devoted to specialists! This is Plant Heritage, which used to be called, rather worthily, the National Council for the Conservation of Plants and Gardens. Yes, quite a mouthful; Plant Heritage is a much better and more precise name. Its members devote themselves to creating national collections of particular groups of plants, especially cultivated garden plants that can become extinct when their popularity wanes. There are more than six hundred national collections throughout Britain, running the gamut of genera from *Abies*, *Acanthus*, and *Acer*, to *Yucca*, *Zelkova*, and *Zingiber*. Big private collections can start from small beginnings.

One of these, the national collection of *Geum* cultivars, is at Brickwall Cottages in Kent. It is a great example of the spirit of amateur collecting that can enhance a garden while also providing a crucial role in plant conservation. The *Geum* collection curator, Sue Martin, had a career teaching cello and piano, but decided to find harmony in her quarter-acre cottage garden by planting a yellow border in 1988. "I wanted to add orange, and put in my first *Geum*," she recalls. The Geum thrived, so she bought more and was given some by a friend in Germany. When an existing national collection of *Geum*, located in Devon, needed a new home, Martin took it on. These warm-coloured herbaceous plants that share kinship with roses are of just the right size, stature, and character for a country cottage garden. "There's something of the herbal, the meadow, and the hedgerow about them," observes botanist Mark Griffiths.

Martin's collection expands in increments and has now reached "probably in the region of 120 cultivars," she says. From the purchase of one plant, to jazz up a border, a new interest, new friends, and, indeed, a new business have flourished.

Among collectors' plants, Geum is an unusual genus to choose as a speciality, but Sue Martin has become so infatuated, her collection of different cultivars is now somewhere in the region of 120. This semidouble one, pale yellow with hints of peach, is 'Dawn,' and of Martin's own creation.

LEFT *Geum* 'Herterton Primrose,' mingling with forget-me-nots, which self-sow all over the garden, dusting it with their soft light blue in spring.

ABOVE RIGHT The shade of an apricot sunset, *Geum* 'Hannays.'

BELOW RIGHT *Geum* 'Bell Bank,' raised by the late and great gardener Geoffrey Smith, at his home in North Yorkshire. It has a particularly fetching and useful shade of rose with hints of copper—or is it copper with hints of rose!

8 OVERVIEW: THE GLASSHOUSE

At first thought, it might be surprising, but in English country gardens today, a Victorian style of glasshouse is still the preferred model, despite various alternative designs having been devised through the twentieth century. There is a good reason for this. The Victorian glasshouse was designed principally for fully operational, hardworking kitchen gardens and was developed with all the practical needs taken into account, from alignment and glass coverage, to flexible aeration, potential for heating, and maximum growing space for the required plants. Numerous variations on them were produced, depending on the plants being cultivated, but essentially the symmetrical design with pitched roof and plenty of air vents is still the one that ticks the boxes for most practical applications even now, whether one's preference is for growing grapevines or gloxinias, tomatoes or tender potted plants.

Development of glasshouses and their wider uptake took longer than it might have done because a punitive tax on glass had been introduced in the eighteenth century, putting glass-rich structures out of the reach of everyone but the seriously wealthy. But with the progression of Queen Victoria's reign (from 1837), a repeal of the glass tax mid-century, and the nation's burgeoning wealth from industry and empire, the costs of owning a glasshouse plummeted, putting them well within the reach of the expanding middle classes. Under the glass of a greenhouse or conservatory, all manner of exotic plants being introduced to the nursery trade from far-flung lands could be cultivated.

Foster and Pearson was one of the first companies to take advantage of the new market for glasshouses, and it rapidly became the world leader in their production. Numerous of the company's creations are still in use today, including in the working areas of some of the historic gardens featured in this book. Robert Jameson, who runs Foster and Pearson today, advises that the designs that have withstood the passage of time were achieved due to very practical considerations.

"Most early glasshouses were made of wood combined with metal, with only a small percentage being made of iron, whether cast or wrought, due to the high initial cost and an intensive maintenance schedule. Solely iron glasshouses tended to be for curvilinear work, because it's difficult to produce the

A gallery of remarkable nineteenth-century creations, developed when iron and glass came of age together.

ABOVE LEFT The conservatory (circa 1855) at Broughton Hall in North Yorkshire.

BELOW LEFT The curvaceous free-standing orangery at Dallam Tower in Cumbria, built around 1826, exquisite and very rare for its design at the time.

OPPOSITE, CLOCKWISE The exotic and over-the-top conservatory at Enville Hall. Paxton's Great Stove at Chatsworth House, smooth and almost modern-looking. A remarkable conservatory that once adjoined the house at Tyntesfield in Gloucestershire.

curves in wood; metal houses were also difficult to seal, though, making them cold and difficult to fumigate," he says. "As cast and wrought irons became more readily available, they were combined with wood to produce rigid and light constructions. For example, the use of trussing enabled far shallower sections of timber to be employed, which reduced shadowing. And, perhaps surprisingly, it increased durability; in humid conditions, small sections of timber are more durable than larger ones, as the deeper sections retain more moisture, making them prone to decay."

Across the country, numerous examples of the great variety of glasshouses that developed in the nineteenth century can still be found. Depending on your particular interest, and purse, you could choose to have a vinery for grapes, a cut-flower house for carnations, a peach house, a camellia house, a fernery, a palm house, a house for growing flowering plants in pots to bring indoors, an orchid house, or probably many other specialisms, as well as raising edibles like melons, tomatoes, and cucumbers. (A craze for alpine houses, which are very extensively ventilated but keep damaging winter rains off the plants, burgeoned in the twentieth century, along with the popularity of rock gardens.) The orangery is something else again; developed in England as early as the seventeenth and eighteenth centuries, orangeries were essentially masonry structures with windows, intended for overwintering citrus trees. Their direct ancestor is the *limonaia* of Italian Renaissance gardens, where the potted lemon trees that ornamented Italian formal gardens were (and are) brought under cover to overwinter in safety from the cold and damp.

Country Life's archive includes photographs of some of the most magnificent glasshouse developments of the nineteenth century; these are long gone, but nevertheless they were wonders of their age. They are the dinosaurs of the greenhouse world: magnificent in their size, design, and ambition, they became irrelevant when the world and its needs moved on. Among them was the Great Stove at Chatsworth by Joseph Paxton (1803–1865). Begun in 1836 and completed in 1840, it was one of the great horticultural wonders of the world, 275 feet long, 121 feet wide, and 62 feet high, with room for two carriages to pass on the main thoroughfare. Its stairs, concealed by "rock formations," led to a gallery so that the tops of palms and other exotic trees could be admired at close quarters. Some seven miles in length of water pipes created a network for heating it, via eight boilers hidden underground. These were fed by three hundred tons of coal each winter, brought to the boilers via

Pelargoniums galore in a traditional conservatory. Note the Lloyd Loom chair with cushions, for relaxing with a cup of tea among the aromatic plants.

an underground railway. It was a casualty of the First World War, however, for without enough coal for the boilers, many of the plants died. Far too expensive to restore and maintain after the war, it was demolished in 1920.

With its sleek, curvilinear design, the Great Stove (page 237) looks almost modern; a different style was preferred by Gray and Ormson for Enville Hall's conservatory built in 1853–55 (also page 237). Housing lovely flowering shrubs such as camellias, azaleas, oranges, and fuchsias among the palms, its presentation was ostentatiously exotic: a cross between the onion-domed Royal Pavilion at Brighton and one of the great railway stations of the age, with Gothic detailing in the glazing and pointy turrets at each end. But, as with Chatsworth's big glass beast, Enville Hall's conservatory was a colossal millstone after the Great War for the same reasons. It fell into disrepair and its whalelike skeleton lasted until the 1950s, when it was dismantled.

From the eighteenth century and particularly from the days of the landscape park and Capability Brown, productive walled gardens had been moved away from the house and when glasshouses became widely used in the nineteenth century, the walls themselves correspondingly became part of the glasshouse's usefulness. A lean-to, or three-quarter span house, could be positioned against the wall—saving on space—and fruit, especially temperature-sensitive plants such as peaches, nectarines, and figs, could be trained neatly against the brickwork. The design for a vinery, producing dessert grapes—then a very high-status fruit for the dining table—would have an arched area in the long side of the brickwork base, through which the vine was carried, to be trained under the glass indoors. The vine's roots were therefore buried just outside the glasshouse, in their own manured bed. It was commonplace to bury horses in the vinery bed, thus enriching the soil with "blood fish and bone" fertiliser over a period of time. Nothing was wasted in those days!

Conservatories were de rigueur from Victorian times onward. Usually, a conservatory was little more than a pretty greenhouse attached to the home, with an internal glazed door providing access without the need to step outside. It could be large or small, but it was a place for growing plants and also, frequently, sitting among them, perhaps to read, or to be sociable. Fashionable conservatories in the twenty-first century, however, are very different beasts. Lightweight metal structures, sheet glass, and smart ventilation enable the conservatory to be somewhere for human enjoyment. These days, the plants are as likely to be admired strictly beyond the glass. Indoors is a clean, uncluttered sanctum, without damp smells of earth, or creepy-crawling insect life lurking among the foliage.

The new, alternative conservatory is a place for people first; plants are still admired, but they are outside the glass, not cosy inside it.

LEFT Outside/inside living, with doors folded back.

ABOVE RIGHT It almost goes without saying that such arrangements require the garden to be worth looking at beyond the glass!

BELOW RIGHT Total transparency.

9 THE KITCHEN GARDEN

In 2018, when I was retiring from my role as gardens editor at *Country Life*, BBC Radio 4's *Today* news show invited me to discuss the state of English gardening. The legendary broadcaset interviewer John Humphrys wondered what key things might have changed in the past two decades, and it seemed clear to me that the two biggest trends that sweep right across the board at every level of gardening are the now almost universal desire to garden sustainably, particularly organically (page 391), and also kitchen gardening.

Inevitably, there is considerable overlap in these two subjects, and it's heartening to see how many people are now growing at least some of the fruit, vegetables, salads, and herbs that they eat. A few years ago one of the seed companies announced that sales of its vegetable seeds had overtaken sales of flowers for the first time. In the Dig for Victory years of the Second World War, everyone learned to grow food out of necessity, but the knowledge ebbed as the wartime generation passed away, and it's fair to say it has largely skipped a couple of generations.

Now, however, the Royal Horticultural Society and others are promoting school gardens nationwide, catching children's interest early on and making food growing fun. And growing something edible, in however small a space— even a balcony window box—is something millennials particularly are very keen on. The reasons for their interest are manifold, but chiefly down to food traceability; it's also part of a more environmentally aware way of life and perceived increased health benefits of homegrown food, from the produce itself, the exercise involved in raising it, and the connection with earth and nature. That all might sound rather worthy, but factor in also the rise of food culture, and the lively exchange of "homegrown" images on Instagram and other social media and we see here a trend that isn't going to go away any time soon.

It's such a different outlook from that of a generation ago, when it was very apparent in the large gardens run by the National Trust that their numerous old walled gardens were chiefly only useful to them as car parks. That they were missing a trick became obvious with the huge success of a charming BBC television series, *The Victorian Kitchen Garden*, first broadcast in 1987. Following a year in the life of the garden, it had two follow-up series, all of them having been repeated multiple times.

In 1990, restorations began in Cornwall in the grounds of an old estate garden, marketed as the Lost Gardens of Heligan. I remember walking through Heligan's lost kitchen garden in the early days with the visionary Tim Smit, the garden's rescuer-in-chief. Slashing through the undergrowth—or should I say overgrowth—which hid an old estate garden that had long ago been locked up, with the key (at least metaphorically) thrown away, was surely a far cry from his glamorous early career as Barry Manilow's music producer. At Heligan, it was obvious that Smit was onto something and, among his talents is certainly the ability to fire up the enthusiasm of potential funders as well as volunteers. The results speak for themselves, with millions of visitors having passed through its doors since they first opened, mid-restoration, in the early 1990s. Despite all the further work in uncovering and rescuing the ornamental grounds, Heligan's walled kitchen garden with its melon yard, pineapple house, and three-hundred-plus varieties of fruits, vegetables, salads, and herbs is still its beating heart.

Another great restored walled garden can be visited at West Dean, near Chichester in West Sussex, where husband-and-wife team Jim Buckland and Sarah Wain redeveloped the gardens over more than twenty-five years before retiring. The walled garden's thirteen Victorian glasshouses nurture an enormous range of fruits, including figs, peaches, nectarines, and grapevines; vast ranges of peppers and tomatoes are raised indoors; and numerous more edibles in the ordered beds outside. As part of the Edward James Foundation, education is part of its remit.

At Osborne House, on the Isle of Wight, Queen Victoria's favourite residence, the walled garden had for long been grassed over, until, at the turn of the millennium, English Heritage raised funds through its Contemporary Heritage Gardens scheme to bring it back to life. Designer Rupert Golby's stylish and opulent reworking of an old theme in a contemporary idiom combines respectful references to Victoria and Albert with abundant planting, within a traditional four-square framework. At around the same time, the National Trust rediscovered the potential in its big walled gardens and has now restored many of them (Knightshayes Court, page 255, is one of them). They have proved to be among the trust's most popular attractions. Nearly everyone these days wants to see where edibles come from, and how they might be grown.

LEFT The potager at Stanton Fence in Northumberland.

ABOVE RIGHT The kitchen garden at Warnell Hall in Cumbria, with pale blue greenhouse.

BELOW RIGHT Traditional crop growing at Jackson's Wold in North Yorkshire.

Lupins and 'Ladybird' poppies at the cutting garden end of the enormous, elliptical walled garden at Gravetye Manor in West Sussex, the former home of the Victorian gardening writer and publishing mogul William Robinson. The walled garden grows a huge range of organic produce for the hotel's restaurant.

GRAVETYE MANOR

WEST SUSSEX

The oval walled garden built in the late nineteenth century has been restored to supply cut flowers as well as food for its renowned restaurant

From the lane, the discreet drive to Gravetye Manor winds its way gently uphill between the trees for more than a mile before you reach the multi-gabled Elizabethan house, built in 1598 by one Richard Infield, a local ironmaster, upon his marriage. This part of Sussex is well wooded—Gravetye itself sits within an estate of a thousand or so acres of field and forest—and it is easy to forget that the region was, during Tudor times, a heartland of industry, with expanses of ancient woodland being felled for charcoal to feed furnaces for smelting iron, for house building, and to supply timbers for warships serving Tudor monarchs. By the time Infield built his sandstone house, the Sussex iron industry was waning, but many who had become rich from it were building fine houses and enjoying more gentlemanly pursuits.

When the Gravetye estate was offered for sale in 1884, the timing couldn't have been better for the firebrand Irishman William Robinson. A gifted gardener, communicator, and publisher of a gardening magazine, he acquired an elegant residence into which he could invest his earnings, and also his ideas on how to create a garden, a home, and the perfect woodland surroundings.

Robinson contributed numerous articles about aspects of his estate to *Country Life* during the first three decades of the magazine's existence (and the last three decades of his). In spite of his very public tirade against formal, architectural gardens, he understood the need for a house to be grounded in its surroundings and laid out the thirty-six-acre Gravetye gardens formally in the immediate environs of his house, spreading out to freer and increasingly more natural landscape as the grounds progressed away from the mansion.

West of the house, a flat, four-square layout (a rose garden in Robinson's day, now featuring lawns but maintaining the pattern) is margined by abundant flower borders of exceptional vigour and inventiveness. It forms a level centrepiece, below which, to the south, meadows run steeply down to a lake. To the north, steep banks of heather and rhododendron rise up to a level croquet lawn and, on rising ground above it, is a shrubby woodland garden with plantings of spring bulbs.

Farther north, and farther uphill, lies something remarkable, and unique to Gravetye: a huge kitchen garden, with twelve-foot-high curved walls built to create a perfect ellipse. Covering some 1.5 acres, its land tilts down gently southeastward, with a main path cutting centrally across from the gate at the southwest end to another in the northeast. A perimeter path, some twenty feet from the wall, traces the oval design, giving access to the beds on either side, which these days are fully productive again, with a wondrous range of fruits, salads, vegetables, and cut flowers.

After restaurateur Peter Herbert took on the house and gardens in 1958, he turned it into a gracious country house hotel and it has stayed that way

ABOVE A brassica party: cauliflowers, cabbages, and kale, all hugger-mugger.

RIGHT Gravetye Manor's fully restored walled garden occupies a site sloping gently to the south. Its location must have been chosen to ensure maximum light and warmth for the produce.

ABOVE Afternoon tea among the tulips and heather bank.

RIGHT William Robinson promoted "wild gardening" with passion and stamina, but this graded area was a formal rose garden in his day. The present arrangement, with its lawn plats and intensively planted yet relaxed beds, adopts the spirit of Robinson, but is more complex and intense than even he could have imagined it.

ever since. The present owners, Jeremy and Elizabeth Hosking, have heavily invested in the property since acquiring it in 2010 and their involvement in the garden has also been unstinted, to the extent that the walled kitchen garden has been fully restored in recent years and supplied with state-of-the-art irrigation concealed under its authentic Victorian "face." The investment has paid off, for the kitchen garden provides year-round produce for the hotel's Michelin-starred restaurant (recently expanded). Head chef and head gardener are in regular conference to select the best varieties of everything, from pears to peas, asparagus to artichokes, strawberries to scorzonera, all of which are raised in six major beds, with the crops rotated annually in the traditional way. Another important aspect of the walled garden is its area for cut flowers, which are used to decorate the public and guest rooms in the hotel.

Although countless old kitchen gardens across Britain fell from use during the twentieth century, there has been a turnaround in the past twenty to thirty years, with many having been brought back into use, sometimes to serve restaurants, as Gravetye's does, or for the benefit of local communities.

As well as providing wind protection, the walls trap the warmth gained from sunshine, aiding crop ripening, and keep out unwelcome animals. The soil is light and rich after receiving regular doses of compost down the generations, warming up quickly in spring and being easily worked in most conditions. Head gardener Tom Coward, who managed the garden's restorations, enjoys its spin-off conservation aspects, too, such as hearing tawny owls calling to each other from the surrounding trees in the evenings, and observing numerous bats swooping and hunting for insects trapped within the walled area.

The 2.5-acre walled garden at Knightshayes Court is divided into themed areas that include vegetables and fruits, herbs, flowers, and foliages for cutting, and also a vineyard. A garden of this size and ambition needs a great deal of maintenance, but some forty or so volunteers help the staff on a rotational basis.

KNIGHTSHAYES COURT

DEVON

The mid-nineteenth century walled garden with its distinctive turreted corners was restored in recent times, providing vineyard grapes as well as food crops

The garden at Knightshayes Court has many points of interest, but only in recent times has its magnificent kitchen garden become one of them. Graham Stuart Thomas, distinguished plantsman, rose expert, botanical artist, and, for many years, gardens adviser to the National Trust, paid many visits to Knightshayes Court while it was still in private ownership. His first visit, though, in 1955 made a lasting impression on him.

After a long train journey, he and a travel companion, "went through the big gates to enter an informal avenue of great trees, including immense Cornish elms and huge Turkey oaks. Suddenly the house came into view: a great Victorian pile of warm-coloured stone on an eminence. I think we both gasped in astonishment … After lunch we started a tour of the garden … I found it difficult to turn myself away from the superb view down the park."

Soon after, he took an advisory role with the National Trust, and then always stayed at Knightshayes as a guest of Sir John and Lady Heathcoat-Amory, when advising on the trust's properties nearby. Gardeners are usually convivial and keen to "talk plants," so Thomas' hosts would naturally show him, on such visits, the latest developments in the garden they were enthusiastically planting, no expense spared. "What lovely visits they were! The walk round the ever enlarging garden was always full of interest, followed by a giant loudspeaker in the drawing-room of an evening, playing magnificent music," Thomas recalled.

The view down the park was indeed stupendous, rolling out like a giant golf course fairway, framed by trees, leading the eye southward toward Tiverton in the distance. Perhaps it was such a view that made Lady Heathcoat-Amory feel immediately at home in the grounds, for, prior to her marriage in 1937, she had been champion golfer Joyce Wethered, the leading British woman player in the interwar period. Did she ever stride out of the house with a driver and hit off a few balls in the direction of Tiverton? At any rate, Thomas recalls that one of the first things the couple did at Knightshayes was to make a little series of putting greens, below the house and garden.

However, creating the garden was all about its ornamental effect and the carefully judged placement of the choicest trees and shrubs over a substantial acreage. To this end, the 2.5-acre walled kitchen garden was actually closed in 1960 and all of its thirteen gardeners were transferred to work in the main garden and woodland areas.

On Sir John Heathcoat-Amory's death in 1972, the Victorian Gothic mansion, the garden he and his wife had made over some three decades, and its surrounding estate were all passed to the National Trust, with Lady Heathcoat-Amory continuing to live there until her death in 1997.

Today's visitors undoubtedly come to enjoy the magnificent ornamental gardens and varied woodland plantings of well-chosen trees and shrubs, reached via beautiful turf walks. These days, however, working kitchen gardens are attractions in their own right; people are now intensely interested in produce and provenance in a way that was much more unusual in the previous generation. So now the huge walled kitchen garden, reopened in 2003, is very much a key part of the visitor experience and indeed, for some people, the main reason they will come to Knightshayes.

Like many kitchen gardens owned by the trust, this one is run on completely organic lines (with Soil Association accreditation) and planted with numerous "heritage" fruit and vegetable varieties, and some thirty volunteers give hands-on help in the processes of sowing, growing, and harvesting. The produce, including wine, is served on-site in the café, with any surplus sold off to the visiting public and in the local market.

OPPOSITE Knightshayes Court, proudly Victorian in the Gothic revival style, by William Burges. Institutional-looking, gloomy, and overbearing? Or theatrical and romantic? You decide. Ironically, the fortune that paid for its building was founded on a newfangled machine process to create delicate lace.

OPPOSITE, BELOW The gardens, however, are wondrous. This quiet pool area is one of many delights.

ABOVE The tradition of the "honesty box'" is a wonderful thing. It is also still often seen at temporary roadside stalls across Britain in the summer months, when home gardeners ask for mere pence in exchange for their surplus salads, flowers, eggs, honey, fruit, etc.

RIGHT The stuff of "medieval" daydreaming: one of architect William Burges's corner flourishes for the walled garden.

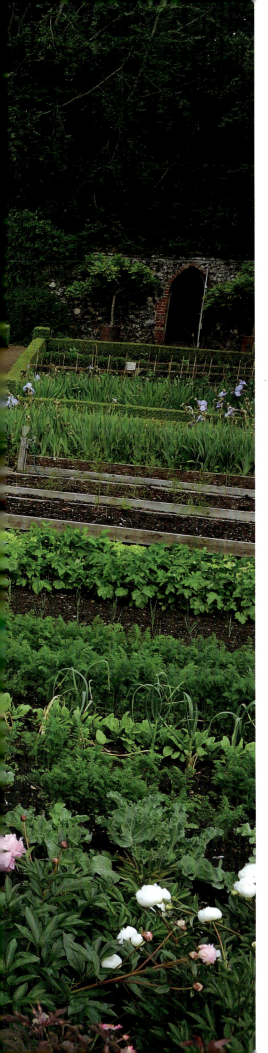

WRETHAM LODGE

NORFOLK

Walls of local flint stones and brick shelter an immaculate kitchen garden where peonies also provide flashes of early summer wonder

The coastline of Norfolk forms a big curve, lapped by the North Sea, to the opposite side of which are the countries of Scandinavia and northern Europe. Norfolk's location and low-lying ground therefore made it vulnerable to further invaders after the Roman period, particularly the Angles, Saxons, and Vikings. In Tudor times a thriving wool industry with links to overseas markets created many rich merchants. All of these things led to an extraordinary number of churches being built in the county and it is said you can't see a horizon in Norfolk without there being a church tower or spire in view. Many parsonages were therefore built to house the clergy (but sold in the twentieth century), so that numerous lovely ex-vicarages and ex-rectories are to be found in the villages and hamlets.

Wretham Lodge is one of the latter, being a lovely former rectory of the Regency period, associated with Wretham Hall (which no longer exists) and the nearby small flint church of Saint Æthelbert. Set well back from the lane down a sweeping gravel drive, the flint-walled house sits in the heart of its 11.5 acres among sweeping lawns and mature parkland trees. For much of the past two decades Gordon Alexander and his partner, Ian Salter, have been refining the gardens. A straight gravel path leads westward from the house, between an avenue of clipped yews to an informal woodland garden full of naturalised narcissi, bluebells, and primulas—a vision of all that is wonderful about spring. And to the northwest, double herbaceous borders, a hundred feet long, sheltered by crisp yew hedging, are glorious in summer with, among other things, many foxtail lilies, daylilies, delphiniums, and regularly spaced tall metal obelisks supporting clematis. The vista along the borders carries on beyond them, over the clipped hedge, to take in the tower of Saint Æthelbert's church in the distance.

By far the most intensive gardening, however, goes on in the substantial, rectangular walled garden east of the house and the drive. Within its high flint walls, the garden has been subdivided into numerous squared-up plots, meticulously edged in each case by a low hedge of box, all of the many hundreds of plants having been grown from cuttings by Alexander. There's something entirely satisfying in seeing well-ordered rows of crops in different stages of productivity as the season gets underway. Although so many trees furnish the garden and form protective shelter, the walled garden is wide open to the light, as it should be. The garden as it is now is a twenty-first-century creation, but a huge old apple tree, of uncertain planting date, occupies a central location; it's dignified by a surrounding rectangle of lawn and some low topiary mounds. Borders around the walls are planted according to what will grow well in each aspect, but a particular pleasure at midsummer is a border full of peonies, whereas another border, devoted to asters, is a highlight of summer's end and the arrival of autumn.

Order in the border: a range of bright, vivid peonies and numerous shrub roses share the kitchen garden with very proper rows of vegetables and salads. The ancient apple tree stands above its own lawn, in the top left section.

ABOVE LEFT Sheltering yew hedges fold around the herbaceous borders on either side of the turf path. The copper beech tree at the end is a fine, dark foil.

BELOW LEFT A view that seems to have been lifted from a Jane Austen novel. The south-facing garden front of the handsome house, seen from the fringes of the wood.

RIGHT 'Goldfinch,' one of the loveliest of rambling roses, tumbles over the flint wall. Its clustered, small, pale-yellow flowers whiten as they mature. Two bonuses: it exudes a strong, fruity fragrance and has almost no thorns—an excellent counterpoint to the ordered rows of productivity.

FRISTON PLACE

EAST SUSSEX

Garden designer George Carter's take on kitchen gardening is to contain it within neat outer and inner hedges and provide further ornament

On the edge of a forest in a fold in the Downs, the atmospheric Tudor house known as Friston Place sits well hidden, at the bottom of a tree-lined, curving drive. To one side of the drive there are sheep pastures; on the other, more pasture and a recently made wildflower meadow. The gardens are arranged all around the house, with some areas planted on gentle slopes, while others have been levelled, accommodating formal gardens and also summer entertainments such as croquet and tennis.

A wonderfully sequestered feel is achieved by the winning combination of numerous old flint walls and more recently planted hedges dividing the garden into manageable spaces, and also the presence of many good trees. It's perhaps a mile from the seashore, as the crow flies, but from within the grounds the sea is not apparent since there are great waves of Cretaceous chalk, ending abruptly in the cliffs known as the Seven Sisters, rising up to the south. Were it not for this proximity to the south coast, the garden would surely be prone to frosts rolling in.

Friston Place is the country home of hotelier Olga Polizzi and her husband, the eminent writer William Shawcross, Shawcross's parents having bought the small estate in 1958. "It is magical," says Polizzi, "surrounded by tall trees, with the sea on one side and the glorious curves of the Downs all around."

There are ancient flint walls everywhere, forming many separate areas and perfect for growing many different species of climbers—roses, wisterias, and vines. Although the gardens had been renovated to some degree by the previous generation, when Percy Cane was brought in to sort them out, since Polizzi's arrival, the sense of order achieved by crisp runs of hedging has been ratcheted up considerably. She has been aided in this by her friend, the garden designer George Carter, whose deft hand can be seen here and there, in the creation of disciplined vistas and whimsical but stylish touches of garden decoration.

The kitchen garden is a case in point. It covers a small area, when compared with the garden as a whole, but it's surely one of the smartest vegetable plots you will find anywhere. Reached through a doorway in a high wall, beyond the drive northeast of the house, it's arranged as a long, rectangular space, carved out of a paddock, containing a symmetrical arrangement of six elongated rectangular beds, each one edged with knee-high, precision-trimmed box hedging.

From its entrance, marked by a stretch of terrace and a pair of stone urns, the eye is drawn to the end of the vista, which terminates in the smartest potting shed imaginable. It's a lovely square building, of blue grey painted weatherboard and shingle-roofed, with a gilded finial crowning the apex; this

Olga Polizzi's kitchen garden is a very well-ordered space. To terminate the view, George Carter designed the smartest potting shed imaginable, square, weatherboarded, and silvery pewter, with a gilded ball finial above its shingled roof.

ABOVE LEFT A lime avenue runs along the edge of a large wildflower meadow.

BELOW LEFT The chicken area and the nuttery occupy a separate enclosure, within old, high walls. The George Carter henhouse is very smart, and surrounded by gilded egg motifs, a gilded cockerel weather vane, and hedges of hazel.

RIGHT Stylish alfresco dining, a Polizzi trademark.

Two views across the kitchen garden: George Carter's obelisk fountains bring height and decoration to the central beds. All the beds are productive—not a square inch is wasted.

is certainly a place whose ordered neatness would inspire the gentle cultivation of salads and herbs. Would a leek or spear of asparagus dare to grow crookedly in such a crisply formal setting? You might think, quite reasonably, that a kitchen garden cannot be fully operational without some sheltering glass, but behind the potting shed, says Polizzi, a not-very-pretty tomato house is lurking, so even that has been thought about.

To avoid any sense of flatness and lend movement to the composition, George Carter also installed a pair of lead obelisk fountains in the central beds and added paired columns of clipped beech at either end. The latter bring their vivid seasonal changes of colour into the garden and visually link the kitchen garden with the runs of beech hedging found through the rest of the gardens.

Part 2, if you like, of the productive element in the gardens, is the chicken run and nuttery, located within an old walled garden northwest of the house. This is an enclosure that Polizzi is particularly fond of, with its elegant square henhouse, avian sculptures, and series of wooden posts, each one topped by a large, gilded lead egg. Few hens can boast such a fine residence as this; their area is enclosed by neat formal hedges that are made, unusually, out of common hazelnut, *Corylus avellana*.

As a busy hotelier and designer, Polizzi is frequently drawn away. But, she says, "The minute I arrive here I want to go into the garden and have a look around. I love creating new interiors, but what I love even more is thinking about and planning my garden."

10 THE CUTTING GARDEN

The Victorian artist-gardener Gertrude Jekyll (page 309), having her house at Munstead Wood built for her by Edwin Lutyens from scratch, was able to make numerous special requests to be woven into his plans. Among them was a ground-floor workshop for her various artistic pursuits. Immediately beyond the workshop was the "garden shop," a small, cool room on the north side of the house, with an oak door opening onto steps leading straight into the garden beyond. As someone who was keen on bringing the outdoors indoors, via cut stems of flowers and foliage tastefully arranged, she probably kept the garden shop regularly busy. With practicality in mind, there were shelves and cupboards installed for her multitude of vases and a sink set into the work top, to wash said vases, and fill them.

A dedicated room for cutting and preparing flowers is still sometimes seen in grand houses today, but for most people, the "utility room" with similar access to the outdoors is a more flexible space, serving several functions, including deep freezers and, perhaps, a shower to wash down muddy dogs after long walks.

Jekyll did however write a great deal about aspects of cutting and arranging plant material, although she doesn't seem to have especially focused on "cutting gardens" reserved strictly for the vase. Her own garden, having so many different borders and trial areas, both colour-themed and seasonal, hardly needed somewhere else separated out for the purpose of cutting.

Traditional cutting gardens are usually connected with the kitchen garden or allotment and are nearly always a practical, utilitarian space set aside for a crop to be harvested at will. Among the finest of this type is the cutting garden within the great walled garden at Parham House in West Sussex (pages 278–83). Parham has a long and continuous history of flowers grown for the house and exceptionally fine displays. Bulbs and plants are grown in orderly rows with paths between each row to enable maintenance and picking; trials are carried out with new varieties each year, to assess their worthiness against established varieties.

The kitchen garden itself is also worth raiding sometimes. During the 1930s, the distinguished garden designer Percy Cane was proprietor and

OPPOSITE Irises have long been grown at Wardington Manor in Oxfordshire. For many years they occupied beds near the house, when the gardens were in the care of Lady (Audrey) Wardington. The tradition of irises continues with the new owners, and there are many more cut flowers besides, grown by florists, the Land Gardeners.

editor of a journal called, not unnaturally, *Garden Design*, which regularly featured the arrangement of flowers. An entry for July 1936 by floristry correspondent Anne Lamplugh notes, "The kitchen garden is full of decorative possibilities—anyone who has used the huge greenish cream plumes of rhubarb flowers, anything from three to five feet high, will look out each summer for this most handsome decoration. Berries too, are attractive—a vase of red currants (leaves removed), green honesty pods, white currants, a branch of tiny apples, and a few spent love-in-a-mist heads is oddly attractive."

The cutting garden within the elliptical walled kitchen garden at Gravetye Manor in West Sussex (page 249) shows admirably how the florist's flowers bring something extra to the workaday rows of organic produce destined for its Michelin-starred restaurant.

Cutting gardens are now so numerous that many people have turned their country gardens into cottage industries serving the cut flower trade, via a nationwide cooperative called Flowers from the Farm. Another enterprise, at Wardington Manor in Oxfordshire, serves a niche market for gorgeous English flowers grown to biodynamic standards by "The Land Gardeners." The florist Sarah Raven has also built a diverse business on the strength of her own interest in growing flowers for the home, producing a useful book on the practicalities of cutting gardens.

There is no doubt that "the cutting garden" is a thriving area of English garden making in the twenty-first century. The following pages showcase some of the best examples of this kind of work presently being arranged in English country houses. These examples were put on specifically for public display, adding a new dimension and liveliness to the historic interiors.

OPPOSITE, CLOCKWISE In the pink. Sumptuous peonies hardly need any company in a vase, so magnificent are their own individual blooms. Camellia flowers are good for small vase arrangements or floating in water. Just five roses, but plenty of impact. Rhododendrons, especially just unfurling, have vase potential, whether pale and pastel or of stronger hue.

CHATSWORTH HOUSE

DERBYSHIRE

Special displays prepared for the house interiors include flowers of many textures and varieties, chiefly drawing on English garden classics

Known as one of the treasure houses of England, Chatsworth, home to the Duke and Duchess of Devonshire, has been passed down through sixteen generations of the Cavendish family. In the late seventeenth and early eighteenth centuries both the house and its gardens were transformed, creating for the first and second Dukes of Devonshire an estate that showed off the eminent position held by its owners. In an engraving by Johannes Kip, dating from 1707, Chatsworth's huge house appears dwarfed by the vast formal grandeur of its surrounding gardens; even by the grandest standards of that day, it was one of the most elaborate gardens in England, a vision of dazzling pattern and complexity.

The popular formal style makers of the day, George London and Henry Wise, designed fabulously intricate *parterres de broderie*. By 1696 Chatsworth's great water cascade, designed by a French hydraulics engineer who had created decorative waterworks for King Louis XIV of France, was tumbling its shimmering waters down a magnificent flight of steps in the hillside. There were square plats of lawn and geometric topiary in variety; mazes, avenues, canals, platoons of trees, and arrow-straight rides through formal blocks of forest. But new generations tend to have a different outlook, and in 1755 Capability Brown began to sweep away most of the stiffly formal and high-maintenance gardens to be replaced by a much more natural looking landscape. Some formality returned near the house in the nineteenth century under Joseph Paxton and Jeffry Wyatville. Succeeding generations have added to the layers of history and beauty outdoors, but the house interiors provide splendid settings to bring Flora's bounty inside.

These photographs show one of the Florabundance events held in June for a number of years, showcasing flowers and foliage chiefly grown and gathered on the Chatsworth estate, with added material brought in from nearby growers. Created by master florist Jonathan Moseley, aided by a team of some forty local florists, the arrangements are fresh and modern, but at the same time have enough "weight" and character to enhance the almost overwhelming grandeur of the house interiors. The Painted Hall, for example, with its chessboard marble floor and grand central staircase, is as awe-inspiring a space as it was meant to be, having been specifically created by the first duke through the early 1690s to impress his guests. It worked. Decorated with scenes depicting the life of Julius Caesar, it is Chatsworth's only remaining original interior and a challenge to decorate meaningfully with flowers. Big, bold arrangements brimming over great stone urns are just the ticket.

In contrast, in the great dining room, dozens of small vases were arranged along the dining table containing bunches of cottage garden flowers such as sweet peas, feverfew, soapwort, candytuft, cornflowers, and sweet Williams (*Dianthus barbatus*), all produced by a local collective of independent flower

On a Derbyshire stone fireplace at the North Entrance, a simple gathering of early summer blooms, with 'Russell' lupins in purple and pink, a bunch of dusky astrantia, white foxgloves, mint, and slender strands of miscanthus grass.

ABOVE LEFT Tall stems of miscanthus and red gladioli, with white delphiniums stand out above dusky pink roses, apricot alstroemeria, pink zinnias, snapdragons, and foliage of plain green hosta. The zinnias are from the glasshouse, the other flowers from the cutting garden, with branches of willow and larch cut on the estate.

ABOVE RIGHT A plain terra-cotta pot from the garden is filled with deepest purple and nearly black irises, filigree *Allium cristophii*, egg-shaped *A. sphaer-cephalon*, lupins, echium, knautia, and cornflowers, plus foliage of box.

growers in Derbyshire and Yorkshire. While bringing midsummer prettiness and gentle fragrance, the arrangements were small and low, so that cross-table dinner conversation wouldn't be interrupted by the flowers.

Nothing is done in a small way at Chatsworth, so it's not only the abundantly stocked cutting garden that supplied flowers and foliage in variety; the Capability Brown landscape park yielded foliage and branches from numerous trees including pine, fir, maple, silver birch, and beech. Woodland and ravine areas have their own simple flowers ideal for picking, while the walled kitchen garden supplied aromatic herbs and dramatic artichokes on long, rigid stems.

Naturally enough, a good cutting garden will have ample stocks of reliable flowers, those at Chatsworth being under the care of Becky Crowley. Herbaceous plants for midsummer include delphiniums, bearded irises, alliums in variety, sturdy 'Russell' lupins, and a great range of peonies, including, naturally, *Paeonia* 'Duke of Devonshire'. Among the annuals, sweet peas are essential for their fragrance and pastel hues; cow-parsley-like *Ammi majus* is delicately lacy, and marigolds in variety sharpen up arrangements with their zesty orange tints.

RIGHT In the Painted Hall, big, statement displays are required. Branches of fir, beech, and field maple combine with tall stems of angelica and just-opening greeny-white lilies. The shot of magenta is from assorted peonies. All come from the gardens.

FOLLOWING PAGES, LEFT A dramatic arrangement reflecting Dutch/Flemish art on the walls. Deep burgundy and lilac gladioli, dusky-mauve roses and soft pink hydrangeas are threaded through with shots of sulphur and lime, from strands of euphorbia and the ripening seed-discs of honesty (*Lunaria annua*).

FOLLOWING PAGES, RIGHT At the foot of the staircase in the Great Hall, one of a pair of stone vases, filled with Spanish oat (*Stipa gigantea*), green angelica, foliage of dogwood, larch, Solomon's seal, and artichoke. Larkspur and peonies bring in the pink notes and *Allium cristophii* the shimmering mauve constellations.

PARHAM HOUSE

WEST SUSSEX

In part of the large walled garden, flowers for cutting are grown together, where they can be assessed for the quality of their blooms

A long drive winds its way through the ancient deer park at Parham, leading toward one of the finest Elizabethan houses in the country, nestled in a valley in the chalk hills of Sussex. The high ridge of the South Downs frowns from a distance and the great stone house, with its courtyards and outbuildings, sits like a little village in its fortunate setting. A long, straight path runs past the house and ancillary areas, going directly to the walled garden, which for many years has been the hub of much admirable and creative horticultural activity.

The gardens are actually older than the house for the estate was owned by the monastery of Westminster until it was seized by King Henry VIII and passed to one Robert Palmer, a London merchant, in 1540. The present house was built in 1577 and has been a family home continuously since then. When Clive Pearson (son of oil and construction magnate Weetman Pearson, 1st Viscount Cowdray) bought the estate in 1922 everything—inside and out—needed investment and repair, which the Pearsons were able to lavish on it.

In the early part of the Second World War thirty children evacuated from London were brought to Parham; most had never seen the countryside before. Clive Pearson built for them a small wooden playhouse and, to encourage them to eat vegetables, he turned a section of the walled garden into small plots and gave the children tools and seeds to start growing things. With this encouragement and a competitive element introduced for good measure, the children became enthusiastic growers and eaters of vegetables! As the war progressed, Canadian troops were billeted at Parham but, after the war Clive's wife, Alicia, wanted to share the house and gardens with the public. She declared that "Parham has a beauty so essentially English that it is a delight to show it to one's own countrymen and a pride to show it to people from other lands." In the lean times of postwar rationing, a joyous day out to visit a beautiful, carefully restored old house, generously ornamented with flowers cut from its own garden, was a surefire success. The tradition, both of welcoming visitors and filling the house with flowers, continues these days via Alicia's great-granddaughter, Lady Emma Barnard.

Certainly, flowers play a very big part within the four-acre walled garden that has numerous, substantial borders. One-quarter of the walled garden is formally arranged in a series of square, box-edged beds where vegetables and flowers are artistically grown together. There are also dedicated cutting beds, where painstaking work is undertaken by the gardening team; each year they trial dozens of varieties of florist stalwarts, such as gladioli, dahlias, tulips, and assorted annuals. Each Monday, some twenty-five to thirty buckets full of flowers are taken up to the house, then more buckets of Friday flowers pep up the weekend vases as required.

Parham House is tucked into a valley below the chalk South Downs. The cutting garden in the walled garden: dahlias and gladioli in great variety. Note the networks of string to restrain wayward stems. Upturned flowerpots filled with straw are a traditional way of catching earwigs, which eat dahlias. Clean out the straw regularly and dispose of, as you see fit.

ABOVE, LEFT TO RIGHT Shades of pink in *Gladiolus* 'Invitate.' Hot hues in *Gladiolus* 'Traderhorn' and 'Peche Melba.' Crushed-plum *Gladiolus* 'Bimbo.'

RIGHT Gathering the blooms: the numbers on the pots refer to the cultivar performance trials.

OPPOSITE A multitude of garden flowers ornament the house in exquisite arrangements. They include many gladioli, delphiniums, and zinnias, plus dahlias, cosmos, alstroemeria, and chrysanthemums.

FOLLOWING PAGES A harmonious composition, including *Ammi majus*, *Ammi visnaga*, and *Echinacea* 'White Swan.'

On the Great Hall Balcony, swags of fir greenery are shot through with fairy lights and between the swags the displays need to be very bold. This was achieved with clusters of burgundy and gold hydrangea heads, the solidity of the decorations lightened up with long, silvered sprays of asparagus ferns.

CASTLE HOWARD

NORTH YORKSHIRE

The grandeur of the palatial interiors require substantial quantities of dried and dyed flowers to make an impact for the Christmas period displays

The magnificence of Castle Howard can hardly be overstated. Its epic designed landscape covers a thousand acres of undulating moorland and park. With its dramatic approaches (one avenue of beech and lime trees runs uphill and down for more than three miles), passing the monument by F. P. Cockerell (1870), Hawksmoor's Carmire Gate (post-1726), Vanbrugh's gatehouse of 1719 flanked by bastioned fortifications, and his Obelisk of 1714, you are steadily prepared for engaging with the magnificent house itself. From there, another succession of buildings rolls into view, carefully placed in the landscape, including the Palladian Temple of the Four Winds, set on a grassy eminence ("the noblest lawns in the world, fenced by half the horizon," gushed Horace Walpole) and Hawksmoor's great Mausoleum, both built in the 1720s. (Of the circular, templelike Mausoleum, Walpole exclaimed it "would tempt one to be buried alive.") As a statement of power and might for its creator, the 3rd Earl of Carlisle (1669–1738), it has few rivals.

So any sort of floral decorations within the great house need to be muscular and vivid enough to complement and enhance the palatial interiors. Christmas at Castle Howard is therefore a splendid event and visitor attraction, a team effort combining the ideas and skills of the Howard family, their in-house team, and also designers and artists engaged from outside for the event. The house is closed for a couple of weeks during preparations and the estate itself provides tree branches, pine cones, and moss to add to other festive finery. Dried material from the gardens includes rosehips, heads of hydrangea, and assorted seed heads that are gathered and hung up to dry as they present themselves through the year, in preparation for the Christmas bonanza.

Not least among the challenges is the raising and decoration of the Christmas tree, reaching some forty feet or so into the cavernous Great Hall. In order to get it safely decorated with vibrant glass baubles and other finery, a scaffold is erected once the tree has been securely installed and deemed to be standing straight. The secret to achieving successful decoration in this sort of environment is, of course, to think big—and then even bigger. Gigantic swags of fir foliage, stitched through with fairy lights, bring an extra layer of grandeur to the finely detailed ironwork of the balcony, in the illustrated example, the swags looping between tight arrangements of deep burgundy and gold-sprayed hydrangea heads, topped off with silver-sprayed asparagus fern. Numerous rooms and corridors are illuminated with decoration through the Christmas period. The mixtures of natural materials—such as trailing ivy, stems of eucalyptus, lichen-encrusted branches, and berried twigs—and glass ornaments (many handed down the generations), fairy lights, tea lights, gilded fruits, and faux roses, all combine to brighten the dark days of December with more than a touch of fairy dust.

LEFT In the Octagon Room, linking the North and South Long Galleries, a huge pendant drop hangs like a gigantic lantern. The arrangement is a built-up mixture of fresh and faux hydrangea flower heads, roses, twigs, and asparagus ferns.

RIGHT Wooden Versailles tubs are used for a simple but effective parade of illuminated Christmas trees, suggesting a "forest path."

RIGHT In the Crimson Dining Room, decoration is focused on the fireplace and the dining table. Fir and holly foliage make the background to a "tree" of sparkling red and gold apples. The fire is surrounded by garlands that include poinsettia, apples, pine cones, and branches of berries.

11 OVERVIEW: THE LAWN

"I shall soon be rested," says Fanny Price, in Jane Austen's *Mansfield Park*. "To sit in the shade on a fine day, and look upon verdure, is the most perfect refreshment."

Lawns as we know them are indeed largely derived from parks, beginning with the earliest. In the deer parks created by the hunting-mad Norman occupiers after 1066 (page 129), there were naturally open spaces between the stretches of woodland, where animals grazed on rough grass and herbage. The Normans called these areas of pasture *laundes*, and the park that had sheep and cattle within it as well as deer would have had quite considerable open areas of *launde*.

Gervase Markham (ca. 1568–1637) observed the "beauty and gracefulness of the parke," which needed to be an artistically composed blend of "view, lawnde and covert" (the covert being the woods and copses, "places of leave for wild beasts"). The game of bowls also became established in Markham's lifetime and necessarily required the "lawnde"—a feature now in the garden as well as the park—to be made of good turf, kept closely cut. Francis Bacon, whose essay "Of Gardens," written in 1625, tells us so much about the arrangement of the grounds in high status properties, recommends closely mowed lawns in the "green" part of the garden: "Because nothing is more pleasant to the eye than green grass kept finely shorn." The formal grass "plats" of that time are pleasant breathing spaces, located between more intensively gardened areas and the roughness of contrived heath and wilderness.

Turf initially had to be cut from wild sources. Heaths, with their acidic, low-nutrient soils, naturally produce very slender grass species ideal for fine turf; heaths were therefore considered the best sources for a lawn, which was kept short by "mowing and rowling." Mowers had not yet been invented, of course, so in the seventeenth – and eighteenth-century garden and park, the lawns—which became very extensive—were always cut by men with scythes. Charles Quest-Ritson observes, "It was hard and tiring work, which was best done very early in the morning when the grass was wet with dew. In large establishments, teams of scythers worked together, keeping the lawns and grasses short. They were not well paid, being treated as semi-skilled workers

ABOVE RIGHT   In the high Victorian garden of Tortworth Court in Gloucestershire, a gardener uses a sharp scythe to trim the sloping lawn on a bank. Photographed circa 1899.

BELOW RIGHT   At Spains Hall in Essex, circa 1900, a boy leads the donkey that provides the "horsepower," while a gardener steers the mowing machine.

OPPOSITE   At Lilleshall in Shropshire, 1898, the pleasure grounds feature flower beds in concentric circles, containing many thousands of bedding plants. Between them, equine power has been pressed into service, but this time the gardener is steering the pony as well as the lawnmower. Ponies often wore flat-soled leather booties when mowing, to prevent U-shaped hoof marks from imprinting the turf.

and ranking below the gardeners, who knew about difficult things like plants and were therefore more highly esteemed." Women helped the scythers by sweeping and gathering up the grass cuttings into baskets.

In *Hints on Ornamental Gardening* (1823), J. B. Papworth defines the lawn as "that portion of the grass plat which lies between the house and the pasture, which is constantly kept mown, forming a verdant carpet on which the building stands ... The lawn is usually separated from the pasture by a light iron fence—from parks by a ha!-ha! or sunken fence." Nobody really knows when the ha-ha (pages 300–301) was invented or so-named, but examples existed long before Walpole credited William Kent. The ha-ha's design clearly suggests its ancestry is the medieval park pale.

Papworth had little sympathy for the poor scythe-wielding worker, toiling with a heavy piece of equipment at the crack of dawn, and little understanding of the constant sharpness required in the blade. He complained of "the silly habit that the mower has of indicating his industry by the frequent use of the grit stone in sharpening his scythe: and generally at the time of the morning when such noises are tormenting." But only for a few more years was interrupted sleep the price to pay for having a fashionable lawn rolling up to your house.

Edwin Budding changed it all in 1830, with his invention of the cylinder or reel mower. An engineer in the flourishing textile trade, Budding must have observed one day how the cylinder of spiral blades, used to trim the nap of cloth, might just as well be put to use on lawns. This was the sort of game-changing, light-bulb moment that all inventors dream of.

Budding's sales pitch was persuasive. "Grass growing in the shade and too weak to stand against the scythe may be cut by this machine as closely as required, and the eye will never be offended by those circular patterns, inequalities, and bare places so commonly made with the scythe, and which continue visible for several days." Budding could also see the advantages of marketing his mower to men, as a novelty gadget. "Country gentlemen may find, in using the machine themselves, an amusing, useful and healthy exercise," he hinted. (Its potential for economy was also therefore implied.) The mower was not yet mechanised, of course, and later 19th nineteenth-century models were also marketed with women in mind. The "Multum in Parvo" brand was offered in at least six blade sizes, starting with a diminutive model of six-inch width.

Mowers were also designed to be pulled by ponies or donkeys in order for large areas to be cut without the operator becoming fatigued. Round, flat-soled leather boots were developed that covered over the pony's hooves, so that no U-shaped imprints were pressed into the turf. Then, as now, the more blades the cylinder had, the finer the cut of turf. In terms of the business part—the cylinder of blades—little has changed since Budding's

LEFT AND RIGHT Ever-decreasing circles: Two views of the quadrangle at Worcester College in Oxford, where the turf is famously fabulous.

BELOW LEFT At Westwell Manor in Oxfordshire, tucked away just to one side of the entrance court, a carefully mowed spiral adds interest to a stretch of lawn, guarded by topiary pieces.

OPPOSITE A croquet tournament is underway in the grounds of the Bishop's Palace at Wells Cathedral (page 85).

ABOVE RIGHT The ninety-minute picnic interval at Glyndebourne Opera House in East Sussex: the extensive lawns and gardens provide the audience with ample choices as to where to settle and open the Champagne.

BELOW RIGHT Real turf courts for lawn tennis are high-maintenance items, therefore few and far between. This one is thriving, however, at the Manor House in Upton Grey (page 411).

FOLLOWING PAGES Different stages of grass: a fine, mowed path is a luxurious surface in a garden, inviting further exploration. Turf paths also cut through the "grown up" very vertical grasses of *Calamagrostis* × *acutiflora* 'Karl Foerster' in a garden by Christopher Bradley-Hole.

original design of nearly two hundred years ago. Cylinder mowers are still the machine of choice for the fine turf of sporting stadia, golf putting greens, croquet lawns, Wimbledon tennis, and the twenty-two-yard pitch of any cricket ground, as well as any private garden owner whose lawn is the object of pride.

One of the best things about summer in England is the amount of leisure and conviviality that is carried out on lawns of various kinds. Garden fetes and village gatherings; tea on the lawn at an "open garden" day; a marquee set up on the lawn for a wedding party: all are ubiquitous scenes of summer.

Open-air events with picnics are very long established, too, of course, but the place that has elevated "picnic on the lawn" to high art is the opera house at Glyndebourne in East Sussex. Across the summer months, attending the Glyndebourne opera festival is a great excuse to have a cultural day in a setting of exquisite countryside, surrounded by the gentle sheep-grazed hills of the South Downs. The opera performance, starting early afternoon, always breaks at a convenient moment for an hour-and-a-half of serious picnicking in the park.

Glyndebourne also has a croquet lawn, but there is a charming reason why it is off-limits to the festival audience. At ninety minutes, the dinner interval is a long time for members of the company to sit around. So, rather than twiddle their thumbs, members of the orchestra (the two that perform at Glyndebourne are the London Philharmonic and the Orchestra of the Age of Enlightenment) relax by playing croquet. The tradition was started by Glyndebourne's founder, John Christie (1882–1962), and continues today.

That the English are very attached to their lawns is a matter of fact, and long standing. In late Victorian times, wealthy English families departed for their villas in the French Riviera in October, chiefly to be in milder air to avoid, or lessen the effects of, tuberculosis, widespread and incurable in those times. Routinely, turfs rolled up like carpets were sent ahead of the owners, so that lawns could be enjoyed through the winter sojourn. It was a one-way ticket for the soft English lawn, which would not survive the Mediterranean summer.

Lawns today are being challenged by some environmental enthusiasts who don't understand their virtues. A garden lawn has its place, however, and not just for visual or leisure enjoyment. It is an ecosystem in its own right and of enormous benefit to foraging birds, especially starlings (whose population is in serious decline in Britain), blackbirds, woodpeckers, and thrushes. Composed of millions of tiny plants, lawns produce oxygen and absorb carbon dioxide, prevent water runoff by carrying it down into the soil, deter soil erosion, and capture and break down air pollutants. Transpiration makes a lawn cooler than paving on a hot day, and lawns do not need watering during prolonged dry spells. However strawlike it appears in an unusually dry summer, the unwatered British lawn is capable of springing back to life and recovering its verdure as soon as rain returns. And as a soft path leading the way subtly through a garden, it has no equal.

OPPOSITE, CLOCKWISE Turf treatments in variety. At the Old Vicarage at Rickling in Essex (2003), stepping-stones suggest the best route to the church. A stepped turf landscape at Dartington Hall in Devon. In a Cornish cottage garden the turf path is a calm foil against the bright border. At Wretham Lodge in Norfolk, a mowed path cuts across the long meadow grass (2015).

RIGHT Lawn order: the gravel drive of this property wraps around an impeccable turning circle of lawn and groundcover *Geranium macrorhizum*, designed by Sean Walter.

Aha! So that's how they do it! Three ways with the ha-ha:

ABOVE LEFT at Bryan's Ground in Wales, a stone wall retains the higher ground.

BELOW LEFT You can't see the ha-ha, but it's there, at Holdenby Hall, where the striped lawn stops. It prevents the elegant White Park cattle strolling over to graze the fine turf and peer in at the windows.

RIGHT A ha-ha is like a turf infinity pool; from within, you cannot see the edge. And livestock on the pasture cannot make the leap to the lawn because of the ditch.

12   THE ARTS & CRAFTS GARDEN

William Morris (1834–1896), a leader of the late-nineteenth-century Arts and Crafts movement, famously declared: "Have nothing in your house that you do not know to be useful or believe to be beautiful." It's a wonderful motto for achieving a clutter-free way of life. Today, the Japanese decluttering expert, Marie Kondo, advises exactly the same thing and clearly many of us still need such steering, since her book *The Life-Changing Magic of Tidying Up*, with its Morris-like mantra, "Does this spark joy?" has sold multiple millions of copies in more than thirty countries, leading to her Netflix series in 2019, which also went viral.

Although the interiors of Arts and Crafts houses were certainly not minimalist by today's standards, one of the aims of the movement was to declutter overstuffed Victorian homes and gardens, using nature as the style guide. It was a timely corrective to the rise of mass production that had come with the Industrial Revolution earlier in the century. The "Pile 'em high, sell 'em cheap" ethos arrived with the development of intensive factory production and inexpensive imports from a global empire. Artisan craftsmanship was correspondingly declining, especially with cities full to bursting, from a booming population that matched the booming economy.

Ideologically aligned with the Pre-Raphaelite painters, Arts and Crafts pioneers such as William Morris and John Ruskin were idealists and social reformers, who saw that nature, art, and society should be intertwined. Craft skills, handed down through the centuries, were in danger of being lost; how much better it would be if the world could be persuaded to look "back to nature" and use things handmade with care and skill. Ironically, craftsman-made things then, as now, were inevitably expensive and well beyond the affordability of the people Morris and his friends wished to help; the pure Arts and Crafts house and garden at Standen in Sussex, for example, with its complete Morris interiors, was owned by James Beale, a prosperous London lawyer.

The Arts and Crafts movement's chief ambassadors in the garden scene were Gertrude Jekyll (page 309) and William Robinson (page 249), both of them prolific and highly influential horticultural writers, with Robinson a particularly successful publisher of books and periodicals. Robinson lived

OPPOSITE Indigenous style, local materials, and well-wrought craftsmanship were hallmarks of the Arts and Crafts movement, championed by *Country Life* since its earliest days. In this instance, a Victorian gateway into the walled garden at Stow Hall in Norfolk delights the eye.

OPPOSITE A two-way exchange: the Arts and Crafts aesthetic brought the architecture of the house into the garden, and inspiration from the garden—such as design motifs based upon flowers—into the fabric of the house. Clockwise from top left: An armillary sphere sundial in the Arts and Crafts garden at Kellie Castle in Fife; roses enhance a window; a symmetrical Arts and Crafts–style arrangement of pergola, rill, and pool; stained-glass tulips and birds bring the garden into the house at Blackwell in Cumbria.

almost within waving distance of Standen on a nearby hilltop and was invited by Beale's wife, Margaret, to advise on planting the twelve acres surrounding the house which was designed by Morris's friend, Philip Webb. With its terraces, straight walks, squared-off compartments, and crafted oak gates in a stylish version of the vernacular Sussex farm gate, Standen is a pure Arts and Crafts garden, well restored now by the National Trust. But it also contains an important contemporary interest: a Japanese garden, or at least an English interpretation of it.

Only from about the 1860s had trade with Japan recommenced, after two centuries of closure due to the country's isolationist foreign policy during the Edo period. Exponents of the Arts and Crafts aesthetic admired Japanese design and culture, perceiving not only its freshness but freedom from the depravities of an industrialist culture. And the plants that started to arrive from Japan were divine! Veitch's Nursery was quick off the mark, distributing Japanese plants from the 1860s onward, and V. N. Gauntlett later set up its "Japanese Nurseries" in Chiddingfold, Surrey, selling acers, magnolias, cherries, peonies, and bamboos. Josiah Conder's *Landscape Gardening in Japan*, published in 1893, offered guidance to their placement, and Yokohama Nursery distributed an English-language catalogue of its wondrous *Iris Kaempferi, newest & rarest, 50 varieties*. The architect and gardener Harold Peto found his way to Japan in the late 1890s and a number of his gardens feature aspects of Japanese planting, woven into the Arts and Crafts framework of his designs. (Nevertheless, at Heale House [page 147] Peto was not involved in its Japanese water garden, which had already been installed by his client, Louis Greville, before Peto laid out the rest of the gardens.)

Country Life was an enthusiastic supporter of the Arts and Crafts house and garden—most famously via its promotion of Edwin Lutyens's work, of course, although there were others, too. Harold Peto's great friend Henry (Harry) Avray Tipping created three Arts and Crafts gardens around a succession of his own houses, the last one at High Glanau Manor, where the garden has recently been magnificently restored by its owners Hilary and Helena Gerrish.

The gardens in this section display aspects of Arts and Crafts design and detail but not all of them are period pieces. The style is still popular today in updated form, especially in the Arts and Crafts heartlands of Sussex and the Cotswolds, as admirably shown by the garden at Temple Guiting Manor (page 329), for which garden designer Jinny Blom, and architect Ptolemy Dean received numerous accolades and critical praise.

OPPOSITE Munstead Orchard, the Lutyens cottage built in 1898 for Gertrude Jekyll's gardener within the grounds of Munstead Wood, Jekyll's home.

CLOCKWISE Goddards, one of Lutyens's most important early houses (1898–1900) with its crazy-paved stone courtyard planted by Gertrude Jekyll, photographed circa 1903; the Lutyens garden at Papillon Hall, circa 1912, (demolished 1950); the Lutyens-designed garden and pergola at Deanery Garden in Berkshire, circa 1903.

MUNSTEAD WOOD

The famous experimental garden of successful Victorian gardening writer Gertrude Jekyll continues to celebrate her methods and designs

Gertrude Jekyll's contribution to gardening literature, to horticultural journalism, and to gardening itself is profound and prolific. For over fifty years, she guided her readers (particularly *Country Life* readers, from 1900) through the processes of garden planning, making available in her books and articles some of the planting designs she had implemented in her own garden and those of her clients.

An artist and also a gifted plantswoman, with the benefit of many years' experience and observation, she wrote from a position of great knowledge and assured confidence. She was also a keen early photographer and the photos taken by her and by others enabled people to see the impressive results of her planting schemes, whether for spring, summer, or autumnal floral effects.

In her book *Home and Garden*, published in 1900, she opens chapter 1 with warmth and empathy. "Does it often happen to people who have been in a new house only a year and a half, to feel as if they had never lived anywhere else? How it may be with others I know not, but my own little new built house is so restful, so satisfying, that so it seems to me. In some ways it is not exactly a new house, although no building ever before stood upon its site. But I had been thinking about it for so many years, and the main block of it and the whole sentiment of it were so familiar to my mind's eye, that when it came to be a reality I felt as if I had already been living in it a good long time."

Jekyll was describing Munstead Wood, her home made of local oak and honey-brown sandstone. It was built for her by the young architect Edwin Lutyens, who became her protégé after their first meeting in 1889, at a tea party given by a local rhododendron expert.

She lived at Munstead Wood for thirty-five years, from October 1897 until her death in December 1932. Even from the early days her home achieved fame but, busy as she was, she was highly selective about visitors and interruptions. At Munstead she was prolific, clearly energetic (already in her mid-fifties when she moved there), and with a sound sense of business; these days, she would perhaps be classified as a "workaholic."

In her new home she perfected her colour theories for planting borders, designed hundreds of borders and gardens for clients, and produced fine craftwork as far as her ailing eyesight would allow. It seems incredible that her output was so prolific in spite of her being afflicted with progressive myopia. She published hundreds of magazine articles (for nearly thirty years she submitted regular pieces to *Country Life*). Jekyll also ran a plant nursery, raising the plants on a plot well away from the ornamental garden, and selling them from a little flower room set into the north side of her house.

Jekyll had actually begun making her garden quite some time before she was able to live on the property. In the early 1880s her family had bought a

A rare autochrome from about 1912 shows in colour Gertrude Jekyll's pale "Iris and Lupin Garden" at Munstead Wood, with a simple mud path down the middle. The weatherboarded "Loft" beyond was used by Jekyll for her nursery business and for storing seeds.

LEFT Gertrude Jekyll in her Spring Garden at Munstead Wood, photographed in 1918.

RIGHT, CLOCKWISE Autochrome images of Jekyll's gardens at Munstead Wood, circa 1912. Blue clematis and *Echinops ritro* among silver-greys and whites in the Grey Garden; gate into the Spring Garden; *Euphorbia characias* subsp. *wulfenii* and yuccas in the Spring Garden; the Michaelmas Daisy Border; the red section of the Main Border.

PREVIOUS PAGES Munstead Wood house, glimpsed from the Woodland Garden.

LEFT Doorway to Jekyll's "Garden Shop" within her house.

ABOVE LEFT The "tank" pool and stone terrace.

ABOVE RIGHT Munstead Wood house, built by Lutyens in the 1890s, showing the North Court, viewed from the gardens.

fifteen-acre plot, mainly heath and woodland, for her to develop, since she was running out of experimental gardening space at the family home. So, unusually, the new house Lutyens was creating had to fit into an existing garden. Mostly it all fitted together quite well, because she had already designated an area to accommodate the house and had some firm ideas of what it needed to include, both visually and for comfort.

The house front sits back from a quiet little lane, tucked among trees and cradled almost all around by woods of oak, birch, chestnut, and *Pinus sylvestris*. An apron of lawn south of the house enlarges as it winds around to the west. Jekyll's woodland garden, with its colourful rhododendrons and Ghent hybrid azaleas, lies to the south, but the more "gardened" areas are to be found north and west of the house. Her famous colour-graded border of summer flowers—14 feet wide and 180 feet long—lies in the western reaches of the garden, facing southeast below a high stone wall. An arched gateway leads through the same wall into the Spring Garden and beyond it lies an area where the productive nursery and kitchen garden used to be.

Of her famous flower border, Jekyll wrote, "The border has a definite colour scheme; at the two ends blue, white and palest yellow, with grey foliage; and purple, white and pink, also with grey foliage, respectively; the colour then advancing from both ends by yellow and orange to the middle glory of strongest reds." Fortunately, some rare autochromes taken in about 1912 by *Country Life* show the border exactly as she planted it, and they have greatly helped in the restoration of this and other areas of the garden.

Over the wall, the Spring Garden was planted in the 1890s and was "wholly devoted to plants that bloom in April or May." The soft colours of spring were captured in the autochromes and, of course, described by Jekyll in detail, so we see pale yellow primroses and daffodils, wallflowers and tulips in purple tones, and the fiercer orange and scarlet tulips set against the matte dark greenery of yew.

"If I had plenty of suitable spaces and could spend more money on my garden I would have special regions for many a good plant," she wrote in *Home and Garden*. "As it is I have to content myself with special gardens for Primroses and for Paeonies and for Michaelmas Daisies." There were also beds for pansies, China asters, irises, lupins, daffodils, and lily of the valley, and further experimental beds. Nearer to the house can be found her (hazel) nut walk and her special strains of primroses (now thriving again).

The advanced age of its maker and reduced funds often see a once great garden go quietly to sleep. At Munstead Wood, large areas became overgrown and, after the Second World War, some outlying portions of the garden and ancillary buildings—such as the gardener's cottage and Jekyll's former workshop—were sold off. But most of the gardens survive and today are in fantastic shape, the owners having spent several decades sympathetically restoring them, aided in recent years by the head gardener, Annabel Watts, who is herself an expert on Jekyll, the Arts and Crafts movement, and its artists.

PERRYCROFT

HEREFORDSHIRE

Created at the very end of the nineteenth century, the house designed by architect C. F. A. Voysey sits within complementary restored gardens

The Malvern Hills, a designated Area of Outstanding Natural Beauty, rise up in a bumpy spine for some eight miles or so along the western fringes of central England. Combining substantial areas of woodland, farmland, and moor, they share, with nearby Wales, some of the most ancient rock formations in the British Isles and some of the most scenic landscapes. For long, the region has attracted artists and musicians, but also walkers and those interested in its numerous sites of archaeological interest. Atop one of those hills lie the carved-out contours of British Camp, an especially highly regarded Iron Age fort of extensive earthworks, believed to have been in use until the Roman occupation.

It is British Camp that looms up across a valley, as the unmissable eye-catcher seen from the house and garden of Perrycroft, a fine Arts and Crafts house. Completed in 1895 for John William Wilson, an industrialist and Liberal Member of Parliament, this country retreat was created for Wilson by C. F. A. Voysey, one of the most fashionable architects in practice in the 1890s. Roughcast-rendered Perrycroft sits on a flattened-out piece of hillside, with a substantial, level entrance court to the north and its sun-drenched gardens flowing out on determined slopes downward to the west and south.

When the present owners, Mark and Gillian Archer, acquired Perrycroft in 1999, the house had been a hostel for the Boys' Brigade for thirty years.

LEFT The garden at Perrycroft, with the house by C. F. A. Voysey, seen beyond the tall yew hedge.

RIGHT Voysey painted the details and woodwork around the house in Light Brunswick Green, now reinstated by the owners. It picks up the fresh shades of new foliage and grass, fitting the house within its garden.

Although parts of the interior had been institutionally modified for their use, a lot of original Voysey features remained and it was a dream project for sympathetic owners such as the Archers to take on. Mark Archer is treasurer to the Society for the Protection of Ancient Buildings and Gillian Archer is a designer and a conservator of historical fabrics who has worked for the National Trust. Their keen eyes for historical detail are evident everywhere and one particular triumph was to be able to pin down and remix the original Light Brunswick Green chosen by Voysey to blend "with the greens of the surrounding trees and hills." This arresting shade, evident in the windows, woodwork, and leadwork, replaces the black gloss previously applied. It seems a perfect match to the vernal shades of fresh grass, tulip stems, and the untainted emerging foliage of spring.

Venture outdoors onto the green-benched verandah, from what Voysey originally designated as the "smoking room" and you step onto a narrow terrace that runs the length of the long south-facing elevation. From here, the land falls away, somewhat dramatically, through wildflower pasture to a woodland and water garden, the latter fed by a natural spring. Here is somewhere for that "green thought in a green shade," perhaps executed from one of the well-made pieces of Arts and Crafts–inspired oak garden furniture that Gillian Archer has designed for the garden.

Very much more intensive gardening goes on west of the house; first, there's the herb garden, with its blocks of santolina and lavender, which lies on its own graded terrace. Beyond it, the tipsy lie of the land becomes apparent again, with a straight path shooting out westward from the house itself, right down through a magnificently restored yew hedge with topiary toppings, to the garden wall and its Voysey-designed gate at the far end. In between are paired box-edged beds precisely square and set into lawn surrounds, marked alongside the path by a procession of topiary yew cones. The beds are infilled with many wondrous herbaceous plants and Gillian Archer's collection of old roses, a magnificent sight, made all the more spectacular by the sloping ground, which swoops down in both the southerly and westerly directions at the same time.

Voysey sketched a design for the garden and here it is, magnificently restored and added to, so that its Arts and Crafts origins are felt and appreciated, while the detail planting is full of zest and colour, featuring the best of modern herbaceous plants, blended in with old stalwarts that maintain the feel and sumptuousness of a thriving old English garden.

Voysey sketched a design for the garden, now handsomely laid out by the present owners so that the house sits very comfortably within its hillside setting.

LEFT A view out from the house shows one of the tall yew hedges, carefully shaped with buttresses.

ABOVE RIGHT The restored main garden as Voysey had sketched it. The ground slopes away in two directions, taking in magnificent sylvan views.

BELOW RIGHT The woodland and water garden on lower ground, fed by a natural spring.

SISSINGHURST CASTLE

One of the world's most famous gardens, owing to the weekly newspaper column written about it for many years by its creator, Vita Sackville-West

Something disturbing happened at Sissinghurst garden in 2013. Newspapers ran articles about it and people took sides. What was this momentous event? After more than fifty years of female gardeners being in charge (or eighty years if you factor in the owner), the National Trust had appointed a man to be the new head gardener.

They could not have made a better move. Nevertheless, the appointment of Troy Scott Smith ruffled feathers among some traditionalists whose views had become as set in aspic as some of the garden's own areas. And that was the trouble. The garden with shrine status across the world was immaculately kept according to the requirements of the trust and the unimpeachable professionalism of its staff. But it somehow needed "something else" in the age of social media. Visitors matter. In this league, status matters. Numerous other high-status gardens were quietly moving on, continuing to be exciting. They were loosely drawing on the experimental visions of their creators and pulling in the crowds. That missing "something else" happened to be understood and suggested by Smith, and he happened to be a man. His mission, with great sensitivity and respect, is to let the garden breathe, loosen the corsets, refresh the planting, and make it romantic and unmissable.

That the garden enjoys such "shrine" status is of course greatly due to the thing itself—its assured design of rooms and corridors is well considered and beautifully proportioned, in the best Arts and Crafts tradition. It has long been inventively and alluringly planted. Sissinghurst's fame is also down to the public profile of its creators, author Victoria (Vita) Sackville-West

LEFT The towers of Sissinghurst Castle, viewed from the Cottage Garden section, where the castle's verticality is picked up by spires of clipped Irish yew. Summer flowers include daylilies, pale yellow *Thalictrum* and *Verbascum*, and deep gold *Kniphofia*.

RIGHT A neatly framed statue, viewed from the plain green circle known as the Rondel.

ABOVE LEFT A view along the White Garden with its varied textures and variations on whites, greens, silvers, and creams, including *Rosa mulliganii* trained over a central frame.

BELOW LEFT Within the orchard, numerous fruit trees rise out of the long meadow grass, some of them having roses trained through them. The little building with clay tiles and white weatherboarding recalls the Kentish vernacular style of steeply pitched "oast" houses.

RIGHT A view from the tower into the Rondel and Rose Garden. From above, Harold Nicolson's disciplined plan becomes more evident.

(1892–1962) and her husband, the diplomat Harold Nicolson (1886–1968). Both were prolific writers and clearly people are fascinated by their loving marriage, which survived numerous same-sex affairs on both sides. This area of their lives has been endlessly written about and turned into dramas, for both television and film.

Ambra Edwards rather winningly described Sackville-West as "Lady Chatterley above the waist and the gamekeeper below … tall, manly, aristocratic … she strode about her garden in top boots, breeches and pearls." Sackville-West wrote a weekly gardening column for *The Observer* newspaper from 1946 to 1961, detailing her experiments and inspiring her readers with persuasive descriptions of Persian bulbs, white lilies, old roses, cottage garden flowers, and her beloved white garden "across which a ghostly barn owl might silently sweep." She spoke of fresh air and optimism in the drab postwar years of mopping up and rationing. It was Nicolson who laid out the disciplined plan of walled and hedged enclosures, and he was especially proud of the pleached lime walk with its underplantings of bulbs.

By 1959, the garden was well known but lacking care. Sackville-West took on two young horticulturists from the highly regarded Waterperry School of Horticulture in Oxfordshire. Pamela Schwerdt and Sibylle Kreutzberger immediately made a difference. Sackville-West approved of "their youth and keenness, and their workmanlike blue jeans." She noticed they "do not stop working while one talks to them, which I like. No time wasted." After their retirement in 1990, the tradition of talented women in charge continued until Smith's arrival. "I'm going to have to be very confident," he said at the time.

TEMPLE GUITING MANOR

GLOUCESTERSHIRE

This modern garden in the Cotswolds has a very Arts and Crafts feel in its divisions of rooms and features of craftsmanship

The fourteenth-century manor house at Temple Guiting is tucked away in one of those secret, timeless villages in the wooded folds of the north Cotswolds. It was for long known as Manor Farmhouse, there having been (unusually) two manors in close proximity at Temple Guiting in medieval times. The "other" manor (in which the Templars had an interest) was owned by the Lacy and Clinton families until the early sixteenth century, when Richard Fox, Bishop of Winchester, acquired it and gave it to the Oxford college of Corpus Christi, which he founded in 1517. Within a century or so it was gone, however, and so Manor Farmhouse became the manor of the locality.

The architect Ptolemy Dean advised on the restoration and refurbishment of the ancient house and its numerous outbuildings; around them, garden designer Jinny Blom has created a ravishing garden, which, though streamlined and contemporary, fits in seamlessly with the property and its rolling Cotswolds landscape.

The garden's design is designed around a splendid broad terrace to one side of the house featuring a long rectangular pool, bordered on either side by stilt hedges of hornbeam, under which are planted abundant flower borders. Above the main terrace, the higher ground is home to a graded orchard lawn, while below the terrace the next level reveals a series of small hedged enclosures running parallel with the long pool. It is a smart and simple concept that allows the glory of the site to shine through (this is a west-facing hillside with idyllic rural views over woods and pastures above a well-watered valley).

On such a site, with its free-draining slope, abundant light, and rich, slightly alkaline soil, it would be easy to get carried away with the planting, but Jinny Blom kept to a disciplined and repeated palette of violet, blue, and white flowers along the length of the pool, stitching in a variety of foliage textures and forms with plenty of silver highlights. The white flowers that illuminate the terrace include *Hydrangea arborescens* 'Annabelle', white foxgloves, and bearded irises, creamy-toned delphiniums, the white form of wall valerian *Centranthus ruber* 'Alba', white *Viola cornuta*, and the repeat-flowering David Austin rose 'Winchester Cathedral'. Blue notes are introduced with the ravishing pale blue iris 'Jane Phillips'—a deservedly popular old cultivar—sky blue *Viola* 'Boughton Blue', inky columbines, and metallic, azure eryngiums. The mauves woven among all of these are provided by plentiful quantities of 'Munstead Dwarf' lavenders and *Allium cristophii* along the front and intermittent silvery volcanoes of cardoon, with their spiky artichoke flowers among the taller plants.

The place is humming with bees across the summer months, especially around the lavenders, eryngiums, and cardoons. The orchard, too, has

Under pleached hornbeams, like a hedge on stilts, views take in the folds of the Cotswold hills, with a run of irises and white *Centranthus ruber* 'Alba' illuminating the garden when spring gives way to summer.

patches of low-growing clover left unmowed in the lawn for the bees, as does a scenic perimeter walk beyond the garden walls.

The small hedged enclosures on the level below the main garden amount to four separate garden rooms, featuring different moods of topiary in box and yew. Nearest the house the "room" known as the Privy Garden humorously acknowledges the existence of a stone garden hut, now used as a handy store, with perimeter beds planted with roses, *Dianthus carthusianorum*, and a handsome *Cotinus coggygria*.

Next to it, the herb garden is entered and exited via most unusual and attractive low gates that had been 1920s balcony railings from an old hotel in France, picked up at a *brocante* in Nice. This garden features parallel waves of purple-leaved sage, acid yellow-flowered rue, 'Hidcote' lavender, and compact silvery mounds of *Artemisia* 'Powis Castle'.

Beyond the two further garden areas at this level, steps lead up and through a stout oak door in a high wall, to a further area known as the

Peacock Garden, which casts aside restraint and formality in favour of a huge and eclectic range of flowering perennials and grasses set out in curved beds that provide ample cut flowers for the house.

Behind a high wall on the east side lies the tennis court, which is edged beyond the tramlines with quantities of large topiary shapes in yew. Close by, a long path known as the Granary Walk is lined on either side with beds of abundant planting. The combined efforts of Jinny Blom and Ptolemy Dean have produced a garden of quality and beauty in the Cotswolds vernacular tradition, aided by dry stone waller Gilbert Stirling Lee and his team, whose skilled work earned them the coveted Pinnacle Award from the Dry Stone Walling Association of Great Britain.

OPPOSITE One of the four small, linked gardens, with box topiary and crimson *Astrantia.*

ABOVE Tall white spires of *Eremurus*, the foxtail lily, among *Calamagrostis* grasses, dark maroon *Cirsium rivulare* 'Atropurpureum,' and silvery foliage of *Lychnis coronaria*, the rose campion.

RIGHT A long view: the gardens run in succession behind the dry-stone wall. Classic estate fencing separates the gardens from pasture that runs steeply down into the valley.

ABOVE LEFT The central garden, with its long canal, formal lawns on either side, and rows of pleached trees, has a slight Dutch flair. Late afternoon shadows cast patterns on the turf and water. Out of view, the ground rises again to the right (east), where an orchard is planted into the grass.

BELOW LEFT The "privy" building is now a useful garden shed. The pale blue iris, 'Jane Phillips,' is a reliable old cultivar, paired here with silvery foliage of cardoons, *Cynara cardunculus*, a close relative of the culinary artichoke.

RIGHT A small garden of box-edged beds, viewed from the higher main garden, between the deeply cut foliage of the cardoons.

GREAT DIXTER

The Edwardian country garden laid out by Edwin Lutyens and made famous by the writer Christopher Lloyd continues to thrive and experiment

Located on the western extremity of Northiam village, Great Dixter includes a collection of ancient agricultural buildings and a most characterful extended house, part of which dates from the 1450s. The property, just 180 feet above sea level, is surrounded by pastures but, appropriately, enjoys the sequestered nature of a Tudor dwelling. Unconcerned with "what lies beyond," the garden is sheltered and made private by its own arrangement of farm buildings and substantial stretches of beefy, tall yew hedge.

Its Arts and Crafts credentials date from when Nathaniel Lloyd acquired the property in 1910. A London printer, Lloyd was successful enough in business to be able to retire in his early forties. He wisely engaged the brilliant young architect Edwin Lutyens to renovate it, splicing in what had been the derelict remains of a timber sixteenth-century house, which was dismantled and imported from a few miles away. Lutyens's additions, with gabled roofs and soaring chimney stacks, blend seamlessly with the whole.

Lutyens also laid out the garden plan, although it has been noted that fewer walls were built in the garden than the architect would have prescribed, Lloyd preferring the greenery—and perhaps the economy—of yew, to create the divisions. Lloyd took an active interest and designed the topiary lawn, dotted with yew sculptures and, in the early 1920s, the Sunk Garden with its octagonal pond. His wife, Daisy, was a knowledgeable gardener keen on wildflowers, which led to the establishment of the garden's famous wildflower meadows.

Although the Lloyds gave Great Dixter a very nice garden, its greatness has been magnified due to the their youngest son's combined talents for gardening, plantsmanship, and writing—a perfect storm for someone with something to say and an engaging, often provocative way of saying it. Following a degree in modern languages at Cambridge and army service through the Second World War, Christopher Lloyd (1921–2006) received a degree in horticulture at Wye College in Kent. After a couple of years teaching, he then returned home in 1950, working alongside his mother in developing the garden and writing about it (his first published article was about *Lobelia cardinalis*, in the long-gone journal *Gardening Illustrated*). For a talented young man to have found his métier in his mid-thirties and surrounded by the means to achieve it was indeed fortunate.

Christopher Lloyd's first book, *The Mixed Border in the Modern Garden* (1957), was a breath of fresh air in the austere years after the Second World War. More books and articles followed, and Lloyd's lively *Country Life* column, In My Garden, began in 1963 (continuing weekly for more than forty years). The 1970s brought his most highly regarded and still pertinent book, *The Well-Tempered Garden*. "It puts him firmly among that rare band

A view of Great Dixter house, which sits comfortably in the middle of its intensively cultivated gardens. Lutyens, who extended the house, wanted to install a number of garden walls, but Nathaniel Lloyd, his client, preferred to plant yew hedges, which are now characterful and shapely.

Seed-grown mauve poppies *Papaver somniferum*, among radiant spires of lupins, including *Lupinus* 'The Page' and 'Noble Maiden' (from the Band of Nobles Series). The variegated bamboo is *Pleioblastus viridistriatus*, while *Persicaria polymorpha* makes its presence known, with huge white plumes, at the back.

of plantsmen that have not only grown, observed and studied a vast range of plants, but are able to write about them enchantingly and with authority … I cannot remember when I enjoyed a book so much," wrote Roy Hay in *The Times*.

Christopher Lloyd always acknowledged that he had been fortunate in having an already well-designed garden to work in. Lutyens's genius for planning took into consideration the best locations for terraces, steps, views, and a circuit that would link one area logically with the next. The gardens wrap around the house offering a progression of different spaces.

From the northeast entrance, a straight path points the way directly ahead to the house and its unique leaning front porch, past the wildflowers of Daisy Lloyd's Meadow Garden. Off to the right, the Sunk Garden ranges around the oval-octagonal pond, shielded on two sides by typical Sussex barns. Eastward lie the topiaries and experimental plantings of the Peacock and High Gardens.

The house sits squarely in the middle of its gardens and meadows and the famous southwest-facing Long Border stretches away from its south corner, terminating beside a yew-enclosed oak bench specially designed by Lutyens. The Orchard meadow, with its wild orchids, buttercups, and narcissi, fans out down a slope immediately south of the Long Border, while the topiary lawn lies off to the west, behind what was for many years the Rose Garden. In 1992, Christopher memorably wrote about replacing the roses with a jungly, subtropical Exotic Garden. This was the first major change to the garden since it was created, likewise announcing the appointment of Fergus Garrett as the new head gardener.

"Thanks to replant disease, newly planted rose replacements ceased to thrive here, so on Fergus's arrival at Dixter, we made a grand alteration, got rid of the roses and created a late summer to autumn garden for tropical effect, though many of the best foliage plants are quite hardy," wrote

Dark-eyed, magenta-flowered *Geranium psilostemon* runs through this broad bed, where poppies emerge here and there among a succession of plants coming through for each season. The tall grass is *Stipa gigantea*, which shimmers in sunlight when its oatlike flowers expand. Blue *Geranium* 'Orion' occupies the middle ground.

Christopher. "This has been a lot of fun. For colour, we are mainly using dahlias and cannas. There is a haze of purple from self-sowing *Verbena bonariensis* … The banana, *Musa basjoo*, is a hardy Japanese species."

Garrett, also an alumnus of Wye College, had much experience and at Great Dixter, a creative working partnership began, which ratcheted up the garden's status yet further. The borders were invigorated and a flurry of new books from Christopher Lloyd attracted a new following and enhanced the garden's international standing.

Christopher died in 2006, but the charitable trust he set up has put the garden on a firm footing for the future. Heritage Lottery funding, grants, and donations have helped enable sensitive restoration for the historic buildings and created a thriving training ground for resident student gardeners.

Exuberance and experimentation are key to the philosophy, the planting everywhere noticeably more complex and free-form, pushing the boundaries between cultivated and wild. "People sometimes say we are quite brave at Dixter," says Garrett, who is the trust's chief executive, as well as the head gardener. "But this is just normal gardening for us, having fun with plants and not being afraid of trying things out. Often our experiments work and sometimes they don't, but that doesn't matter so much, as long as we learn from them and keep moving forward. That's what the place is about."

PREVIOUS PAGES In the Topiary Garden planted more than a century ago by Nathaniel Lloyd, the grass has been allowed to establish into a wildflower meadow, giving an overall softer feel to this area than in his day.

BELOW Letting them do their thing: summer's abundance with a floral and foliage tapestry that includes *Persicaria polystachya*, scarlet dahlias, violet-blue wands of *salvia patens*, orange helenium, and the small Michaelmas daisy, *Symphyotrichum* (a.k.a. Aster) 'Little Carlow.'

RIGHT A joyful high summer greeting for every visitor: pots are overflowing with a changing display of plants, such as *Amaranthus*, *Rudbeckia*, dahlias in variety, canna, pelargonium, fuchsia, and *Actaea* (*Cimicifuga*).

13 THE EXOTIC GARDEN

In 1990, Angus White, a cabinetmaker, built a colonial-style bungalow on the edge of his garden, complete with red oxide corrugated roof, and beside it opened his Sussex nursery, Architectural Plants, focusing on exotic things he couldn't find elsewhere at the time. He sold cycads, palms, beschorneria, bamboos, bananas, and other leafy things, many of them on the border of hardiness, or just looking that way. He was—and is—among a curious band of individuals who wanted to live among jungly, exotic plants that have big personalities and speak of warm climates.

Four years before, Myles Challis had made an exotic garden at the 1986 Chelsea Flower Show. It was "the first garden of its kind [at the show]," he recalls, filled with hardy palms, bananas, hostas, and bamboos. His follow-up book, *The Exotic Garden* (1989), showed how to do it, and his own small London garden was featured in numerous periodicals, admired for its junglelike approach. Meanwhile, Will Giles, a talented illustrator based in central Norwich, was working away at his own subtropical and acclaimed paradise—one with a distinctly Victorian sensibility. And in the North Downs where rural Surrey meets London, Brian Hiley had filled his garden and very eclectic nursery with cannas, palms, aeoniums, agaves, and aloes, much of which he transported regularly to the Royal Horticultural Society's shows. (Later, he removed the lot to the milder climate of Cornwall.)

These people and their kind were collectively known at the time as "The New Exoticists" and much of what they grew is now surprisingly easy to find, as people have taken again to showy things like loud dahlias and leafy colocasia. Even "houseplants" have rolled back into fashion too after long absence, aided by millennials' enthusiasm for growing shapely succulents and 1970s retro "Swiss cheese" plants (*Monstera deliciosa*) indoors. However, English passions for the unusual and exotic go back several centuries, of course, and the further back you go, the more rarefied those enthusiasms become.

For example, at Hampton Court Palace beside the River Thames, Queen Mary (1662–1694) and her retinue of royal gardeners tended a distinguished range of "Foreign and curious Trees and Shrubbs." They were nurtured in the heated Lower Orangery and displayed outside it in pots for the summer.

OPPOSITE Conjuring up thoughts of subtropical islands: an exotic border in 2008 at Lower House in Hay on Wye, featuring scarlet *Crocosmia* 'Lucifer', hand-shaped foliage of *Ricinus* Carmencita, *Kniphofia caulescens* with its glaucous leaves, bronze and striped foliage of cannas, and a fan palm.

OPPOSITE, CLOCKWISE Originally, collections of "Exotick" plants were the prerogative of royalty. In her short life, Queen Mary II (1662–1694) displayed at Hampton Court Palace a distinguished range of "Foreign and curious Trees and Shrubbs," brought from distant lands. Today, exotic gardens are widespread and may include fabulous things such as: waterlilies; Indian peacocks; bright cactus-flowered dahlias such as 'Tahiti Sunrise'; or prehistoric-looking foliage such as cycads.

Wooden tubs, painted terra-cotta pots, and decorative Delft pots contained what were then undoubtedly "stupendious Rarities" that only royalty could obtain: species such as prehistoric-looking cycads from Japan, spiky agaves from Mexico, the silvery succulent *Cotyledon orbiculata* from South Africa, and clipped orange trees. The royal collection under Queen Mary was probably the finest in England, perhaps in Europe, too; she was the original New Exoticist.

Plant exploration in the early days was exciting but perilous. It required physical stamina, endurance, diplomacy, a strong gut, and a healthy dose of luck. One of the greatest explorers was Sir Joseph Banks (1743–1820). Young, rich, and privileged, he had shunned the Grand Tour to Italy that was expected to round off the education of men of his class. "Every blockhead does that. My Grand Tour shall be one around the Globe," he declared, presciently. His initial voyage was a seven-month journey surveying the coastline of Labrador and Newfoundland in 1766, where he catalogued the plants, birds, and wildlife he found. But his next expedition was truly round-the-world, aboard HMS *Endeavour*, skippered by James Cook. The three-year voyage, from 1768 to 1771, took *Endeavour* to Brazil and Tierra del Fuego, across the Pacific to Tahiti, thence to New Zealand, Australia (the *Terra Australis Incognita*, or Unknown Southern Land), Indonesia, Java, and South Africa. It yielded more than 1,300 species new to Western eyes and advanced Banks's stellar scientific career. As scientific adviser to King George III he worked hard to establish the royal gardens at Kew (page 219) as the world's premier botanic garden; his influence on its collections was profound, and he was one of the founding eight members of what became the Royal Horticultural Society (page 475). In the gardens that follow, numerous species were collected by Banks and by the subsequent plant explorers he sent out into the far corners of the world.

TRESCO ABBEY GARDENS

ISLES OF SCILLY, CORNWALL

Located in one of the mildest parts of the country, Tresco often has some two hundred different species in flower outdoors in midwinter

Flung out at sea, in the far southwest of England, some thirty miles or so from the westernmost point of Cornwall, Tresco forms part of the Isles of Scilly, a remarkable archipelago. Five of the islands are inhabited, but there are some 140 more islands and islets that are the domain of maritime birds and sea life. Several lighthouses bear witness to the fact that sailors have long needed to steer carefully when approaching the Scillies; in times past there was regular trade in items salvaged from wrecked ships.

Generally, the islands have only low hills or none at all, and although they can be subject to storms and all the weather the Atlantic Ocean can throw at them, their climate is mild, benefiting from the warming influence of the Gulf Stream. It's not uncommon to have weeks of sunshine broken only now and then by squally showers; the beaches of the larger islands typically have long crescents of white, powdery sand of the sort you might expect in the Caribbean, often basking under clear blue skies. The Scilly Isles therefore receive many summer holidaymakers and also attract artists, as well as birdwatchers during migration seasons.

In order to spend time in the Abbey Garden on Tresco, the second largest of the islands, visitors must undertake a slightly adventurous journey. Many take a train to Penzance, taxi to the little domestic airport at Land's End, and board a Twin Otter plane for the fifteen-minute flight to Saint Mary's, the largest and most populated of the isles. From there, a five-minute taxi ride to the harbour puts visitors in the right place to take one of the "RIB" boats that ferry among the islands. It is all very well to land on Tresco, with its various forms of luxurious seaside accommodation; people walk or cycle everywhere, for motor vehicles are used only to serve the holiday cottages and farm.

All of which should see visitors settled in to explore the renowned exotic garden, which covers seventeen acres. The Abbey lies within the garden, a somewhat romantic-looking ruin, dating back to when King Henry I (ca. 1068–1135) enabled the monks of Tavistock Abbey to build a priory on the remote island. There had been a monastic settlement on the island since 946 AD, but the monks struggled to survive on Tresco in the long term, due to raids by bands of pirates. In 1351 most of the Abbey property was destroyed and within two hundred years, with the dissolution of the monasteries under Henry VIII, the priory was abandoned, though it may have already closed before then.

It was one Augustus John Smith (1804–1872), lord proprietor of the Isles of Scilly for more than thirty years, who took a lease on the islands in 1834. Smith was living in the age when plant hunters were voyaging far and wide, bringing back to England all manner of exotic plants from warmer climates. In order to make his garden in the south of the island, Smith first had to create shelter by

LEFT The mild climate of the Isles of Scilly, off the western coast of Cornwall, enables many plants that would perish in most other parts of the British Isles to survive and thrive outdoors.

FOLLOWING PAGES A view from the upper terraces reveals how tall evergreen hedges filter the winds coming off the sea, enabling palm trees to grow around the ruins of the old abbey.

planting trees on the barren, windswept site. After that, an infrastructure of stairways and horizontal paths to access the rising ground was required.

The spine of the garden is a long, straight staircase rising up a steep hill through the middle of everything. From its direct north-south axis, paths lead off left and right, enabling exploration of the subtropical plantings. The garden is very rich in species from Mediterranean climates around the world, especially from Australasia, South Africa, and the Americas. Therefore, it's not unusual for the gardeners to count more than two hundred different plant species actually in flower on New Year's Day. It's an annual assessment and in fact, the garden proudly announced a count of 306 species on New Year's Day 2018.

Mature Monterey pines and cypresses supply much of the shelter and have a Mediterranean look about them, which provides a convincing

backdrop for the species of *Leucadendron*, *Leucospermum*, *Clethra*, protea, *Jovellana*, homeria, and much else besides. Although the garden is certainly of interest to plant enthusiasts, it also has much more general visitor appeal, being one of the most pleasant places imaginable to stroll among unusual and colourful flowers and beautifully planted pots; to chance upon statues and fountains carefully positioned; and to eat well in the garden café.

Another point of interest is Valhalla, a covered area in the far south of the garden, where a collection of ships' figureheads has been assembled. Most of them date from the mid-to-late nineteenth century and came from merchant sailing vessels or early steamships that were wrecked on the rocks nearby. Now beautifully restored, the figures of busty ladies, sailors, and animals lean out strikingly from their permanent stone perches, referencing another aspect of the history of these fascinating islands.

OPPOSITE FAR LEFT Canary Island date palms *Phoenix canariensis* have achieved "champion tree" status among the different species of trees growing in the British Isles.

OPPOSITE LEFT With its crevices partially occupied by creepers and succulents, the old abbey ruin makes a striking if slightly melancholy feature in the middle of the gardens.

RIGHT Planted in the nineteenth century and added to ever since, Tresco's subtropical garden is home to species from across the world's Mediterranean climate zones, from Brazil to New Zealand and Burma to South Africa. Thriving among the palms are numerous *Dasylirion acrotrichum* from the deserts of Mexico.

FELBRIGG HALL

NORFOLK

Part of the old walled kitchen garden at Felbrigg is given over to displays of southern hemisphere plants which are also light on water requirements

James Lees-Milne (1908–1997), aesthete, diarist, and the National Trust's country house expert from 1936 to 1973, shone a slender beam of light on life at the splendid seventeenth-century mansion of Felbrigg Hall, recalling a moment in September 1946: "Went on to Felbrigg for dinner. Wyndham Ketton-Cremer's mother is staying, a sweet, white-haired old lady … he is mentally stimulating. Plenty of serious talk. House huge, but Wyndham is well looked after by his couple, and lives comfortably. No electric light, and I had to walk miles with a candle from my bedroom to the w.c. at the far end of the Stuart wing."

The Windham/Wyndham family took over the manor of Felbrigg in the fifteenth century, expanding their landholding in the succeeding centuries while also making both the house and the grounds larger, more important, and more fashionable, as people do, in times of enhanced status. Humphry Repton might have contributed to the late-eighteenth-century alterations, being a neighbour and a good friend of the William Windham then resident, but no archival evidence exists to confirm it. Both the house and grounds saw fluctuating fortunes across subsequent generations and the property was left to the National Trust in the will of Mr. R. Wyndham Ketton-Cremer in 1969.

Graham Stuart Thomas (1909–2003), the National Trust's gardens advisor for many years, wrote that, "If you drive through the park at Felbrigg on a still autumn day you will be struck by its expanse and peacefulness, and the mellow tones of trees and buildings. The sea is but a mile away. The house and garden are sheltered by the Great Wood planted by William Windham in the last quarter of the 17th century. Many of the great oaks and sweet chestnuts date from that time … the orangery, which houses some remarkably large camellias, was built in 1705."

All of that rings true today, but the walled garden is a much more exciting place than when Thomas knew it. He noted some old fruit trees survived but relatively little in the way of kitchen garden productivity, the main interest of the walled garden being a clutch of modest seasonal eruptions—of lilacs in spring, some edible herbs in the summer, a bed of tree mallows (*Lavatera*) for late summer, grapevines and belladonna lilies in the autumn. Precious little, in other words, to put the garden on a must-see list, although it has a charming octagonal dovecote, set into the middle of the northernmost wall.

Thomas began a process of making the walled garden a little more interesting, within the confines of what the minimal staff could cope with, which was continued by his successors. Perhaps it was helpful that there was so little historical precedent to take notice of, for it gave the trust a freer hand to reinvent the walled garden with some imaginative planting. For many years, this has been down to the efforts of Felbrigg's head gardener, Tina Hammond, who spent much of her childhood in Australia and, in the process, absorbed

Located near the north Norfolk coast, Felbrigg Hall is in one of the driest locations in Britain. Within the sheltering walled garden, its exotic plants from the southern hemisphere include the spectacular Australian scarlet bottlebrush, *Callistemon laevis*. Its vibrant red is picked up in bedded-out begonias at the front of the border and set off by the bronze-black succulent *Sedum* 'Purple Emperor'.

LEFT Presided over by a Chusan fan palm *Trachycarpus fortunei*, one of the exotic borders glows with *Kniphofia*, *Callistemon*, and 'Purple Emperor' sedums.

BELOW The east-west border in July, with lilies in full flush and dahlias just coming into their own. The dahlia in the foreground is 'Moonshine,' then come *Lychnis*, *Anthemis* 'E. C. Buxton,' all mixed in with a liberal dose of *Eschscholzia californica*.

an interest in the colourful and shapely flora of the southern hemisphere.

In replanting much of the walled garden at Felbrigg over the past fifteen-plus years, Hammond has also drawn on her earlier experience at another National Trust property, Saltram, in the mild microclimate of Devon's south coast, where subtropical plants in great variety are long established.

Felbrigg's light soil is ideal for such a venture and the straight gravel paths are margined by several borders where one may come across azara, agave, aloe, and astelia; beschorneria, corokia, *Hakea*, and *Hedychium*; puya, fascicularia, *Dasylirion*, olearia, *Callistemon*, melaleuca, and pittosporum—certainly a departure from the traditional lineup of English border plants. In most parts of the country it would be unthinkable to attempt growing such things outside year-round. Nevertheless, species such as the tender aloes get glass protection here in winter, to keep out the dampness that can be their nemesis.

The walled garden is not the only part of the grounds to nurture plants of borderline hardiness, however. On the other side of the house, in the woodland shrubberies of the West Garden, mature trees filter out the cold winds to give protection to the mountain pepper, *Drimys lanceolata* and crimson-stemmed, May-flowering *Drimys winteri*; Chilean *Desfontainea spinosa*, with tubular orange flowers, and *Crinodendron hookerianum*, the red lantern tree of Chile. Truly, the world within a garden can be found at Felbrigg Hall.

CLOCKWISE One of the greenhouses in the walled garden displays further tender treasures—chiefly things that are just too delicate to survive year-round outdoors, including some substantial cacti; a close-up view of the Brazilian plume flower, *Justicia carnea*; seen through a veil of *Echium* flowers, the glowing red-hot pokers of *Kniphofia* 'Nancy's Red.'

In the far north of Scotland, overlooking Little Loch Broom, Durnamuck's exotic South African bed includes fiery *Watsonia pillansii* and red-hot pokers or torch lilies, *Kniphofia uvaria*. The exotic plants and their startling colours have a surprising affinity to the otherwise subtle, tweedy landscape.

DURNAMUCK COTTAGES

In spite of its location in the far north of Scotland, its west coast location and the Gulf Stream give this garden a mild enough climate for exotic planting

For anyone truly smitten with exotic, subtropical flora, taking on a plot of land on Britain's west coast can be a good start; the warming influence of the Gulf Stream from the Atlantic Ocean brings with it relatively milder winter temperatures. It has long attracted garden makers to settle on the west side, even as far north as the Highlands and islands of Scotland, where the fjord landscape is romantically beautiful and untamed—the haunt of the majestic golden eagle and its white-tailed cousin.

Professional gardeners Will Soos and Sue Pomeroy, both originally from England (although Soos grew up in Scotland), met when they worked at the National Trust for Scotland's Inverewe, a famous plantsman's garden, also located on this rugged and remote stretch of coast. An opportunity to create their own garden from scratch came in 2009, when they took on the croft at Durnamuck with its four-acre plot sloping away to the shore of Little Loch Broom. They designed and built the cottage themselves, creating a stylish hybrid of two overseas houses they admired, one a former chapel in South Africa and the other a friend's house in the United States. It's very much a homegrown place, its walls made with chunky, water-worn stones found on their land and at the lochside.

Although it's surrounded by mountains, their property is on lowish ground near the loch. Therefore, building raised beds to lift the plants away from a somewhat high water table was one of the first things to be done, along with planting trees and hedges to create some wind shelter. The beds around the house are all set into an area of gravel, but as one progresses into the garden, the gravel is left behind transitioning to an open lawn and turf paths winding around a pair of long irregular beds. These follow the sloping land as it proceeds southeastward in a gentle gradient down to the loch's deep, dark waters. Assorted grasses—always a graceful choice for a breezy location—mingle with South African bulbs planted in bold, drifts, stitched through with silver-leaved shrubs and characterful boulders.

One of the things one will notice is how "right" the plants look in this setting. Many, of course, come from similar habitats and climatic challenges in their own lands and therefore look "at home." Despite the richly saturated colours of crocosmia, kniphofia, agapanthus, watsonia, and gladiolus—a much showier palette than the tweedy local flora—their bright hues are absorbed by the enormous landscape so that the plants enhance their surroundings of looming mountains and rapidly changing skies, milky silver one moment, lowering pewter the next. And likewise, the backdrop of basalt greys, peaty browns, and subdued, shifting greens enhances and gives definition to every bloom and leaf.

It would be misleading, however, to say that the garden is only concerned with exotics. Soos and Pomeroy live thirty-six miles away from the nearest

shop, which is across a mountain range. Popping out for a loaf of bread is not an option! They therefore bake their own and in fact are self-sufficent year-round, having hens and sheep on the croft and growing all their own organic fruit and vegetables. Of course, there are also sea fish in the loch.

The couple's shared passion for southern hemisphere flora and the aromatic herbs of Mediterranean lands has taken them across the world on numerous occasions, to discover more about plants in their natural habitats. In this location, where winter's days are dark and long, heading south like the swallows sounds like a fine idea. The upside is that on summer evenings daylight lasts well into the night, and even then seems in a hurry to return, illuminating the little house with the red oxide roof and its jewel box of precious summer flowers.

ABOVE RIGHT The South African Bed against a backdrop of Sail Mhor and a glimpse of Little Loch Broom. Glowing with heat, despite the overcast sky: *Watsonia pillansii*, *Helichrysum populifolium*, *Kniphofia uvaria*, and *Crocosmia* 'Emberglow.'

BELOW RIGHT Apparently illuminating the water's edge: the South Africa Bed with wind-blasted eucalyptus and silver birch trees to the left. The orange crocosmia is 'Mars,' the blond grass to the left is *Chionochloa flavicans*. There is a band of *Watsonia* 'Tresco Hybrids' farther back in the bed and *Kniphofia uvaria* in flower behind.

In the heart of the city of Oxford, Worcester College's exotic border is sheltered by high walls that give protection to substantial banana plants *Ensete ventricosum* and the floppy-leaved giant reed, *Arundo donax*.

WORCESTER COLLEGE, OXFORD

OXFORDSHIRE

A long, burgeoning border of big-leafed plants such as bananas, and rich summer flowers enjoy the protective shelter of high walls

Among the colleges of Oxford University, Worcester College enjoys the reputation of being very much like a country house, within what is now the central part of the city. Its grounds are exceptionally spacious, covering some twenty-six acres, including exceedingly plant-rich gardens, an orchard, a substantial lake of a roughly inverted L-shape, and beyond it, much-used playing fields.

At the heart of the college, the quadrangle (with immaculate lawn and enviably trim, grassy banks) is enclosed by the main buildings along two sides (north and east), a row of former cottages to the south, and an actual garden wall on the fourth, west side. The walls themselves are clad with creepers including roses, *Campsis*, and wisteria, a sort of amuse-bouche, just hinting at the verdure and plantsmanship that lies beyond.

As with much of Oxford, the college has ancient origins, but its grounds are especially fascinating since researchers suggest it is likely that the garden has been under continuous development for some 730 years, making it one of England's oldest continuously cultivated gardens. It began with the aforementioned row of cottages along the south side, founded in 1283 as a college for Benedictine monks and continuing as such until the dissolution of the monasteries under Henry VIII, in about 1539. What did the monks grow in the surrounding grounds, strung out in the countryside on the edge of town but close to the river? Nothing as exotic as can now be seen; from the meadows and willow beds close by, they created a typical *hortus*, a monastic garden for raising vegetables and medicinal herbs.

What was in the monks' day known as Gloucester College, became annexed to Saint John's College after the dissolution, and renamed Gloucester Hall around 1560. It stayed that way until Sir Thomas Cookes (ca. 1648–1701), a very wealthy but childless Worcestershire baronet, came into the picture, albeit after his own lifetime. In his will, he left £10,000 in trust to endow a new college at the university. But the haggling and squabbling by interested colleges making claims on the funds meant that it wasn't until 1714 that the money was settled on Gloucester Hall, to be renamed and repositioned in the hierarchy as Worcester College. (By that time Cookes's endowment had usefully swelled to £15,000.)

All of which preamble leads to Worcester College's tercentenary celebrations in 2014, for which Edward Wilson, emeritus fellow and the college's former garden master, dug around for clues to piece together the garden's key moments of development. Maps and drawings from the sixteenth, seventeenth, and eighteenth centuries show lots of squared-up plots around the buildings of the times. A lot of extra land was bought in the eighteenth century, however, and numerous trees and shrubs were planted, including species quite recently introduced from Japan. Influenced by Richard Payne

OPPOSITE FAR LEFT Worth closer inspection: silvery *Plectranthus argentatus*.

OPPOSITE LEFT × *Chitalpa tashkentensis* 'Pink Dawn.' Chitalpa is unusual, being a hybrid of plants belonging to two different genera: *Chilopsis* and *Catalpa*.

RIGHT A medley of summer flowers from *Cleome* 'Colour Fountains,' 'Cosmos Purity,' *Echinacea purpurea*, and bronze foliage of *Ricinus communis* 'Carmencita' (the latter is a cultivar of a striking but entirely toxic species, much used in Victorian bedding schemes).

Knight's Picturesque aesthetic sometime after 1800, the grounds achieved, and still possess, the feel of a spacious park.

Eminent gardeners of the late nineteenth and early twentieth centuries connected to the garden included Alfred Parsons (whose design for the provost's rose garden has been recently reinstated), as well as the unstoppable force that was Ellen Willmott, of Warley Place in Essex (page 16), Tresserve in the French Alps, and Boccanegra, on the Italian Riviera, who donated plants and seeds.

"Each generation has left 'some impress' on the gardens and grounds," says Wilson. "There has been from the beginning an adventurous policy of plant acquisition, echoed in our own time, for example, by the purchase of two first generation Wollemi pines."

Wilson's involvement through the early years of the twenty-first century, together with the exceedingly talented Simon Bagnall, head of gardens, saw the gardens achieve new heights of excellence everywhere. These lovely photos show Bagnall's skilled planting of the long mixed border, which lies back-to-back with the ancient monastic cottages. In late summer it's an exotic tour de force of textures, flowers, foliages, and colours, with banana plants, *Aeonium*, *Bomarea*, and fiery dahlias, stitched among marigolds, *Crocosmia*, and very much else besides.

LEFT Dramatically illuminated in the low-angled sunlight, a crimson dahlia echoes the violet-and-scarlet-flowered *Fuchsia genii*, which has bright, golden-lime foliage, and the bronze-rosetted succulent *Aeonium* 'Schwarzkopf' in a large vase.

OPPOSITE ABOVE The mixed border in summer is an exotic tour de force of textures, flowers, foliages, and colours, with banana plants, *Aeonium*, *Bomarea*, and fiery dahlias, among marigolds, montbretia, and very much else besides.

OPPOSITE BELOW Orange-flowered *Dahlia* 'David Howard,' *Acanthus mollis*, and zesty, lime-coloured foliage of *Cornus alba* 'Aurea' have dignified presence among wispier subjects.

14 THE ROSE GARDEN

Roses appear in the writings of ancient Greece and the Roman Empire and later were adopted into Christian iconography (the five petals of the wild rose suggesting the five wounds of Christ). Several wild roses occur in the British Isles, but those most admired are chiefly derived from species and cultivars originating in the lands of the Persian Empire and East Asia. Owing to their very long time and value in cultivation, roses have associations with Brahma, Buddha, Muhammad, Vishnu, and Confucius. In other words, human admiration of the rose is ancient and universal.

Likewise, rose gardens exist and are loved all over the world—nothing quite matches a rose garden in full sail and scent at the height of early summer, especially at sunrise, or as evening approaches and the soft light is accompanied by what seem to be extra layers of intoxicating "rose" fragrance, perhaps mysteriously blending with, but not resisting, the scents of nearby plants.

Indeed, the rose in perfumery has the most venerable of origins. *Rosa × damascena* is especially prominent in the making of scent. Even now, it is the rose of choice among growers of essences for the fragrance market. Long established plantations are cultivated in pockets of Asia, Turkey, and the Balkan Mountains of Bulgaria. As dramatic as anywhere is El Kelaa M'Gouna, Morocco's Valley of Roses, an oasis tucked among the gorges and fortresses where the Atlas Mountains rise up from the western fringes of the Sahara.

Rose fragrances are blended to varying degree into the majority of manufactured perfumes. Luca Turin, perfume specialist and author of *The Secret of Scent: Adventures in Perfume and the Science of Smell*, recalled being captivated decades ago by the original Nombre Noir by Shiseido, which he found enchanting. "A perfume like the timbre of a voice, can say something quite independent of the words actually spoken. What Nombre Noir said was 'flower.' But the way it said it was an epiphany. The flower at the core of Nombre Noir was half-way between a rose and a violet, but without the trace of the sweetness of either, set instead against an austere, almost saintly background of cigar-box cedar notes. At the same time, it wasn't dry, and seemed to be glistening with a liquid freshness that made its deep colors glow like a stained-glass window."

OPPOSITE In the Rose Garden at Mottisfont Abbey in Hampshire, *Rosa gallica* var. *officinalis* and the raspberries-mixed-with-cream flowers of Rosa *gallica* var. *officinalis* 'Versicolor' (syn. Rosa mundi), are part of the Graham Thomas collection of old roses. Thomas designed the rose garden with enormous flair.

OPPOSITE Roses bewitch the beholder with their fragrances, beauty, richness, and abundance of flowers in many shades.

ABOVE LEFT An American shrub rose of Floribunda type, 'Apricot Nectar,' introduced in 1965.

ABOVE RIGHT Maroon-crimson 'Chianti' was the first red rose from the David Austin nursery, carrying an old rose fragrance and flowering just once in due season.

BELOW RIGHT Delicate pink 'Gentle Hermione,' a fragrant David Austin rose from 2005.

BELOW LEFT The sumptuous Gallica rose 'Charles de Mills,' dating from around 1790, prepares to unfurl its multitude of purply-crimson petals.

The Romans had a passion for roses and imported them from Egypt. Large acreages were devoted to cultivation for rose oils and for rose petals, to be used in decoration. The Romans also developed *rosaria*: gardens made specifically for the growing of roses. Thereafter, for many centuries roses in Europe were chiefly apothecaries' plants, grown for medicines, rose water, and rose oil. The first Chinese rose species arrived in Europe only in the 1750s, after which time crossbreeding increasingly occupied the interest of rose breeders.

Rose gardens in the modern world took off in the nineteenth century in Europe, largely driven by the collection of roses gathered by Joséphine Bonaparte at the Château de Malmaison, which she purchased in 1799. Many of her roses were painted by Pierre-Joseph Redouté, and the idea of the rose garden spread from France to other parts of Europe and beyond.

Among Victorian enthusiasts propagating the virtues of rose gardens was Samuel Reynolds Hole (1819–1904), canon of Lincoln and later dean of Rochester Cathedral. His own epiphany occurred one summer's evening in 1846, when he was relaxing in the garden of his family's home at Caunton in Nottinghamshire with book and cigar. Resting his eyes on a crimson rose, he became "overpowered by the conviction that the rose was the loveliest of all the flowers." Thereafter, roses began occupying the gardens at Caunton in ever greater numbers, increasing to a hundred, then a thousand, then five thousand. With no space left in the garden, his collection advanced like an occupying army into the home farm, prompting his father to request that he leave a *little* space for the wheat.

Dean Hole became the first president of the Royal National Rose Society, established in 1876, a time when English rose gardens were in the ascendant. In those days, and for another century or so, most rose gardens were monocultures, with the plants set into earthy isolation. These days, people prefer a more naturalistic approach, for roses often benefit from a supporting cast of complementary plants, as the following gardens demonstrate.

BORDE HILL

Its famous woodland gardens of trees and shrubs are magnificent in spring, but the elegant rose garden was added for summer interest

Tree-lined roads, often margined by extraordinarily handsome specimens of English oak, undulate through the High Weald of Sussex to bring the visitor to the gates of Borde Hill. The two-hundred-acre garden counts itself among an elite cluster of Victorian/Edwardian plant collectors' gardens in an especially interesting part of the county (nearby are Wakehurst, Nymans, Leonardslee, and the High Beeches). All of them became dedicated woodland gardens on a grand scale, taking advantage of—and sponsoring—the plant-gathering explorations in China, the Himalayas, and elsewhere of Wilson, Forrest, Kingdon Ward, and others (see Plant Collectors' Gardens).

Colonel Stephenson Robert Clarke, whose family fortunes were created via shipping and railway engineering, bought the Borde Hill estate in 1892. His passion was for rare trees and shrubs (the garden's collections are especially significant in this respect), and succeeding generations have added to the gardens in other ways. For several decades, the garden has been under the care and development of his great-grandson, Andrew John Stephenson Clarke, and his wife, Eleni, who drives forward the development of the garden and its associated enterprises with energy and imagination. They have widened the two-hundred-acre garden's appeal into other seasons, planting new areas of summer borders and, with particular gusto, a traditional rose garden of generous proportions, created by garden designer Robin Williams in 1996 and subsequently revised by his son, Robin Templar Williams.

LEFT The rose garden at Borde Hill was created by garden designer Robin Williams in 1996 and subsequently updated by his son. Roses from the David Austin stable predominate, including the clear yellow 'Graham Thomas' and paler primrose yellow 'Jayne Austin.'

RIGHT Pale pink rose 'Kathryn Morley' bears its fragrant blooms on upright stems.

Billowing purple hedges of *Nepeta faassenii* separate some of the rose beds.

Borde Hill house, with its multiple tall chimney stacks, makes a fine backdrop. The rose garden was developed to enhance summer interest in the gardens as a whole, which have a large woodland area full of spring treasures and champion trees dating from the days of the late-Victorian and Edwardian plant hunters.

From its centrepiece, a brick-edged pool and fountain, turf-margined paths fan out to display a harmoniously colourful display of shrub roses—chiefly, but not exclusively, English shrub roses bred by David Austin—themselves decorously hemmed in by low hedges of lavender and catmint. It's a glorious sight through the weeks of midsummer, although a number of the plants will carry on blooming for much longer.

David Austin's English roses include stalwarts such as 'Gertrude Jekyll', one of the nursery's most popular hybrids, in a lovely warm pink, with a powerful old rose fragrance wafting from largish, well-formed flowers—characteristics that also make it an excellent rose for cutting and taking indoors. Also present is 'Graham Thomas', reliable and soft, buttery gold, named for the great plantsman and rosarian who did so much for reinstating the nation's affection for classic old roses. There are representations from Austin's collection of Shakespearean-named roses, including the excellent

'Falstaff', with fruity fragrance, cupped, rosetted flowers of deep, cerise-crimson hues. 'Falstaff' produces "some of the most magnificent blooms of any that we have bred," says Austin. Among the departures into old roses, we find 'Rose de Meaux', an old centifolia type, believed to been raised in 1789 (a date firmly etched in the mind of every schoolchild as the beginning of the French Revolution!). 'De Meaux' speaks of more appealing things, being the essence of prettiness, with small, pink pom-pom flowers on a dainty bush only some three feet high and therefore popular in small gardens, although with the characteristically short flowering season of its kind.

A high brick wall and some stout chunks of yew hedging and topiary separate the rose arena from the family home, but the roses, grouped in harmonious shades of cream, various pinks, cerise, apricots, and pale yellows, provide a complementary foreground to the mellow sandstone elevations and steep gables of the late-sixteenth-century house.

Culland Hall, abundantly clothed in summer with white rose 'Seagull' and, further along, shades of pink and apricot from the rose 'Albertine'. Between them is deeply fragrant 'Wisteria Caroline', flowering earlier in shades of mauve to violet. The pink rose in the foreground, planted long ago, is unidentified.

CULLAND HALL

The charms of roses are fully exploited in this garden: clothing the house walls, tumbling over a pergola walk, and filling out the beds

Lucy Thompson acknowledges the influence of Sissinghurst Castle gardens (page 321) on the work she has done at Culland Hall, since she and her husband, Simon, moved to Culland in the mid-1990s. Simon's parents lived there previously, and his mother made a garden around the house, but by the time Simon and Lucy settled in, little was left of what had been created long before. It was time to start again and, once the chainsaws and mechanical diggers had done their work in opening up the "lost" areas, Lucy took up the trowel, as her mother-in-law had done before her.

Having grown up in Kent near Sissinghurst and been inspired by its formal arrangement of discrete areas separated by walls and yew hedges, Lucy felt this was the way forward in remaking the garden at Culland Hall. Early on, she engaged the expertise of garden designer Mark Anthony Walker to get things started, and later the help of Simon Johnson to make sense of the entrance area.

The house looks directly south, across a stone terrace and a formal rectangular lawn. Straight on, a short flight of steps leads to another lawn, which gives way to a ha-ha at its far end, overlooking pleasantly undulating sheep pasture that runs down to a tree-fringed lake. The south-facing wall of the house itself is festooned with climbing plants that peer in at the windows through the growing season, providing flower-and-foliage-framed views from indoors, along with the scents of roses and wisteria. Pruning the specimens on this wall must be an ongoing and mighty task, albeit a worthwhile one for the charming effects achieved through spring and summer. In between the dependably rapid colonization by violet-flowered *Wisteria* 'Caroline', the mutable apricot pink rambler rose 'Albertine' jostles for wall space, along with the rampant rose 'Seagull', with its little clusters of gold-centred, pure white flowers.

Roses are at the heart of most areas of the garden. Between the two formal lawns that lie south of the house, a border runs along either side of the central steps. Lucy is fond of colour schemes and in this area the chosen hues are shades of blue and yellow that blend smoothly into the landscape, yet complement each other so well, especially when other, upstart hues are excluded. The 'Pilgrim', a softly pale yellow rose with characteristic dense flowers, holds its own in the border in the company of Turkish sage *Phlomis russeliana*, creamy *Sisyrinchium striatum*, and airy wands of *Thalictrum flavum glaucum* and *Cephalaria gigantea*; shots of contrasting violet blue are contributed by *Iris sibirica* 'Silver Edge' and spires of blue delphiniums. Other notable yellow roses stitched through the border are the taller, deeper yellow 'Graham Thomas' and the early flowering, tall shrub rose 'Fruhlingsgold', carrying plentiful simple, palest primrose flowers among very dainty foliage.

ABOVE LEFT Midsummer abundance in the box-edged beds includes roses 'Fantin-Latour,' 'Prince Charles,' 'Rose de Rescht,' '*Königin von Dänemark*,' and 'Charles de Mills.'

BELOW LEFT A view down the brick path leads to roses 'Hansa,' 'Comte de Chambord,' 'Prince Charles,' 'Fantin Latour,' and 'Rose de Rescht.'

OPPOSITE A classic combination for midsummer: the white rose 'Adélaide d'Orléans' on the pergola, with *Nepeta* 'Six Hills Giant' providing a hazy mauve margin along the path. Also, just visible and reaching into the pergola walk is the dusky bluish-mauve rambler 'Veilchenblau,' bearing clusters of tiny flowers.

The rose garden itself lies west of the house, with brick paths running between box-edged beds. This is a garden for midsummer, containing mainly old-fashioned, once-flowering cultivars in the classic, traditional colours that range through many shades of pink (in 'Comte de Chambord', 'Fantin Latour') through cerise ('Rose de Rescht', 'Hansa') to deeper, magenta-crimson and purple hues ('Prince Charles', 'Charles de Mills').

An adjacent garden of white and near-white flowers is formal and symmetrical, with straight paths cutting between half a dozen rectangular beds edged with box hedging. Certainly inspired by the famous white garden at Sissinghurst, its long season of bulbs and herbaceous plants are also joined by roses here and there, such as the creamy 'Macmillan Nurse'; the pergola, draped in *Rosa mulliganii* is, of course, another reference to Sissinghurst's white garden.

A gateway from the central path of the white garden leads further westward, to a pair of deep borders, separated by a generous strip of lawn. A wall on one side and a yew hedge on the other provide the requisite enclosure as well as shelter. Shrubs supply plenty of the borders' interest through the seasons but there are also roses—pink, shaggy-flowered 'Fritz Nobis', crumply crimson moss rose 'Capitaine John Ingram', tough-as-nails nineteenth-century shrub rose 'Gipsy Boy', and David Austin's shell-pink shrub rose 'Gentle Hermione'.

Another squared-off area to the north is home to the kitchen garden and greenhouse as well as a magnificent rose pergola, margined on one side with a spectacular border of herbaceous peonies. All of the spaces have been carefully planned and joined up to provide a continuous and logical sequence through what many people would consider to be a quintessential English country garden.

ELSING HALL

NORFOLK

An existing and substantial collection of roses had romped away uncontrollably but was recently reined in and nurtured by the present owners

Whoever first called moats "quiet mirrors of history" got it exactly right. And of all areas in England, Norfolk and Suffolk are especially rich in moats attached to houses, for various defensive, social, and geographic reasons. They were often dug around manorial and ecclesiastical buildings, but also gardens, where they usefully provided a barrier to wild animals or thieves.

Old moated manors can also be deeply romantic—often the house is charmingly reflected in its surrounding waters. So when Patrick Lines and Han Yang Yap saw moated Elsing Hall in 2006, they were spellbound by the "Sleeping Beauty" gabled and flint-walled manor, with its barley-twist chimneys reaching to the sky and the potential of its reed-filled moat. "Ignorance can sometimes be a blessing," recalls Lines. "We had no real idea of what we were undertaking." Two years passed while the Grade 1 Listed house was undergoing careful refurbishment, before they were able to start looking at the garden.

And here indeed was another sleeping beauty: before Lines and Yap bought the property, it had been empty for some while, and the garden had not been tended in any conventional way for many years. On starting to tackle it, they discovered that there were hundreds of unpruned thorny roses variously cascading, romping, languishing, and generally creating mayhem: in the substantial walled garden, in the long borders between house and lawn, over the house walls, and along pleasant waterside walks. And the moat itself had become a reed bed across, which, says, Lines, "one could walk with barely the need of wellies."

How do you take in hand years of overgrowth in herbaceous borders and 250-plus roses of all shapes and sizes, most of which, although decades old, have almost never been pruned? The thing to remember is that anything surviving by this stage is by definition "a survivor." Weaklings have long gone. Therefore, ruthlessness is the answer: chop, chop, chop. It's the only way back. Lines and Yap engaged an experienced gardening couple, Robin and Alison Mahoney, who remain with them to this day.

Meanwhile, they read a lot, visited many gardens to develop their understanding and knowledge, and experimented. With the help of the Mahoneys, Lines and Yap have refined the borders, created new ones, and disciplined the climbers and ramblers on the house walls. Roses cascade into the waters of the moat. Roses of countless kinds share numerous borders with complementary companions—foxgloves, geums, campanulas, foxtail lilies, delphiniums. The walled garden has been revived with box-edged beds for peonies, fruit and vegetables in great variety, a restored greenhouse, and numerous roses trained along its walls.

Elsing Hall wears its roses well. The ground floor windows are garlanded with numerous roses including 'Fantin Latour,' '*Königin von Dänemark*,' and 'Madame Alfred Carriere.' The herbaceous border in front contains delphiniums, bronze fennel, poppies carrying silvery-green seed heads, and short yellow foxtail lilies.

It would be quite natural, however, to wonder how on earth there came to be all those roses—and indeed, the fine fifteenth-century house itself. Elsing Hall was built in about 1470 for one John Hastings, replacing a much earlier house built by his ancestor, Sir Hugh de Hastings, who enjoyed a successful military career and an advantageous marriage. Elsing Hall stayed within the family for seven generations and then passed across to the Browne family, where it stayed for the next four hundred years. It was sensitively extended and upgraded in the eighteenth and nineteenth centuries, but only reached the open market for the first time in its history in 1958.

The big moment for the roses came with the arrival of David and Shirley Cargill, who bought the property in the 1980s. Shirley's inspiration was a garden called Lime Kiln, owned by rosarian Humphrey Brooke, who had assembled a very significant collection of several hundred varieties. Shirley's own collection of some 250-plus varieties grew naturally, with scarce interference from secateurs or twine. The Cargills also planted beds of roses and herbaceous plants along the south side of the house, a formal display of topiary, an arboretum of choice flowering trees, and a pinetum in old pasture.

When they first saw the house, Lines and Yap "hardly noticed the garden." But, of course, as every gardener knows, once you do notice it, the garden is the thing that daily keeps calling you back. Therefore, their renovation and developments continue, with new sculptures and rose pergolas, more plants (including roses!), and plans for further water interest, via a fountain and rill.

OPPOSITE The south side of the house, seen from across the moat. In the nineteenth century the terraces by the house were restored and the moat widened, giving it the effect of a broad lake on this side.

ABOVE RIGHT Roses adorning the house wall here include dusky crimson-violet moss rose 'William Lobb,' lilac 'Veilchenblau' with clusters of small flowers, extrovert mutable pink 'Handel,' and in the distance, unimpeachable 'Albertine.'

BELOW RIGHT A bewitching view along the moat in the more distant gardens with layers of green around a cascade of the 'Kiftsgate' rose, reaching out of its tree into the reflective waters.

The romantic nature of the property immediately captivated Lines and Yap when they first saw Elsing Hall. Its trees, such as the weeping willows, undeniably contributed to the atmosphere. Rescuing the garden from its wild state has taken many years; these photos, from 2013, show a "midway" stage, and much refinement has been done since.

Midsummer in the walled garden, and its door is almost disappearing under an exuberant explosion of foliage and flowers, including *Salvia turkestanica* in the foreground and a froth of white geraniums around the statuesque stems and globular green seed heads of *Angelica archangelica*, with a 'Seagull' rambler rose tumbling over the wall.

One of the remaining fruit trees in the walled garden gives support to a deep red rose, frequently admired and commented on by visitors. In the distance, a moon gate installed by Lines and Yap can be seen.

WEST WOODHAY

BERKSHIRE

Finding that the big old walled garden had more than enough space for kitchen produce, the owners installed a bewitching new rose garden

Many hundreds of roses are planted into a large portion of the huge walled garden at West Woodhay in Berkshire. Their exuberance is contained within a formal arrangement of eight very substantial box-edged beds, with four beds surrounding each of two impressive, timber fruit cages, full of burgeoning berries of various kinds, ripening right through the growing season. The walls and the surrounding trees all help contain the distinctly rosy and fruity fragrances wafting about through midsummer, and the roses themselves—old-fashioned and modern shrub roses in great variety—relish a deep and fertile soil, which, being in the kitchen garden, has been manured for centuries.

That is just as well, for this part of the countryside is not the easiest location for rose growing. The Berkshire downland is a classic chalk landscape: highly alkaline, very freely draining, and consequently rapidly leaching away any nutrients it comes by. The best way forward is to do as gardeners have done for centuries in their kitchen gardens: pile on the compost and manure to enable the soil's texture and structure to improve and thus hold onto its fertility. Roses are greedy, but they repay the gardener who takes trouble to get the soil right.

The walled garden, which was redesigned by country garden designer Veronica Mackinnon, has other outstanding areas, too. An orderly portion is dedicated to a wide variety of produce for the kitchen, supported by polytunnels and greenhouses. Its eastern side is ornamental, being devoted partially to a grassed area for free-ranging bantams and chickens rescued from intensive farming; there are numerous trees and flowering shrubs, and all is maintained to the highest standards by the gardening team.

Nevertheless, there is a great deal more to West Woodhay, both in its wider gardens and park, developed with real verve in recent decades by the Henderson family, but also because of the fascinating history of the place itself.

The seventeenth-century manor house was built in 1635 for the polymath Sir Benjamin Rudyerd (1572–1658), a poet, wit, lawyer, and Member of Parliament. It stayed with his family for some seventy years until his grandson sold to one William Sloper. Some of the park's oldest trees date from these earlier times, but little evidence survives that can be traced back to the seventeenth-century formal gardens.

West Woodhay (pronounced "Woody") remained with the Slopers for some 170 years, during which time another artistic flowering occurred, in the lifetime of William Sloper (1709–1789), who fell in love with the celebrated singer and actress Susannah Cibber. Though both were married to others (resulting in scandalous lawsuits, avidly reported in the press), the arrival of Mrs. Cibber—muse of George Frideric Handel, David Garrick's leading lady at

The walled garden at West Woodhay celebrates the rose in a multitude of ways, having been replanned by garden designer Veronica Mackinnon in 1999 to include substantial areas devoted to roses.

Drury Lane, and friend of the music historian Charles Burney—ensured that West Woodhay was a popular country salon among the artistic elite until her death in 1766, whereupon she was buried in Westminster Abbey.

Though it is pleasant to conjecture the arias, rehearsals, and concerts that must at times have wafted through the avenues and wildernesses of the eighteenth-century gardens, succeeding Slopers erased all traces of Mrs. Cibber. When William's great-grandson, the Reverend John Sloper, inherited in 1821, he used his shotgun to persuade villagers to attend church.

Like many other country estates, West Woodhay was turned into a hospital during the First World War, and a school in the Second. Henry Henderson, a railway magnate, bought the house in 1920 and his grandson, John, demolished Victorian extensions in 1948 to reveal the original seventeenth-century house. He also turned his attention to the garden, engaging James Russell of the renowned Sunningdale Nurseries in Surrey to advise on new plantings, particularly in the pockets of acidic clay soil, which fortunately occur here and there in the grounds, widening the range of what can be comfortably grown. Exotic trees and shrubs were deployed in John Henderson's Arboretum; it forms a long band west and south of the house where mature beeches and oaks have long brought shelter from winds whipping over the nearby hills.

Harry Henderson and his wife, Sarah, came to live at West Woodhay in 1995 and, since 1997, Harry has been making a new arboretum in the park, around a sequence of pools he created south of the main lake. There are further ornamental gardens near the house, particularly a paved and colon-naded Italian Garden unveiled in 2018, with "altar and font" flowing water sculptures linked by shallow rills, created by William Pye. This imaginative feature has been laid out on the footprint of a church, long gone, built by Vanbrugh for William Sloper in 1716 but demolished in 1883.

"My style is delegation!" says Harry Henderson with a laugh, when he is asked to sum up his involvement, but it's much more than that, of course. His enthusiasm for new projects is coupled with an appreciation of the special nature of this exceptional landscape for, like all great beauties, West Woodhay is somewhere that requires few adornments to succeed.

The large walled garden is divided into several areas of productivity, with its south-western section devoted to masses of roses and also a pair of substantial wooden fruit cages, protecting soft fruits from animals and birds.

LEFT A cottage adjoining the walled garden is enhanced by the abundance of rambler roses tumbling over the high walls. 'Rambling Rector' is a classic rose for such purposes, being extremely floriferous but flexible enough to cascade.

ABOVE RIGHT The east front of West Woodhay house with its driveway courtyard, seen from high ground, across a lake in the shallow valley.

BELOW RIGHT The west garden, where a formal arrangement of rectangular beds, edged with nepeta, meet at a central pond. Since these photographs were published in 2009, the gardens have continued to develop with new areas, enhanced planting, and an expanding arboretum.

15 OVERVIEW: ECO-GARDENING

For a number of years Dame Miriam Rothschild (1908–2005) hosted a delightful annual event at her Northamptonshire home, Ashton Wold. It was timed for early summer, when the fields of her estate were awash with wildflowers and the bees and other insect life that attend them. Her family and friends from across the worlds of conservation and natural history packed into the Arts and Crafts house that her father had built, to network and celebrate, wander through the garden with its mowed paths lined by waist-high cow parsley *Anthriscus sylvestris*, and perhaps wave at the herd of Père David's deer, an extraordinary creature hailing from the Chinese wetlands, extinct in the wild.

Aside from Dame Miriam's numerous scientific discoveries and her wartime stint as an Enigma codebreaker, she gardened according to her own principles as an environmental campaigner, and her influence has been far-reaching. Dame Miriam's epiphany was complete by the 1970s, when she recalled that her taste in gardening "had undergone a complete and drastic metamorphosis. I had become a wildflower and grass gardener." Seeing the roadsides and fields denuded of the flowers that sustained insect life, she developed her own wildflower seed mixture of poppies, corncockles, marigolds, cornflowers, and flax, and marketed it as "Farmer's Nightmare." That her campaign took off is evident from the plethora of assorted wildflower seed mixtures available today, which are now a significant industry in themselves.

Others had similar postwar environmental concerns, and there were reasons for them to feel that nature was being sidelined at much too great a cost. In 1946 a group of farmers, scientists, and nutritionists, dismayed by the intensification of agriculture in the war years and the likely effects that continued escalation would have, formed the Soil Association. Their stated concerns were the loss of soil through erosion and depletion; decreased nutritional quality of food; exploitation of animals; and farming's impact on the countryside and wildlife (not least through the expanding use of pesticides and other agrochemicals).

Rachel Carson's *Silent Spring*, published in 1962, was a wake-up call based on scientific evidence of the devastating side effects of pesticides such as DDT.

OPPOSITE Bees forage over the spires of tiny flowers on *Veronicastrum virginicum*. Choosing plants that support wildlife with pollen and/or nectar has been a big trend for the last three decades or so, as gardeners have stepped in to do more to help vulnerable creatures whose populations are declining.

It had become the go-to farming insecticide worldwide, and was routinely used by gardeners, too. In the first half of the twentieth century, pesticides were marketed to people in ways that assumed Nature was a foe to be conquered. *Amateur Gardening* and similar journals carried advertisements for a multitude of insecticides and applicators. A substance called "Katakilla … the most powerful insect killer ever discovered" was illustrated with a man holding a pump sprayer as if it were a rifle. An advert for Derrothan "Anti-Pest Defence" carried images of slugs, caterpillars, and beetles—wearing swastikas! The combative approach to weeds and insect life persisted for decades after the war, but it marched in opposition to a burgeoning movement focused on more holistic husbandry.

In 1954, horticulturist and writer Lawrence Hills (1911–1990) founded the popular non-profit group now known as Garden Organic. His associated books sold well to a new tribe of vegetable gardeners and smallholders. (In 1975, reflecting the trend, the BBC broadcast a hugely popular television sitcom, *The Good Life*. Its characters, Tom and Barbara Good, parodied the "grow your own" followers of Lawrence Hills's organic methods.)

Various events in the 1970s helped open people's eyes to the frailty of nature. The wholesale loss of elm trees from the English landscape due to Dutch elm disease was a tragedy. In 1976, a prolonged hot summer and severe drought caused serious setbacks to gardens and nurseries. In 1978, Beth Chatto responded with a book called *The Dry Garden*, full of practical advice about selecting attractive plants that cope with drier habitats, gleaned from experiments in her own Essex garden.

The 1980s saw steady progress in gardening more sustainably. Environmental adviser Chris Baines created the first wildflower garden at the Chelsea Flower Show in 1985, and published the influential guide *How to Make a Wildlife Garden*. John Stevens's *National Trust Book of Wild Flower Gardening*, subtitled, *The New Way to Create a Naturally Beautiful Garden*, appeared in 1987. In the same year, television's most popular gardener, Geoff Hamilton, published *Successful Organic Gardening* and his role as key presenter on the BBC's *Gardeners' World* television show enormously ratcheted up interest in chemical-free methods. Subsequent lead presenters Alan Titchmarsh, then Monty Don, followed suit. The influence of such television endorsement cannot be overstated and its eco-friendly approach is now matched on the hardy perennial BBC radio series, *Gardeners' Question Time*.

In 1995, the first solar-powered robotic lawn mower was launched at the Chelsea Flower Show, perhaps a little ironically as the concept of the wildflower meadow was rapidly gaining ground. The then Marchioness of Salisbury (1922–2016) had for long been an advocate of both organic

A naturalistic tapestry of grasses and wild/wild-type flowering plants that support a range of wild creatures, by Christopher Bradley-Hole. Plants include *Eupatorium maculatum* (Atropurpureum Group) 'Riesenschirm,' *Persicaria amplexicaulis* 'Fat Domino,' *Verbena bonariensis*, and the fountain grass *Pennisetum alopecuroides* 'Hameln.'

gardening and wildflowers, in the grandest of settings. Having signed up to organic methods back in the 1970s, she encouraged others to do likewise. Her Hatfield House garden was an irresistible promotion for its benefits, and both she and Miriam Rothschild helped the Prince of Wales establish organic gardening at Highgrove, his Gloucestershire home.

In the new millennium, concerns about genetically modified (GM) crops led to activist protests at trial grounds as Britain, in common with a number of other European nations, rejected "Frankenfood." Environmental concerns also focused on the continued extraction and availability of peat, a limited resource from scarce and shrinking habitats, routinely used for potting composts in the horticulture industry. Numerous peat alternatives were developed and widely adopted.

Encouraging wildlife into gardens is a big trend of the past twenty years. (The bird food industry is now enormous.) The Royal Society for the Protection of Birds, a huge wildlife conservation charity, widened its remit in recent times, to love all manner of creatures. It even changed its magazine's title from *Birds* to *Nature's Home*. Likewise, the Royal Horticultural Society has steadily shifted its axis over the years to focus on sustainable gardening as a key principle.

The triumph of the 2012 Olympics in London included universal praise for its setting. The Olympic Park, as it was called at the time, showcased to the world the potential for "pictorial meadows" in themed plantings. These days, nearly everybody with the space has a meadow of some sort, sometimes beefed up in a Robinsonian kind of way, with camassias, but more frequently, just awash with oxeye daisies, pretty flowers of June and July that councils also now encourage along roadsides and roundabouts. (This must be a win-win situation; everybody loves them, and the councils save on mowing bills.)

Miriam Rothschild would have reason to feel encouraged, I think, and so would her father, Nathaniel Charles Rothschild (1877–1923), who was a dedicated amateur naturalist, passionate about nature and conservation. As long ago as 1912 he steered the creation of the Society for the Promotion of Nature Reserves, now better known as the Wildlife Trusts. It is an enormous volunteer group, with some 2,300 nature reserves spread across the whole of the United Kingdom. Nevertheless, in spite of the good news, the situation isn't rosy. Numerous formerly common species of bird, butterfly, and bee are in steady decline. Therefore "eco-gardening" has an increasingly important role to play, to some extent providing rescue resources, in places where agriculture continues to fall short.

OPPOSITE Enhancing the wilderness: the brilliant scarlet shrub rose, *Rosa* 'Scharlachglut' (Scarlet Fire) invigorates the pastoral scene and its open, single flowers will produce orange-scarlet, urn-shaped hips for autumn. It is grown here among ox-eye daisies (*Leucanthemum vulgare*) and foxgloves *Digitalis purpurea*.

CLOCKWISE A water-wise approach: gravel garden planting by Sarah Price, for the M&G garden at Chelsea Flower Show in 2018, with *Helichrysum arenarium*, *Tulbaghia violacea*, *Ridolfia segetum*, fescue grasses, and airy *Briza media* floating like miniature confetti. Hand-watering by can prevents wastage. Lutyens included rainwater butts in his house designs. This butt was at Goddards, one of his early Surrey houses.

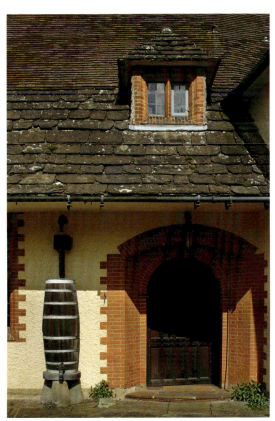

LEFT Blue camassia and butter-cups in the wildflower meadows at Highgrove, home of the Prince of Wales.

OPPOSITE, CLOCKWISE Floral foragers: a Painted Lady butterfly on *Buddleja davidii*; a bumblebee works its way over the globular flower heads of *Buddleja × weyeriana* 'Sungold;' a Painted Lady butterfly dips her proboscis into the deep tubular flowers of a white *Buddleja davidii* cultivar; "where the bee sucks …" a bumblebee dines out on black-berry flowers.

16 RESTORATIONS AND REINVENTIONS

The first page of house advertisements in the very first edition of *Country Life* (January 8, 1897) offered a selection of extraordinary properties for sale, including "Stowe House, Buckingham, the stately ancestral home of the Dukes of Buckingham and Chandos." As discussed at the start of this book, by the close of the nineteenth century, such places had become obsolete and irrelevant, with many houses and gardens already showing signs of decline. Stowe was being offered with eleven hundred acres of deer park, stabling for twenty-five horses, and a park with lakes "of considerable area, further beautified by numerous charming waterfalls and bridges, temples and statuary." (The downturn that caused a deluge of fine properties put up for sale had some mileage left before the late-twentieth-century "age of restoration" would turn around the fortunes for such places.)

The "golden afternoon" of the Edwardian period, with its stupefyingly lavish house parties, was a "last hurrah" that met an abrupt full stop with the First World War. Wars are cripplingly expensive and high postwar taxation only added to the appalling loss of a generation of young men. Across the country, whole villages of able-bodied conscripts did not return from the carnage of the trenches to tend the farms and gardens, and neither did their horses. Countless gardens and parks were ploughed up to grow food, which was scarce in wartime, and many homes were turned into military hospitals.

Therefore, in the 1920s, many gardens needed restoring or redesigning in low maintenance ways. The "woodland garden" idea ticked many boxes, being informal in design (so anyone with land could do it) and with fairly low maintenance needs. A woodland garden of newly available shrubs and trees from distant lands also nicely fed into the English love of collecting, while having an essential element of clubby competitiveness with one's peer group. The great age of plant hunting in the between-the-wars decades of the 1920s and 1930s saw plant hunters such as George Forrest (with sponsored collectors Frank Ludlow and George Sherriff on his heels), working in western China, or Frank Kingdon-Ward, scouting for irresistible woodland treasures from Burma, Assam, and Tibet, send back tens of thousands of new plants from far and wide.

OPPOSITE Windswept sheep pastures separate remote Lindisfarne Castle on Holy Island from its distant walled garden, redesigned in 1911. Its then-owner, *Country Life*'s proprietor, Edward Hudson, had commissioned the garden plans from Gertrude Jekyll. The National Trust restored Jekyll's plantings as in her original drawings in the early years of the new millennium.

OPPOSITE, TOP LEFT AND BOTTOM RIGHT The walled garden at Arundel Castle in West Sussex is an imaginative restoration/reinvention of a once productive area, which had been a car park since the 1970s. Julian and Isabel Bannerman created a bold new garden that celebrates the life of Thomas Howard, the 14th Earl of Arundel (1585–1646). The "Collector Earl" was one of the earliest "Grand Tourists" and an art patron on the grandest scale.

Conversely, faithful restorations through the mid-century decades were scarce, although some were too important to ignore. In the 1930s, for example, Geoffrey Jellicoe was engaged at Saint Paul's Walden Bury to restore and spruce up its important early-eighteenth-century park. In 1946, William (Bill) MacKenzie, newly appointed curator at the ancient Chelsea Physic Garden in London, began restoring its glasshouses, rock garden, and order beds, all ruined during the Second World War.

In 1954, Nancy Lancaster, the Anglophile American socialite and decorator, took on Haseley Court (page 43) and restored its garden, which had been devastated by war. "The avenues I remembered when I had been there fifteen years before had been cut down—there was now a wide horizon of fields," she recalled. She replanted the avenues and paid Russell Page to plan the square beds in the walled garden, but then set his plans aside "because I thought they were too fussy."

In 1948 the National Trust took on the garden at Hidcote (page 20) and started to think about its many gardens that were underfunded and underwhelming. With the appointment of Graham Stuart Thomas as its first gardens adviser in 1955, numerous partial restorations and re-creations "in the style of … " were undertaken over succeeding years. Thomas also became a founder and keen supporter of the Garden History Society, which was to have a profound role in documenting and steering restorations of "lost" and damaged gardens from the 1970s onward. Hestercombe, in Somerset (pages 18–19), was a rare, early beneficiary of a new mood to restore in the 1970s.

Nevertheless, such things need money, and the boom years of the 1980s are when restorations really took off and by then, they were soundly underpinned by academic research. The creation of the Heritage Lottery Fund helped enormously. Private individuals drew upon Nancy Lancaster's boxwood-and-roses approach to re-create formal gardens suited to their old houses and this time, mechanical tools made light work of keeping parterres and knot gardens trim, with minimum effort. Stowe, with its "numerous charming waterfalls," was eventually saved. Its palatial house became a school in 1923; its park was passed to the National Trust in 1989 and three decades of painstaking restoration have reinstated its glories. The 1980s and 1990s are now seen as the "historicist" period during which restoration took priority over innovation.

The gardens that follow reveal stories of exemplary restoration and occasional reinvention, by a diverse range of inspired and dedicated individuals and groups.

OPPOSITE, TOP RIGHT AND BOTTOM LEFT Details from the restored Edwardian Japanese Garden at Kingston Lacy in Dorset. Created in the early twentieth century, when Japanese gardens were very fashionable, the one at Kingston Lacy had disappeared over subsequent decades. The National Trust decided to restore it in the early twenty-first century. Archaeological ground radar surveys and searches in the estate's archive enabled the trust to form a picture of how it may have looked.

BIDDULPH GRANGE

STAFFORDSHIRE

One of the National Trust's earliest and longest-running garden restorations has seen Biddulph's "world garden" returned to glory

Among the fine restorations achieved by the National Trust in recent times, the garden at Biddulph Grange is certainly one of the most exciting and atmospheric. Biddulph has been compared with an *Alice in Wonderland*-like, counterintuitive, and spatially distorted experience, although Brent Elliott has suggested its inception might have expressed a strand of Victorian sentiment that identified geology and archaeology as portents of "the second coming" and the end of history.

Whatever its origin, restoration has largely focused on an early plan and, as Stephen Lacey engagingly described, "the meandering paths have you squeezing between rock faces, crossing water by stepping stones and plunging down dark tunnels; you enter a half-timbered cottage and find yourself in an Egyptian tomb, clamber through a Scottish glen and come out in a Chinese water garden; at every turn, there are strange beasts, flamboyant flowers, eruptions of rock, or soaring exotic conifers in ambush."

Three people were involved in its creation. The owner was James Bateman, whose family wealth had come from the coal and steel industries; he was aided by his wife, Maria, and a friend, the esteemed landscape and marine artist Edward William Cooke.

The Batemans moved to the former vicarage at Biddulph in 1842, whereupon they transformed the house into something very much grander in the Italianate style. The garden wasn't only about creating theatrical set pieces, however. All three of its makers were seriously interested in plants. Bateman was an orchid expert and the author of three sumptuously illustrated volumes on the genus; rhododendrons were another passion and he was a member of the RHS Plant Exploration Committee. His wife (the sister of Rowland Egerton-Warburton, who was then creating the famous double herbaceous borders at Arley Hall) was keen on hardy herbaceous plants. Cooke, who was married to the daughter of the great nurseryman George Loddiges, shared Bateman's fascination for orchids and rhododendrons, but his natural history interest also extended into the realms of zoology and geology. It's tempting to speculate on the fun these creative people must have had in dreaming up a veritable Eden of multiple cultures and floras.

Bateman was not the first, however, to discover how expensive it can be to create and maintain a house and garden of such ambitious scale. In the 1860s he could no longer afford it and by 1871 he had sold up and moved south.

From 1923 to the mid-1980s the property was a hospital, with wards built over part of the fifteen-acre gardens. The National Trust acquired it in 1988 and began restoring the lost garden, which had succumbed to vandalism during more than fifty years of decline. Today we see it as a wonderfully preserved and lively example of eccentric mid-nineteenth-century taste, the garden's creation inspired by the excitement of growing hitherto unknown species, arriving as ships' cargo from far-flung parts of the world.

One of the National Trust's most complex and interesting garden restorations was carried out at Biddulph Grange, from the end of the 1980s onward. The remarkable garden takes the visitor on a "world tour" created by a trio of natural history enthusiasts. This area, with its stepped and buttressed yew hedges, is the Dahlia Walk, containing its vividly hued collection, in flower from high summer to autumn.

OPPOSITE A view of "China," one of the exotic gardens, which today benefits from the maturity of its tree collection. The National Trust's restoration has aimed to be as close as possible to the original concept. Fortunately, an 1862 detailed description in *The Gardeners' Chronicle* was able to support the archaeological evidence that was uncovered as the trust searched for clues within the lost gardens.

ABOVE RIGHT Carved stone sphinxes guard the gateway set into crisp yew hedging, suggestive of a stepped pyramid, in the garden known as "Egypt." Once you are inside, chambers "inside the pyramid" focus on a stone carving of the "Ape of Thoth" perhaps referencing science and botany in Egyptian mythology.

BELOW RIGHT Massive chunks of cut stone create one of the portals to "China." One of the great benefits of the gardens as seen today is that many of the original trees—rare new treasures collected by plant hunters in James Bateman's day—are now mature and add to the garden's otherworldly atmosphere.

LEFT This spectacular temple was in a parlous condition when the National Trust took on Biddulph Grange. Its details include gilded dragons, seahorses, and grebes; it is the star turn at the heart of what for most visitors is the whole garden's star turn—China. Its elaborate ceramic roof-tiles are replacements, based on originals found at the bottom of the pool.

ABOVE RIGHT Peering out of what looks like a shrine, a magnificent gilded water buffalo. Like the other garden sculptures, it was created by Benjamin Waterhouse Hawkins (1807–1894), a specialist in natural history subjects. Water buffalo have a number of mythical and philosophical references in Eastern cultures, which might be a reason for its presence in "China" at Biddulph Grange.

BELOW RIGHT With a lugubrious expression and surrounded by ivy, a plant much enjoyed by Victorian gardeners, an enormous carved stone frog greets visitors to the water garden that is "China."

UPTON GREY,
THE MANOR HOUSE
HAMPSHIRE

The availability of the original planting plans inspired the owners to restore a lost garden designed by Gertrude Jekyll in 1908

Upton Grey is a picture-postcard village in the gently rolling chalkland hills of north Hampshire. It was here that Charles Holme, an energetic and dedicated champion of the Arts and Crafts movement, decided to settle, following his earlier residency near London at Red House in Bexley, William Morris's own former home, built for him by Philip Webb.

Holme had enjoyed a sufficiently successful career trading silk and wool textiles to be able to retire from business in 1892, aged forty-four. His next career can be seen as taking his interests in art, crafts, and architecture a stage further, as he founded (in 1893) and for some years edited *The Studio: An Illustrated Magazine of Fine and Applied Art.*

Holme acquired a number of properties in Upton Grey, one of which was a farmhouse of Tudor origin known as the Manor House, that he engaged architect Ernest Newton to extend and update in 1907. Holme lived elsewhere in the village and let the house to a tenant, but Gertrude Jekyll was engaged in 1908 to design a suitable garden to wrap around it. It's believed she didn't visit Upton Grey. By this stage of her life, she preferred a sort of postal design service, preferably with plans sent in by architects, to which she could add the planting schemes.

The front of the house faces west onto its entrance drive, beyond which is a substantial wild garden, accessed via an attractive iron gateway through a wall. One first notices a lovely detail at ground level, where everything is curved: a stone-terraced threshold at the gateway, beyond which lies a series of broad, but extremely shallow, semicircular turf steps. It's a stylish and deliberately low-key preamble into what is clearly an unarchitectural space. A grass walk sashays through the middle, between longer grass, planted sparingly and randomly with large shrubs and cascading shrub roses. This lovely walk, studded with Jekyll's daffodils in spring, culminates in a distant corner, where a fishpond, half covered with waterlilies, is lushly planted around the edges with yellow iris, meadowsweet, and tansy. It's a romantic spot, framing a glimpse of the medieval church next door.

The long, east side of the house looks out over the formal garden, which drops away down a gentle hill. "Many a garden has to be made on a hillside more or less steep," wrote Jekyll in *Wall and Water Gardens*, published in several editions since 1901. "The conditions of such a site naturally suggest some form of terracing, and in connection with a house of modest size and kind, nothing is prettier or pleasanter than all the various ways of terraced treatment that may be practised with the help of dry-walling."

The slope of the hill at Upton Grey enabled the creation of several such descending terraces, so that steps down from the pergola by the house led first to the rose lawn, inset with a parterre design of trapezoid beds arranged

The transformation of the space since the Wallingers arrived in the early 1980s has seen the complete restoration of the Gertrude Jekyll garden, according to her Edwardian designs. In the upper garden, a pergola is swathed in roses and plants grow among the crevices of the dry-stone walls.

around two central raised stone beds. The specialties of this area are roses, peonies, and lilies, with an edging of felty, grey-leaved *Stachys lanata*, or lamb's ears.

Below it, a bowling green also spans the width of the house, and below that, a lawn tennis court, the ensemble enclosed by yew hedges, with an informal nut walk (for hazelnuts and their useful branches) beyond. Chiefly north of the main garden and running down the slope in long beds perpendicular to it, Jekyll designed further areas devoted to herbaceous borders, and a medium-sized Victorian greenhouse was installed. These photos show the garden's almost overwhelming summer abundance as Jekyll planned it, with its bright borders and colour drifts, inspired by her own two-hundred-foot-long border at Munstead Wood.

That we are able to see all of this as a living garden today is down to the extraordinary efforts of John and Rosamund Wallinger, who, as a young London couple in 1983, bought the house and were subsequently astonished to learn that the overgrown, uninteresting grounds had once been a Gertrude Jekyll garden and that detailed plans for it still existed, in the Jekyll archive at the University of California at Berkeley.

Many years of painstaking effort by the Wallingers, with Rosamund fully hands-on, resulted in the reemergence of a living, working, true-to-plan Jekyll creation, complete with high-maintenance herbaceous borders and the rare bonus of a genuine Jekyll wild garden. The story of the garden's resurrection was candidly and movingly told by Rosamund in *Gertrude Jekyll's Lost Garden* (1999). Since the 1990s, thousands of visitors have come from all over the world to experience it and perhaps meet the woman who had no previous experience of gardening but painstakingly brought this masterpiece back to life.

ABOVE LEFT Jekyll's signature white lilies in the restored parterre terrace. Note the grass tennis court beyond, which also featured in her plans.

BELOW LEFT Rosamund Wallinger and assorted pets at work in the garden.

OPPOSITE Jekyll's recommended herbaceous plants fill one of the nursery/cut flower borders. The gardens feature several other restored herbaceous borders.

ABOVE An English cottage garden
classic combination as recommended
by Jekyll, with old-fashioned hollyhocks
and cascading roses.

RIGHT The Wild Garden, also fully
restored, with the nearby village church
glimpsed in the background.

RYCOTE PARK

OXFORDSHIRE

Following the virtual building of a new house with references to Tudor designs, the owners turned to restoring the gardens and park

Rycote Park sits in gently undulating, open farming country just west of the fine market town of Thame. Geographers call this region the Upper Thames Clay Vales, giving a clue as to why brickwork and clay tiles are the prevailing building materials hereabouts. Yet few, if any, places in the region can compete with Rycote for its stylish and sympathetic use of brick. In Tudor times it was a vast palace, frequented by royalty. When viewed from above, Rycote, like the Tudor pile at Knole in Kent, appears more like a small village than a house. A fire, which started in the bakery, engulfed the palace in 1745 and subsequently most of the remains were auctioned off as building materials in 1807, but its rebirth in the twenty-first century has returned much of its magnificence.

Not a great deal is known about the early formal gardens, though a bird's-eye view of the estate by Kip and Knyff published in 1714 reveals a complex seventeenth-century garden of avenues and plats, courtyards, long rides, topiary trees, and a moat. All was swept away in the mid-eighteenth century by Capability Brown, and certainly the presence of the clay would have made his trademark creation of a majestic lake a viable proposition.

"What we've sought to do is just to give a taste of what was here before [the fire], but in a way that is reasonably manageable today," says Bernard Taylor, a banker who bought the Rycote estate in 2000 and immediately set about repairing and reinstating the grounds while the house was being extensively rebuilt.

For the gardens and creation of a long-term historic landscape strategy, the Taylors turned to the landscape architect Elizabeth Banks, who is familiar with period restorations and indeed is the author of a seminal book on the subject, *Creating Period Gardens* published in 1991. Banks's interpretation perfectly fits into the Taylors' careful reconstruction of Tudor aspects of the house, notably on the east side, where Banks plotted a broad terrace for a formal rose garden. Height is brought into it with the use of treillage obelisks within the beds, echoed by slender stone obelisks as finials along a new stone balustrade.

David Austin's English roses occupy the flower beds in great profusion; pink, peach, and crimson tones predominate, sharpened by shots of yellow here and there, the blend complementing the mutable warm tones of the brickwork. In the choice of roses, Tudor connections—so evident in the house—are subtly acknowledged in cultivar names, such as the deep-crimson 'William Shakespeare' and also his character 'Falstaff'; in soft, pale pink 'Sceptre'd Isle' and the classic rose pink 'Mary Rose' (the latter named after Henry VIII's renowned warship).

The first landscape project, however, was the "pond"—a thirteen-acre lake, which probably had not been cleared since Capability Brown excavated it in

LEFT AND FOLLOWING PAGES
The rebirth of Rycote in the twenty-first century has seen the house substantially rebuilt with references to its Tudor origins and new formal gardens laid out alongside it. Assorted roses occupy the box-edged beds and the classic Anduze vases of Provence were specially made and imported from France.

BELOW Two views of the walled kitchen garden. It was rebuilt in the traditional manner, with high walls and criss-crossed by paths of Breedon gravel, which beds down to a hard surface and has a timeless look. The new aluminium glasshouse in the Victorian style has three different climate zones.

OPPOSITE A sheltered courtyard facing southwest is a warm and sunny location for the herb garden, which is conveniently located next to the kitchen and an outdoor dining area. Its herbs include lavender, thyme, sage, rosemary, santolina, and nepeta.

the eighteenth century. Over some twenty years, Brown extended the medieval fishponds into a serpentine lake, which makes a more-or-less boomerang shape lying northeast of the house, as well as converting the formal gardens into parkland stretching down to the house. Reinstatement of the lake and its two islands has greatly increased the habitat for the varied wildfowl that paddle the waters, along with swans—fiercely protective of their cygnets—and geese with their goslings, while the fish stocks include rainbow and brown trout. The water is aerated by two large floating fountains, which also help prevent overgrowth of pond weeds. At the west end of the "boomerang," water flows under a handsome new oak bridge into a calm area devoted to waterlilies—presently some five different varieties—and a walk around the lake perimeter takes in other features, too, such as a fine new weatherboarded and thatched boathouse, and the remnants of a 1920s woodland garden among old oaks, where double daffodils and shrubs, including some rhododendrons and mahonias, erupt into flower in their due seasons.

Rycote Park has many fine trees, but two are especially noteworthy: one, which dominates the lawn near the walled kitchen garden, is an Oriental plane, *Platanus orientalis*, of massive girth. Although its top has been blasted out by gales from time to time, it has made up for what it may have lost in height by creating a great, buttressed trunk with low-sweeping branches that have rooted themselves around it protectively. The other notable specimen, a great yew, is across the park beside the little Rycote chapel, and is believed to have been planted by monks in 1135, predating the existing chapel by some three centuries.

After substantial restoration, the walled garden has been reinstated as a traditional, productive kitchen garden, formally laid out and crisscrossed by compacted Breedon gravel paths and with a fine glasshouse. Apart from general salads, vegetables, and soft fruits, more unusual vegetables such as salsify, scorzonera, and sea kale are raised, as well as cutting flowers for the house. Some of the glazed Anduze pots the Taylors had made for them in Provence line the kitchen-garden paths, and there is another French touch in a collection of elegant wire cloches, deployed wherever pigeons or pheasants could be a nuisance.

Elsewhere, the range of buildings forming the house and entrance courtyard enclose a glorious herb garden, facing southwest and butted up against the kitchen wall. Humming with bees, and redolent of Mediterranean hillsides, it nurtures billowy cushions of lavender, thyme, sage, and santolina in great variety, plus nepeta, rosemary, *Convolvulus cneorum*, and many other sun lovers. With its proximity to the kitchen through one door, and access to another wing of the house through another, this is a favourite al fresco dining area for the Taylors, under the watchful gaze of a magnificent swooping bronze barn owl by artist Stanley Dove.

ORPHEUS, BOUGHTON HOUSE

NORTHAMPTONSHIRE

A modern land form of turfed banks and water was installed within the seventeenth-century park as part of ongoing renovations

At Boughton House, reinvention is certainly a key word beside restoration, where the landscaped grounds have been smartened up in the past three decades. The present Duke of Buccleuch (pronounced Ber-kloo) has made it his mission to restore within reasonable (i.e., affordable) parameters, an extremely rare "transitional" garden of the late-seventeenth/early-eighteenth century, while adding new ideas and vigour that enhance its long history.

The late-seventeenth-century landscape was created by the duke's ancestor, Ralph Montagu (1638–1709), whose family had settled there in 1528. Ambitious and fashion-conscious Montagu, who had been an ambassador in France to Louis XIV in the 1660s and 1670s, had seen Versailles being developed with its power statement avenues and its wondrous baroque uses of water and elegant buildings.

In the 1680s, Montagu began an enormous series of works at Boughton, building a new north front on the house in the French style, with staterooms and a formal landscape garden to match its grandeur, inspired by what he had seen on the Continent. He took the straggling course of the River Ise and altered it, in a disciplined series of straight lengths and turning it through right-angled corners. A vast area of formal gardens was created, with a framework of canals and cross waters and a series of terraced parterres and fountains, which took advantage of the naturally sloping ground. Ralph's son John inherited in 1709 and developed it further (he created twenty-three miles of avenues at Boughton, excluding the rides he cut through local woods). Landscaper Charles Bridgeman is believed to have been involved sometime around 1730. The formal landscape enjoyed about sixty years of glory until 1749, when John died.

Had it been a more important property in the eyes of its owners, Boughton might well have undergone radical alterations by Capability Brown. That didn't happen, says the Duke of Buccleuch, because "at that point, the house passed through the female line twice in succession, to families who already had lots of houses, including my own Buccleuch family. Boughton became a fringe property and the whole thing was basically allowed not to be spoiled; instead, it was allowed to go to sleep. It grew over and it disappeared, virtually, and the plug was taken out of the sluice gate."

Since the 1970s, there has been intermittent restoration of some of the early features, beginning with the Broad Water, a big square reservoir that fed numerous fountains in the long-lost lower gardens. Since the millennium the duke has initiated more restorations, most recently the Grand Etang near the house, a one-acre rectangular lake with sloping sides containing 1.5 million gallons of water. Its *jet d'eau*, sending up a plume of water between seventy-five and 100 feet, recalls (and, with modern technology, exceeds in height) its wondrous predecessor of the 1690s.

Orpheus is a new earthwork by Kim Wilkie within the partially restored seventeenth- and eighteenth-century landscaped park at Boughton House in Northamptonshire, a home of the Duke of Buccleuch. Orpheus was unveiled in 2010; its measurements, proportions, and gradients were worked out carefully by computer, then transferred to laser survey equipment, to guide the digger precisely.

Boughton is also about looking forward, however, and contributing something new for future generations. In this spirit, the duke commissioned landscape architect Kim Wilkie to create a new landform, sympathetic to the existing features in the park. The result is Orpheus, an alluring stepped earthwork that mirrors an original adjacent mount that survives from the early landscape. Unveiled in 2010, Orpheus invites the visitor to walk down its steady gradient to examine its watery depths. Pure spring water from another part of the park wells up within an open cuboid structure, then follows a curved channel to feed into the void.

"Within the whole landscape, I hope it's quite discreet," says Wilkie. It is. It seamlessly fits into its setting. The measurements, proportions, and gradients were worked out very carefully by computer and then transferred into laser survey equipment, so that the digger was guided very precisely to create the desired gradients and slopes. Today's is a very different world from the one of plumb lines, theodolites, and discernment by eye that would have been employed in creation of the eighteenth-century earthworks. It has been suggested as a metaphor for the mythical story of Orpheus and Eurydice, an idea that suits it well, playing on the Age of Enlightenment, poetry, politics, and reflecting planes of water that underpinned early-eighteenth-century thought in landscape garden creation.

LEFT The park at Boughton has many fine trees; its avenues carry the view into the distant horizon. Elaborate landscape and water gardens were created in the 1680s and the next generation developed the park further from 1709, when some twenty-three miles of avenues were created over the enormous estate.

OPPOSITE In the upper section of Orpheus, pure spring water from another part of the park wells up within an open cuboid structure. It then flows along a slender curved channel before feeding into the pond at the bottom of the turf-banked excavation shown on pages 422–23.

PAINSHILL PARK

SURREY

There had been a tale of wonder and woe in the creation of this unique mid-eighteenth century park, now restored to glory

"I am convinced that much good Wine might be made in many parts of the south of England," wrote Charles Hamilton, creator of Painshill, in a contribution to Sir Edward Barry's *Observations, Historical, Critical, and Medical, on the Wines of the Ancients* (1775). He might wonder now at the steady increase of land in southern counties, which, year by year, are being taken out of arable use and instead turned into vineyards. English wine, particularly English sparkling wine, is up there with the best—perhaps not so surprisingly, since areas of the South Downs share their calcareous geology with the Champagne region of France. In this spirit Hamilton, inventive, creative, and independent minded, planted a vineyard on unpromising ground at Painshill. It is, however, a mere sideshow to the main event—his unique and uniquely wonderful landscape garden.

Painshill was created in the naturalistic style between 1738 and 1773. That it survives at all is down to the willingness of the former Esher Urban District Council and a group of local activists to have the will to rescue, back in 1975, what was no longer visibly a garden, but a lost landscape: hostage to scrub, bracken, forests of self-sowed trees, and under it all, the bare ruins of a few scattered little buildings.

Yet, in its day, Painshill must have been a marvel of imagination and determination. Hamilton, a young milord of means (but alas, as it turned out, not enough means), bought a tract of land expressly to make the landscaped park that fired his imagination. From the outset it was going to be an uphill task, and not only because it was on rising ground. The setting is actually wonderful, with its views into a gentle valley, but it was rough, sandy heath, fast-draining, acidic, and devoid of nutrients. Just improving it was a slow process; in difficult areas the ground had to be sowed with turnips, which were fed to sheep, whose manure in turn helped to raise the fertility of the soil. (Later, Horace Walpole was to praise Hamilton for creating "a fine place out of a most cursed hill.")

Like the garden at Stourhead, created by Hamilton's old school friend, Henry Hoare, Painshill is the inspired creation of its owner, with a walk following a prescribed route to enjoy its buildings and statues, its references to the ancients and the thrill of its crystal-encrusted grotto. From the entrance, the historic route twists and turns past the Fir Walk and the top of the vineyard, which slopes gently down to a lake, stretching east/west along the valley. A succession of features follow: an amphitheatre, then an exquisite Gothic temple focused on the lake spread below; a twisty route through the trees leads to a Chinese bridge and little islands in the curvaceous lake. The island grotto is a wondrous cavern of tufas, spars, and stalactites, but there is still a long way to go.

Glory has returned to Painshill, which was a lost landscape buried under scrub and self-sowed trees around a muddy bog in the 1970s. More than forty years of hard work and fund-raising have resulted in the restoration of a unique Picturesque landscape garden dating from the mid-eighteenth century.

ABOVE LEFT Bridge over calm waters: Hamilton chose a site widely regarded as very poor ground to start a garden. It did, however, have a natural valley, something that he exploited with supreme artistic taste.

BELOW LEFT The Turkish Tent sits on another hill and also enjoys views down the lake. This is, of course, a reconstruction of the original one created in the 1750s. It is undeniably exuberant and exotic, evoking distant lands and cultures.

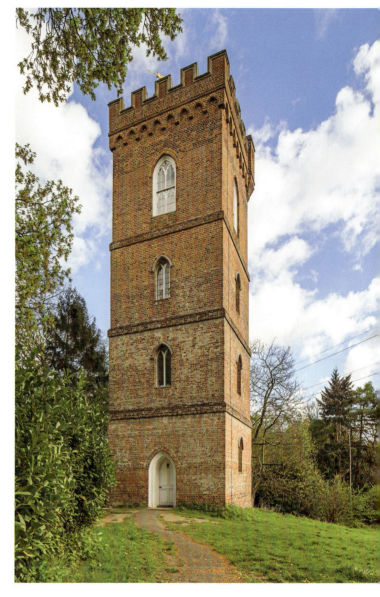

The restored Grotto has openings onto the lake and its ceilings of "stalactities" were clad with pieces of shiny, sparkling feldspar. Originally a gardener was engaged to wait in the dark for visitors to approach the subtly illuminated cave. He would turn on a pump to set off dripping water, while a pool of still water created perfect reflections.

On the lake's other side, reached by a different bridge, the path stays with the water's edge, leading to a Mausoleum, then following a curve formed by the River Mol to reach the Cascade and an area of plantations and open glades, with various tracks through the Alpine Valley to the most distant folly, the Gothic Tower. From here, the return route across the open grasses of the "Elysian Plains" leads on to the Temple of Bacchus (Hamilton's celebration of the god of wine, who presided over the vineyard) and along the high ground to the Turkish Tent, which enjoys views down the lake and up again to the aforementioned Gothic temple on a hill in the far distance. From here, there is still a fair stretch of park to enjoy via the bathhouse and icehouse but by now one's pace is likely to quicken since there's a tearoom at the end of it all.

That any of it is here today is down to the magnificent efforts of the Painshill Park Trust and volunteers, steadily restoring and remaking it all over more than forty years. Hamilton, tragically, ran out of money before he could build his house and sold the park that had taken him thirty-five years to create. His creation, however, now delights us all.

The Gothic Tower is located at the far western end of the garden. It is believed that Charles Hamilton was his own architect for all the garden's imaginative buildings. Hamilton was a cultured man, but not rich enough to maintain his expensive creation. By 1773, the money was gone and he had to sell Painshill. Its magnificent restoration, however, enables us to appreciate the marvel it is today.

17 MODERN GARDENS

The Chelsea Flower Show of 1959 included, among its show gardens, "The Garden of Tomorrow," featuring the very latest gadgetry, such as an aluminium greenhouse with a mist-propagation bench and automatic soil heating and watering. There was a "Webb radio-controlled lawn-mower," an ancestor of the robot mowers that are now so popular. But since it required the operator to be present to direct it via a handheld remote control, it wasn't going to change the world any time soon. (The 1964 invention of the air-cushioned Flymo, on the other hand, was a game changer.) But, despite the gadgets, the Garden of Tomorrow was itself stuck in the past, its design being the familiar suburban central lawn with flower beds pushed back around the edges—and full of rhododendrons, the show's standard fare for most of its gardens from the 1920s until the early 1990s.

The young landscape architect John Brookes offered an alternative, modernist garden in 1962 that spoke of the approaching age of the Beatles, Mary Quant, miniskirts, and Mini cars. With its clean, straight lines, cuboid pergola suspended over a square pool, and modern furniture, stylistically it was certainly an advance on "The Garden of Tomorrow."

In country gardens through the 1960s and 1970s, the emphasis was still on reducing maintenance, with easy-care rhododendrons and ground-covering plants—heathers, pachysandra, and ivy—papering over the high taxation and staff shortages. Change happened in the boom years of the 1980s under Margaret Thatcher's Conservative government. Important exhibitions in the 1970s and early 1980s highlighted the plight of the English country house, its gardens, and also the work of Edwin Lutyens. A big historical restoration phase emerged, coupled with a Gertrude Jekyll revival. Suddenly, much attention was focused on knots and patterns found in old herbals and herbaceous borders. Traditional styles prevailed, and modernism still had very little uptake in the English country garden scene, but people started to love roses again because they could be fitted into Sissinghurst-inspired gardens, and David Austin was producing wayward, old-fashioned-looking ones, which (sometimes) had better disease resistance.

Tim Richardson, chronicler of English gardening in the twentieth century and director of the Chelsea Fringe (an iconoclastic, now international event,

OPPOSITE "Hortus Conclusus," a garden at the Chelsea Flower Show in 2004, designed by Christopher Bradley-Hole for the late Sheikh Zayed bin Sultan Al Nahyan, then-ruler of Abu Dhabi and a keen gardener and conservationist. It won Best in Show for its coherent modern design and innovative planting.

OPPOSITE, CLOCKWISE Pine trees and pumice: a gallery of modern details. Charlotte Harris's Royal Bank of Canada Garden, Chelsea Flower Show 2017, with *Pinus banksiana*. A bonsai pine on a sea of *Hakonechloa macra*, in a garden by Christopher Bradley-Hole. Basalt pyramids in the RBC Garden, Chelsea Flower Show 2016, by Hugo Bugg. Basalt paving contains pools and rills in "Hortus conclusus", as before.

taking place at the same time as the RHS show), observed that "the early 1990s saw the continuation of the historicist theme of the mid- to late-1980s, with restorations proceeding apace at estates and larger gardens ... In the last decade of the century, everything that could be restored was restored ... Restoration was politically uncontroversial and apparently backed up by public opinion in surveys, whereas new design was liable to be railroaded at any moment (Kathryn Gustafson's aborted design for Crystal Palace Park in the late 1990s was a case in point). This way of looking at gardens self-consciously through the prism of the past was given legitimacy by an ultra-historicist strain in garden history, which dictated that 'newness' as a concept was fundamentally flawed."

But, as the novelist L. P. Hartley, author of *The Go-Between*, famously observed, "The past is a foreign country; they do things differently there." The 1990s were pre–social media, of course, with its free exchange of ideas. Also pre-smartphones, pre-iPads, and indeed, for all but the geeks, pre–World Wide Web. From here, late-twentieth-century restoration obsession now appears as a last hurrah, before English gardening decided to move on and embrace the new millennium.

Numerous analyses point at two events in the 1990s that seismically shifted the direction of English garden design away from the default Arts and Crafts. First, in 1994 a symposium held at Kew Gardens introduced British designers to the naturalistic and matrix herbaceous planting styles with wispy grasses, which had rejuvenated public parks in Germany; along with Piet Oudolf's rolling waves of grasses-and-perennials, these freer-seeming planting styles chimed with our concerns for nature and the environment (page 391). And in 1997 the Latin Garden designed by Christopher Bradley-Hole for the *Daily Telegraph* at the Chelsea Flower Show was the show's first truly successful modern garden, winning Best in Show. It combined semi-naturalistic ideas suited to dry, gravel gardening, serious plantsmanship appreciated by the RHS judges, and deft modernist design, with a narrative that was both ancient (telling the life story of the Roman poet Virgil) and brand new.

In their different ways, the gardens that follow in this section illustrate the new, modern mood in English gardening. Britain has a unique and flourishing Society of Garden Designers, a professional group that continues to grow, and the younger people coming through have the talent, confidence, vision, and connections that will help them succeed in an environmentally challenging world. English gardeners will continue to make beautiful gardens in a multitude of styles. That's part of our diversity. The difference in the twenty-first century is that a credible alternative to historicism has emerged and it will be interesting to see how English gardens shape up in the future.

Cut-leaved stag's horn sumac *Rhus typhina* 'Dissecta' kicks off the autumn tints at Denmans. The garden's flowing forms and structural trees were put in by Joyce Robinson starting in the mid-1940s. John Brookes refined and replanted the garden in the 1980s.

DENMANS

WEST SUSSEX

The home of the late John Brookes, foremost British twentieth-century garden designer in the modern style, reveals wonderfully balanced spaces

In 1969, an important new book changed the way that many people saw their gardens and indicated the direction that garden design would take thereafter, particularly in small and town gardens. The book was *Room Outside: A New Approach to Garden Design*, by the modernist garden designer John Brookes (1933–2018), which he published because of his conviction that a garden must work as a stylish, outdoor room to be used and enjoyed by all the family. By now, it is difficult to understand how revolutionary his guidance was, but since England had largely turned its back on the modernist movement that had influenced garden styles in America and much of Europe, Brookes felt that people—especially people living in cities and suburbs—were missing out on how to really enjoy the patch of ground outside their house. *Room Outside* showed, with copious drawings, details, monochrome photos, and no-nonsense text, how to put together a stylish space with places to sit out and to dine; it described where to put paving, how to choose fencing, how to organize plants, and how to use colour.

By the time Brookes arrived at Denmans, with its light, open-feeling garden, a few miles northeast of Chichester, he was a very well-established landscape designer, having begun in the design offices of Brenda Colvin and Sylvia Crowe. Thereafter he had developed his own thriving design practice and had been for several years the director of Garden Design studies at the Inchbald School of Design in London.

Brookes had known the garden at Denmans and its owner, Joyce Robinson, for a few years before he took over its clock house and former stables in 1980, setting up home there and running a garden design school. Robinson passed the garden to Brookes to develop in his own way, although for some years she would venture out from her cottage in the garden to stop and chat with some of the garden's numerous visitors.

What Brookes had admired when he first saw Denmans was how "rambly" it was—and different from anything else he had seen. The Robinsons had been at Denmans since 1946, and Joyce thought its gently south-facing slope was ideal for making a garden in a natural way. She created a gravel "stream" in 1969, using water-worn gravel from the seabed at nearby Littlehampton, artistically spotlighting areas here and there with larger seabed stones and planting "only things that might be found growing in a dry stream bed; grasses, iris, thistles, mint, willow and elder," she noted in her garden memoir. "Under the banks and in the grave everywhere I planted violets, water forget-me-nots, musk and lamiums."

Brookes recalled later, "When I first came here I took over the garden slowly, getting used to Joyce and Bertie [Reed, her gardener]. Joyce thought it took ten years to feel that I was running the garden and it certainly took

LEFT The garden is very naturalistic in form and gently guides the visitor through episodes of tree-dappled glades and calmingly curvaceous routes.

RIGHT John Brookes was very keen on creating compositions of form and texture, using the contrasting natures of plants. In this exemplary view, a clipped box globe is juxtaposed with the strappy leaves of *Phormium tenax*; the under-plantings of flat-flowered sedum, perennial wallflower, and furry-leaved *Verbascum bombyciferum* balance the weightiness of the larger plants.

LEFT Both John Brookes and Joyce Robinson were keen on showing plants in a contrived natural setting at Denmans. In the Picturesque manner of the eighteenth century, Brookes composed a series of serene views within the garden, sparingly using props such as large pots or sculpture—a technique that works in the hands of a master.

RIGHT A view down the lawn, showing how the birch trees planted into it bring changing patterns with their filtered shadows. The geese are models that help animate the scene.

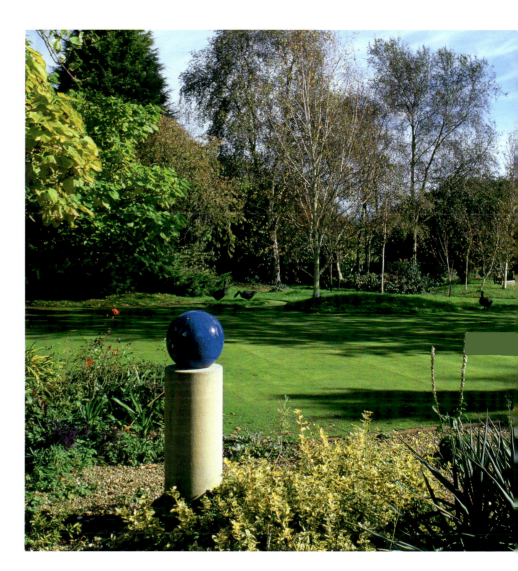

ten years for me to feel that her garden was mine! The big trees were hers, the bones were in and she had done the dry gravel stream. But she was a plantswoman and a collector of plants, while I liked arranging the plants and getting the shape right. Mrs. Robinson was beginning to think ecologically very early on and wanted to use Mediterranean plants to create a glorious disarray, but her dry gravel stream didn't seem to go anywhere so I put a pool in to finish the garden with a positive statement." In subsequent years Brookes continued to develop the garden, strengthening its curvaceous design and sharpening up the planting, while being respectful of its creator's earlier vision.

These softly autumnal pictures by Andrew Lawson, taken in the early 2000s, capture the richness of texture and contrasting plant structures that were so important in Brookes's planting designs and continue to be a hallmark of the garden today. Denmans is partly contained by the high brick walls of a former estate kitchen garden, which give added shelter to the Mediterranean plants of its gravelly areas. Substantial curvy areas of lawn are edged by interesting mixed shrubs and herbaceous plants and plenty of trees. It is one of the most soothing and relaxing gardens around, calmly expressing the remarkable talents of its makers.

SCAMPSTON HALL

NORTH YORKSHIRE

Desiring to make a visitor attraction out of their large walled garden, the owners called in fashionable designer Piet Oudolf to revamp it

In fertile Yorkshire farmland midway between the city of York and the North Sea coast, Scampston Hall is a fine Regency house with several important names attached to its grounds. Charles Bridgeman (1690–1738) was engaged to work on the park in the early eighteenth century, followed by Capability Brown, who advised on some adjustments a generation later. Like many of Brown's clients, Sir William Saint Quintin of Scampston used his own workmen to implement his suggestions, made in 1772–3. Pleased with the results, Sir William wrote to Brown in March 1773:

> *I have rec'd the favor of your letter with the plan inclosed for the Cascade, which I like very much … I have made the sunk fence on both sides of the gate-way, which has a most charming effect … I shall be in London some time next month, and will certainly wait on you. I beg your acceptance of some Yorkshire Hams …*

North of the mansion house is a magnificent 4.5-acre walled garden, also built in the eighteenth century, and this was no doubt in full food production through the eighteenth and nineteenth centuries. But, as with so many other walled gardens, it was unsustainable as a traditional working kitchen garden in the twentieth century and became, instead, an unloved area for the raising of sheep and crops of Christmas trees.

Following their move to the family home in 1994, Sir Charles Legard and his wife, Caroline, spent years painstakingly upgrading and restoring the house. In 1998, they attended a talk at John Coke's celebrated garden Bury Court in Hampshire, given by the Dutch garden designer and nurseryman

LEFT Sitting comfortably: framed by the heart-shaped leaves of a multi-stemmed *Cercidiphyllum japonicum*, wooden seats in the Perennial Meadow are surrounded by violet spires of Nepeta racemosa 'Walker's Low' and *Salvia nemorosa* 'Amethyst,' with pink splashes from *Geranium psilostemon* in the foreground and dots of deep claret *Knautia macedonica* behind.

RIGHT A view over the Perennial Meadow to the roofs of the old coach house and former stable.

PREVIOUS PAGES The dipping pond in the Perennial Meadow. Plants include *Salvia* 'Amethyst', *Nepeta* 'Walker's Low,' Geranium 'Rose Clair,' *Knautia macedonica*, and *Dianthus carthusianorum*.

BELOW *Phlomis russeliana* among *Rudbeckia occidentalis*, *Salvia* 'Amethyst', *Stachys officinalis* 'Hummelo', and *Allium cristophii*.

RIGHT The Silent Garden, with some of the twenty-four yew columns reflected in its pond and casting dramatic shadows across the lawn.

Piet Oudolf, who revealed his own take on how to use herbaceous perennial plants in big, bold drifts, incorporating ornamental grasses. It sparked in them an idea that their walled garden could be retrieved and made beautiful, in an interesting and modern way. From the outset, it was to be a visitor attraction and was among the first of Oudolf's British projects, following Bury Court and the nature reserve garden created in 1997 at Pensthorpe in Norfolk.

The appetizer at Scampston is a perimeter path leading from the walled garden's entrance, giving views into the main event, between beech hedges topped by pleached lime trees. The path has its own border by the wall, planted with tree peonies, hydrangeas, hostas, lilacs, ferns, epimediums, ligularias, and much else.

Aerial views best show the thinking behind the walled garden's design. Its formality hints at the Anglo-Dutch garden of William and Mary's time, here brought into the twenty-first century, with a nod to both traditions in its largely symmetrical layout, subdivided into nine or so rectangular spaces of different emphasis. Many of them are cushioned with lawns between the topiaries and beds of swishy, modern grasses. At the garden's heart, aligned with the restored glasshouses, is a four-square garden with central pond, crossed by gravel paths. Here, the substantial beds are abuzz with bees across the season, enjoying Oudolf's trademark herbaceous perennials.

These days, the next generation is in charge at Scampston, with Christopher and Miranda Legard finding new ways to make their ancient estate pay for itself. The walled garden is a much loved and successful part of its adaptation to the twenty-first century.

BROUGHTON GRANGE

OXFORDSHIRE

A new, partially walled and partially hedge-enclosed garden on three levels was created for the owner by designer Tom Stuart-Smith

April in England is blossom time. It is also tulip time, and there is not a lovelier month in the year, unless it is May (which is also blossom and tulip time!). Every year the British become more and more enraptured by tulips—almost as much as the Dutch. And to prove it, more gardens each year prepare long in advance to host "tulip festivals" to celebrate the virtues of a special and much-loved flower, or if not an actual festival, they at least put on a good show.

Despite their cheerful springtime ubiquity in parks, gardens, seafront displays, roundabouts, pots, and window boxes, tulips are not native to these isles, but descended from bulbs of Central Asia and the Levant, stealing the hearts of gardeners in Northern Europe well over four hundred years ago. In *The Tulip*, her magisterial homage to the bulb, Anna Pavord wrote "in the second half of the sixteenth century, Protestant Huguenots most probably brought the tulip into England from Flanders, for, long before the Dutch cornered the market, Flanders was the most important centre of tulip breeding in Europe."

One of the traditional ways of displaying garden tulips is in beds edged with box. But at Broughton Grange, this classic combination—with the fresh greens of box foliage setting off the jewel-bright hues of tulips—took on a whole new dimension under the guidance of landscape designer Tom Stuart-Smith in 2001. Engaged by owner Stephen Hester to make extensive alterations and new areas in the garden, Stuart-Smith took advantage of land that falls away steadily to the south to create a squared up area, divided into three broad, stepped terraces. Each of these is further divided into three distinct sections, so that the central one—the x of the oxo, as it were, in any direction—is occupied by a square pool, with stepping-stones lined up to create a straight path over the water on its west side. The whole garden is walled only along its western and northern perimeters (its splendid stepped and buttressed stone walls are by the architect Ptolemy Dean), so that the lovely views of rolling Oxfordshire countryside can be enjoyed to the east and south.

The upper two terraces are concerned with herbaceous perennials and grasses in Stuart-Smith's take on the contemporary "New Perennials Movement" naturalistic method; the middle terrace is also populated by large, slightly Dalek-like topiary figures in beech (*Fagus sylvatica*). The spring spectacle of tulips-in-box lies in the lowest terrace, which as immediately evident from these photographs is unusual in its design. Stuart-Smith took for his inspiration the leaves of the surrounding beech, oak, and ash trees and looked under a microscope at the leaf-cell structure to arrive at his ordered-but-complex abstract design. Some five thousand tulips are grown within the irregular, hedged pattern, the plantings being composed of repeated groups of bright mid- and late-season cultivars. Triumph, Lily-Flowered, and Viridiflora

Tulips rise out of the unusually shaped box parterre, where the pattern is based upon magnified leaf cell structures. Although the tulips are in a rich assortment of shades, varieties are kept separate, in their own quarters, intensifying the effect of their multiple hues.

BELOW A detail of the tulips in the lowest terrace of the walled garden.

RIGHT From the upper terrace of the walled enclosure, a channel heads southward to spill water into the pool that sits in the middle of the garden.

groups predominate, says Stuart-Smith. Zingy reds, purples, and yellow with red stripes all work well against the fresh greenery of emerging young foliage on the box plants, but also oranges and strong pinks, so the planting is refreshed with new ideas and different cultivars every so often.

This is only part of the greater garden, however, which is now regularly open to visitors. Stephen Hester's own great interest is the arboretum, which he has been adding to for many years; it now represents a very significant tree collection, planted over some eighty acres. Traditional formal gardens near the house relate to the Victorian era, and there are also wildflower meadows and a plant nursery.

VILLAGE GARDEN

A large garden on London's margin has been designed to blend seamlessly with the open land beyond it, creating a wildlife haven

"We think loosely of the countryside as 'village England' but it is vastly more complicated than this," wrote W. G. Hoskins, painstaking chronicler of England's landscapes, both existing and vanished. It is easy to forget that London is a collection of hundreds of villages, settlements, and farms, drawn into the conurbation and steadily built upon for the past two thousand years.

The disappearance of agriculture from London's doorstep was substantially ratcheted up in the late nineteenth century with the arrival of the railways, extensive new housing, and cheap food imports. By the 1930s, concern was being raised about unchecked urban spread and sprawl. The idea of Green Belt was mooted, whereby a ring of countryside around the cities could be protected from building development but provide public access for leisure pursuits, as well as forestry and agriculture. A number of London's outer villages thus gained conservation protection, at least in part, and have naturally become sought after, owing to the undoubted benefits of open space, alongside easy access to the capital.

Garden designer Christopher Bradley-Hole was brought in by the owner of one such village house, to "make something special," of a long and steeply sloping garden that appeared disconnected from both its house and the open landscape beyond. Glorious views to the south took in native oak and hawthorn woodland, part of the Green Belt common land. Bradley-Hole noted that, among the area's many charms are the generous punctuations of open space, given over to simple cultivation with native trees and long grass.

LEFT Smooth stone paving forms a substantial terrace on the south side of the house, looking into the garden. The timber path leads to steps down into the garden, between blocks of yew hedging.

RIGHT The garden echoes the simple modernist lines of the house.

Aerial views also revealed the wider landscape beyond the village: a typical pattern of lowland English fields. The field pattern became the inspiration for the garden's design.

Large blocks of native hedges (yew, beech, field maple, and hawthorn) were planted to suggest, in an abstract way, the "fields," but also to reflect the changing seasons. (Hawthorn's May/June blossom, and the mellow autumn colour on the beech and field maple are particularly attractive.) Other "small-scale fields" of the composition are planted with a mix of tall grasses and flowering perennials to create a new, naturalistic landscape.

The design was drawn to be geometric and formal closest to the house, visually creating a seamless connection with new, stone-paved terraces. Plants were chosen to be suggestive of the native flora but not tied to being so. New areas of native woodland as well as extensive beech hedges and beech blocks were planted on the perimeter; existing hazels were coppiced, and trees of hornbeam and English oak were planted in key positions. Hornbeam hedges, extending to the front, were planted to frame groups of multi-stemmed *Amelanchier lamarckii*.

"The grasses and airy herbaceous plants sway and catch every breeze, bringing movement into the garden," says Bradley-Hole. "Early season flowers are a mix of bright and subtle colours but by autumn, more muted tones come to the fore. Then, the accents are plumes of grasses which continue to flower through to February, when they are cut down to allow the spring garden to re-emerge."

The design continues to evolve. A grassy mound, created to arrest the slope of the ground, provides a raised vantage point from which to see the garden; elsewhere, Bradley-Hole designed a cedar-clad pavilion that rotates to take in different views. Although it wasn't part of the brief, the garden has also become a valuable ecosystem, with dramatically improved bird and animal life, including owls, all too rare now in London postcodes.

PREVIOUS PAGES The design of the garden is an abstract interpretation of field patterns in the landscape. Mowed paths take various routes through the planting, which includes blocks of native tree hedging, assorted ornamental grasses, and herbaceous perennials.

RIGHT A tapestry of summer perennials mingle together. They include *Gaura lindheimeri* 'Whirling Butterflies,' orange and blood-red daylily *Hemerocallis* 'Stafford,' crimson-red *Persicaria amplexicaulis* 'Taurus,' *Aster lateriflorus* var. *horizontalis*, *Veronicastrum virginicum* 'Album,' and dusky-mauve *Eupatorium maculatum*.

BELOW A view across the garden from the house terrace toward a grass mount, which itself gives elevated views back over the garden.

WEST PROMENADE, BEXHILL

EAST SUSSEX

The long seaside promenade at Bexhill leads the way in how to garden for more water-wise times, with low-maintenance and salt-tolerant species

Bexhill-on-Sea lies in the southeasternmost corner of the British Isles, lapped by the Pevensey Marshes to the west, and sheltered to the north by the wooded hills of the Sussex High Weald. With its languorous miles of south-facing beach, numerous golf clubs, and a benign microclimate in the sunniest corner of England, the formerly ancient hamlet that became an Edwardian seaside resort has long been established as a popular place for retirees.

Perhaps something in the air gives its residents a reputation for longevity. The comedian Spike Milligan, once a Bexhill resident, used to say that "all the old people retire to Eastbourne—and their parents live in Bexhill." Fans of Agatha Christie's crime stories will recall the seaside town's appearance in one of the author's more unsettling mysteries, *The A.B.C. Murders*. When it was published, in January 1936, the resort was already in the news, however; just a month earlier, there had been the grand opening of Bexhill's dazzling De La Warr Pavilion: an audacious, modernist public building beside the sea—all chrome and glass, with the horizontality of a Cunard passenger liner.

Through the second half of the twentieth century, with more and more people jetting off to find reliable sunshine and sangria in far-off lands, the coastal resorts of home suffered—and eventually something had to be done. Under the Commission for Architecture and the Built Environment, a "Seachange" funding scheme was set up in the early 2000s to help some of the nation's ailing seaside towns. At Bexhill, it enabled much-needed restoration of the seventy-year-old De La Warr Pavilion, followed by the regeneration of the seafront promenade. What was formerly a tired half-mile of tarmac punctuated by dreary low walls of concrete "bricks" was transformed into an innovative, linear series of herbaceous gardens, right next to the sea.

To make the replanted promenade interesting and engaging to people of all ages, discreet objects (such as timber and rope climbing paraphernalia) are stitched in, and there are plenty of seats. The overall impression is of a light, airy landscape suited to the maritime location, with an abundance of hardy, cushiony Mediterranean flora, selected and arranged by planting designer Noel Kingsbury. Choosing from the lists he made, of plants which are known to thrive alongside extreme coastal exposure, Kingsbury whittled down his choice to a limited palette, arranged in random groupings. Thus, you get a feeling of harmony and unity across the scheme, but with different selections of plants coming to the fore in each of the numerous flower beds along the route.

With "staycations" becoming popular once more, and a surge of renewed interest in Britain's handsome coastal towns, this unique and appealing solution to low-maintenance planting in a challenging location has inspired the replanting of a number of private gardens on the seafront.

Plants fit for a promenade: just a few steps back from the huts on the beach, naturalistic plantings of *Helichrysum italicum*, purple *Osteospermum*, *Ballota pseudodictamnus*, *Cistus* × *argenteus* 'Silver Pink,' and *Hebe albicans*.

LEFT Shimmering and shapely by the sea: *Stachys byzantina*, *Eryngium bourgatii*, and *Hebe albicans*.

ABOVE AND BELOW RIGHT Areas of turf and the gravel-mulched beds are crossed by decking paths. Planting includes *Santolina chamaecyparissus*, *Nepeta* × *fassenii*, *Salvia nemorosa*, *Eryngium bourgatii*, *Stachys byzantina*, and hebe.

THE OLD RECTORY, NAUNTON

High walls, built in the local "dry" style without mortar, separate and shelter a sequence of garden spaces thoughtfully planted

The Edwardian architect Harold Peto, himself the creator of numerous wonderful gardens, wrote that "Old buildings of masonry carry one's mind back to the past in a way that a garden of flowers only cannot do. Gardens that are too stony are equally unsatisfactory; it is a combination of the two in just proportion which is the most satisfactory." Peto wasn't talking about the Old Rectory at Naunton and its garden, but he could have been, so well do the house, the garden walls, its pavings, and the richly varied plants all interact with each other in perfect balance.

Angela Cronk and her husband, Michael, had enjoyed numerous stays in the Cotswolds before they actually decided to make the move from London. When they looked over the Old Rectory that was for sale, it was a daunting prospect, for the previous owners had been absent and both house and garden were showing signs of neglect. They saw the potential, however, and Angela, who had followed the work of garden designer Dan Pearson over the years, was in no doubt that his was the help she needed. There was refurbishment work to do on the house, but concurrently they started laying out the garden's new pavings and dry-stone walls according to Pearson's plans. In the end, she recalls, owing to several periods of very bad weather, Steve Swatton, the master stonemason, was occupied at Naunton for more than a year. Even so, the results were clearly well worth the time and effort.

Occupying a squarish plot of about one acre in the middle of the village, the Old Rectory is enclosed by high walls, although part of the wall is dropped

LEFT Oak "arrow slits" were inserted into the new dry-stone walling. They enable enticing glimpses into other parts of the garden. These yellow flowers on *Ligularia* 'The Rocket' flourish in wet soil at the side of the pond.

RIGHT A doorway off the courtyard is framed by deep-yellow-flowered *Clematis* 'Bill MacKenzie.'

PREVIOUS PAGES The end of the walled Canal Garden terminates with a loggia and seat, which looks back to the outdoor dining area and the house.

BELOW Across the South Terrace multi-stemmed specimens of *Amelanchier lamarckii* rise out of cubes of boxwood.

RIGHT Wisteria engulfs the ground floor windows on the south side of the house. Flat-topped cuboid box provides calm interventions of greenery among a cast of changing herbaceous flowers and the upright stems of the fashionable grass *Calamagrostis* × *acutiflora* 'Karl Foerster.'

on the north side to access the River Windrush, which flows right past. The gardens wrap around the house to the north, east, and south, with a series of shallow steps leading from the house straight into a sunny terrace on the south side. In this area, Pearson used cubes of box topiary to create structural accents, around which he put in softer planting and multistemmed trees of *Amelanchier lamarckii*, which delight in three seasons, with spring blossom, delicate green summer foliage, and rich autumn tints before leaf fall. The South Terrace leads eastward through a small wildflower meadow and lawn area to the swimming pool, which is largely screened off by trees and shrubs planted in a natural way.

Head north from there and you enter a walled sanctuary where the eastern half contains a long canal with richly planted beds on either side; the western end is next to the house and has space for outdoor dining. In the northeast corner, close to the river, Pearson created a pond with bog garden surround, beyond which lies the small kitchen garden in a formal arrangement of raised beds.

It is an idyllic situation, and each part of the garden has its own purpose and atmosphere. If pressed, however, Angela Cronk says that she is especially fond of the pond and river area: "Water is hugely attractive; the fish, the herons, the birds nesting around the edge; there is so much going on there; I am always drawn back to it."

HAUSER & WIRTH, BRUTON

SOMERSET

The nurseryman and garden designer Piet Oudolf was commissioned to create a stimulating landscape beside a leading contemporary art gallery

Somerset and Dorset are adjoining western counties with many old places bearing quaint names. Wyke Champflower, Kington Magna, Stour Provost, Shepton Montague, Weston Bampfylde, Sandford Orcas, and Ryme Intrinseca—who could fail to be enchanted by such names, which seem as if they have spilled out of the stories of Thomas Hardy or Anthony Trollope?

Tucked into delightfully rolling hills amid these poetic places is Bruton—less euphoniously named than others in the area, for sure, but nevertheless an ancient small town. The Domesday Book of 1086 tells us it was Bruuetone, meaning "vigorously flowing river." For long it has attracted New Age and artistic types and its coolness, for those who care about such things, was finally sealed with the arrival of the Hauser & Wirth art gallery at Durslade Farm on the edge of town in 2014.

Beside the gallery buildings, a long, hedge-margined pasture was designated for Oudolf Field (after its creator, celebrated Dutch garden designer Piet Oudolf), a 1.5-acre "perennial meadow" of island beds, through which runs a gravel river, footprinted with circular islands of turf.

Oudolf's signature "look" is very identifiable—much use of herbaceous perennials, planted in generous, merging drifts, with muscular prairie grasses erupting here and there. It's an impressionistic, uncorseted approach that has found many followers. Indeed, his influence on twenty-first-century planting design has been profound, as can be seen in other gardens featured in this section.

Oudolf's plants are chosen largely for their character, leaf shape, and texture; their individual flowers are often small, although numerous, and there is a leaning toward plants that "die well," leaving statuesque seed heads held aloft through winter. Oudolf has almost an "impressionist" style of mixing and blending that seems to make disparate colours work together; even when the brick reds, say, of *Helenium* are shoulder-to-shoulder with magenta *Lythrum* or metallic blue *Echinops*. Gertrude Jekyll might have reached for the smelling salts, confronted with Oudolf's apparently laissez-faire attention to clashing shades. But since she was very interested in the art of the impressionist movement—so topical in her day—perhaps she would enjoy his fearlessness. Think of Dutchman Vincent van Gogh's textured garden views at Arles, alongside the serene, carefully composed paintings of Hercules Brabazon, Jekyll's friend and mentor, whose beautiful landscape paintings were only shown publicly late in life at the encouragement of John Singer Sargent, or, indeed, Jekyll's own exquisite paintings. They all have their place. You don't have to like all the art displayed at the gallery; but outside you would need a heart of stone not to be moved by the changing Somerset light dancing across Oudolf Field and the myriad butterflies that attend it all summer long.

Oudolf Field at the Hauser & Wirth gallery is a long, rectangular hedge-margined pasture of 1.5 acres. The planting is impressionistic, as befits an art gallery, with a medley of grasses and summer-to-autumn flowering herbaceous plants including *Echinacea*, *Lythrum*, and *Helenium*.

PREVIOUS PAGES In close-up, pink-mauve pokers of *Liatris spicata*, a North American prairie plant, with creamy-white achilleas, round-headed *Allium* 'Summer Beauty,' and deep-bronze-stemmed *Sedum* 'Matrona.'

RIGHT Midsummer mergers: big sweeps of colour appear like bold brushstrokes on a canvas, with assorted herbaceous perennials, including terracotta-red *Helenium* 'Moerheim Beauty,' *Echinops*, sedums, *Allium* 'Summer Beauty,' and *Origanum* 'Hopleys.'

WISLEY ROYAL HORTICULTURAL SOCIETY GARDENS

SURREY

The flagship of Britain's premier horticultural society is undergoing considered improvement and updating, raising its standards of excellence

The sun-soaked tropical coconut groves of Sri Lanka seem a million miles from the sandy heaths and pastures of Surrey, but these two disparate locations were brought together in an interesting way to produce Wisley, the flagship gardens of the Royal Horticultural Society. The story starts with one George Fergusson Wilson (1822–1902), a London chemist whose father founded Price's Patent Candle Company in 1830. The Wilsons developed a candle wax that was less expensive than beeswax, but gave cleaner, brighter light than cheap tallow, which was smoky and smelly. Made with coconut oil (for which the Prices' company leased a thousand acres of coconut plantations in Sri Lanka), the new candle was a mid-range product that had an enormous market with numerous spin-off products added to the list over time, selling worldwide.

In 1878, George Wilson (who had also developed a popular insecticide) purchased Glebe Farm with sixty acres in the Surrey countryside at Wisley, where he created an experimental garden he named Oakwood. He developed a Wild Garden at Oakwood, planting lilies in the wood and bright flowers on the hillside beside it, in the free-style, loosely naturalistic manner promoted by William Robinson. In the lower ground he planted irises and lupins; a pinetum was planted to the north; and vegetable gardens and an avenue of trees along the approach road were established. Lilies and primroses were two of his special interests, and his trial garden was visited by Gertrude Jekyll, William Robinson, Edwin Lutyens, and many others.

LEFT The Winter Walk at Wisley Gardens wraps around an informal pond. This area lies alongside Oakwood, the physical and metaphorical heart of the garden, which started under the care of George Fergusson Wilson in 1878.

RIGHT Always the gardener's companion, a robin redbreast pauses for thought.

PREVIOUS PAGES This scene through the dogwoods in the Winter Walk resembles the exciting brushwork of a Jackson Pollock painting, the plants being a medley of *Cornus amomum*, *Cornus sanguinea* 'Midwinter Fire,' a sapling tree of *Taxodium mucronatum*, and white stems of the ghost bramble *Rubus thibetanus* in the background.

Actively involved in the RHS, Wilson was its treasurer for a number of years and when he died, Sir Thomas Hanbury (of the famous La Mortola botanical garden on the Italian Riviera) bought the Oakwood/Glebe Farm property and donated it all to the society. Wisley expanded with further acquisitions of land and today stands at some 240 acres, with every square inch devoted in one way or another to expanding horticultural knowledge, advancement, and appreciation. Its core areas include ravishing mixed borders and numerous gardens of special interest, such as a cottage garden, exotic garden, and vegetable, rose, and walled gardens. Its rock garden, alpine meadow, and alpine house are outstanding showpieces for diminutive treasures. There are borders by Piet Oudolf and a huge recently built glasshouse and lake, with surrounding plantings by Tom Stuart-Smith. Its fruit collections occupy huge orchards and the trial grounds form part of the day-to-day judging of cultivated plants.

Inevitably, a garden that has expanded piecemeal over more than a century but has such a wide scope requires "the bigger picture" to be looked at from time to time. Presently, Wisley is in an exciting moment of development, in the middle of a £160 million investment initiative, including a new welcome building, a national centre for horticultural science, and a master plan for the gardens steered by Christopher Bradley-Hole, whose redesign of the arrival area includes a dramatic cherry colonnade of *Prunus × yedonensis* and a versatile "Town Square" meeting place as a flexible event space, opened in 2019.

Recently the Royal Horticultural Society celebrated its landmark of half a million members, which suggests it has come a very long way from its foundation in 1804, when the "Horticultural Society of London" was formed (its seven founders aspired to build a membership of twenty-eight—certainly it was an exclusive club). Wisley now welcomes some 1.2 million visitors per year and the society's satellite gardens around the country bring its educational efforts to the regions at Rosemoor in Devon, Harlow Carr in North Yorkshire, Hyde Hall in Essex, and a new 156-acre garden at Bridgewater in Greater Manchester, opening in 2020.

The Winter Walk, shown here, lies beside Wilson's original Oakwood. It wraps around an informal pond, weaving through bold plantings of dogwoods, fragrant witch hazels, winter bulbs, and nodding hellebores. Planted in the past few years, it has become a popular part of a very impressive year-round garden.

OPPOSITE, CLOCKWISE Reasons to be cheerful, the brightest jewels of late winter at Wisley: *Narcissus* 'Twinkling Yellow'; *Helleborus* (Rodney Davey Marbled Group) 'Anna's Red' with burgundy petals; *Chaenomeles × superba* 'Coral Sea'; *Crocus vernus* 'Grand Maître' among garnet stems of *Cornus sericea* 'Coral Red.'

19 ↑

2

32

Newcastle-upon-Tyne

Carlisle

56

13 **48**

York

Manchester

14

27

4

Stoke-on-Trent

Nottingham

16

22

20 Norwich

33 **39**

Leicester

62

17

Birmingham

41

42

Cambridge

31 **45**

35

10

52 **40**

Cheltenham

11

6 Oxford

3 **26**

61 **47**

1

28

55

GREATER LONDON

Bristol **21**

46

12

58

59 **43**

Bath

54

9

5

38

49

29

30

37 **36** **7** **24** **25**

8

Southampton

60

44

57

34

15

18

Brighton

50

51

23

Exeter

53

THE GARDENS
KEY TO MAP

VISITOR INFORMATION

Many of the gardens in this book are private and offer only very limited opportunities for visitors, sometimes just on special open days to raise money for charities such as the National Garden Scheme and local nonprofit groups. Therefore, contact details are given below; websites are useful for guidance to opening dates, but it can be advisable to call and confirm an opening before setting out on a long journey. Factors such as adverse weather conditions or other unexpected events can cause closure at short notice, in spite of opening times published online or elsewhere.

ALLT-Y-BELA
Private but periodically available as a bed-and-breakfast
Llangwm Ucha
Usk
Monmouthshire NP15 1EZ
E-mail: alltybela@icloud.com
www.alltybela.co.uk

THE ALNWICK GARDEN
Regularly open to visitors
Greenwell Road
Alnwick
Northumberland NE66 1HB
Telephone: (01665) 511350
E-mail: info@alnwickgarden.com
www.alnwickgarden.com

OPPOSITE A stroll in the gardens at Glenae, near Dumfries, which opens for the Scottish Gardens Scheme.

RIGHT Tea and cake on mixed fine china, one of the pleasures of a National Garden Scheme open day at Lowder Mill in West Sussex.

BARNSLEY HOUSE
Open to guests of the hotel, spa, and restaurant
Barnsley, Cirencester
Gloucestershire GL7 5EE
Telephone: (01285) 740000
E-mail: info@barnsleyhouse.com
http://www.barnsleyhouse.com/

BIDDULPH GRANGE
Open to visitors as part of the National Trust
Grange Road, Biddulph
Staffordshire ST8 7SD
Telephone: (01782) 517999
E-mail: biddulphgrange@nationaltrust.org.uk
www.nationaltrust.org.uk

THE BISHOP'S PALACE GARDEN, WELLS
Regularly open to visitors
Wells
Somerset BA5 2PD
Telephone: (01749) 988111
www.bishopspalace.org.uk

BLENHEIM PALACE
Regularly open to visitors
Woodstock
Oxfordshire OX20 1UL
Telephone: (01993) 810530
www.blenheimpalace.com

BORDE HILL
Regularly open to visitors
Borde Hill Lane
Haywards Heath
West Sussex RH16 1XP
Telephone: (01444) 450326
E-mail: info@bordehill.co.uk
www.bordehill.co.uk

BRAMDEAN HOUSE
Private but open to visitors on a few selected days, via the National Garden Scheme
Bramdean
Alresford
Hampshire SO24 0JU
www.ngs.org.uk

BRICKWALL COTTAGES
Private but plants available by mail order
Brickwall Nursery
1 Brickwall Cottages
Frittenden
Kent TN17 2DH
Telephone: (01580) 852425
www.geumcollection.co.uk

BROUGHTON GRANGE
Open to specialist groups by prior appointment
Wykham Lane
Broughton
Banbury
Oxfordshire OX15 5DS
Telephone: (07791) 747371
E-mail: enquiries@broughtongrange.com
www.broughtongrange.com

BURFORD PRIORY
Private
Oxfordshire

CANTERBURY CATHEDRAL PRECINCTS
Open to visitors on special event days only
11 The Precincts
Canterbury
Kent CT1 2EH
Telephone: (01227) 762862
E-mail: enquiries@canterbury-cathedral.org
www.canterbury-cathedral.org/whats-on/event/open-gardens-weekend/

CASTLE HOWARD
Regularly open to visitors
Slingsby
North Yorkshire YO60 7DA
Telephone: (01653) 648333
www.castlehoward.co.uk

CHATSWORTH HOUSE
Regularly open to visitors
Bakewell
Derbyshire DE45 1PP
Telephone: (01246) 565300
www.chatsworth.org

COTTAGE ROW
Open to small groups, by prior appointment only
School Lane
Tarrant Gunville
near Blandford Forum
Dorset DT11 8JJ
www.ngs.org.uk

CULLAND HALL
Open for charity once a year and private tours by appointment
Culland
Ashbourne
Derbyshire DE6 3BW
Email: lucy@culland.co.uk

DEENE PARK
Regularly open to visitors and prearranged groups
Corby
Northamptonshire NN17 3EW
Telephone: (01780) 450278
E-mail: info@ deenepark.com
www.deenepark.com

DENMANS
Regularly open to visitors
Denmans Lane
Fontwell BN18 0SU
Telephone: (01243) 278950
E-mail: office@denmans.org
www.denmans.org

DURNAMUCK COTTAGES
Open to visitors as part of Scotland's Gardens
2 Durnamuck
Little Loch Broom
Wester Ross IV23 2QZ
www.scotlandsgardens.org

ELSING HALL
Private, but open to prearranged groups by appointment
Elsing
Dereham
Norfolk NR20 3DX
www.elsinghall.com

EURIDGE MANOR FARM
Private, but available for hire for special events
Colerne, Chippenham
Wiltshire SN14 8BJ
Telephone: (01637) 881183
E-mail: enquiries@euridge.net
www.uniquehomestays.com

FELBRIGG HALL
Open to visitors as part of the National Trust
Felbrigg
Norwich
Norfolk NR11 8PR
Telephone: (01263) 837444
E-mail: felbrigg@nationaltrust.org.uk
www.nationaltrust.org.uk

FRISTON PLACE
Private
Wealdon
East Sussex

GRAVETYE MANOR
Open to guests of the hotel and restaurant
Vowels Lane
West Hoathly
Sussex RH19 4LJ
Telephone: (01342) 810567
E-mail: info@gravetyemanor.co.uk
www.gravetyemanor.co.uk

GREAT DIXTER
Regularly open to visitors
Northiam
Rye
East Sussex TN31 6PH
Telephone: (01797) 252878
E-mail: office@greatdixter.co.uk
www.greatdixter.co.uk

GREYHOUNDS
Private, but usually opened during biennial Burford Festival
Burford
Oxfordshire
www.burfordfestival.org

GWAENYNOG
Private
Dolanog
Welshpool

HASELEY COURT
Private
Oxfordshire

HAUSER & WIRTH, BRUTON
Open during gallery opening times
Durslade Farm
Dropping Lane, Bruton
Somerset BA10 0NL
Telephone: (01749) 814060
www.hauserwirth.com

HEALE HOUSE
Regularly open to visitors
Middle Woodford
Salisbury
Wiltshire SP4 6NT
Telephone: (01722) 782504
E-mail: info@healegarden.co.uk
www.healegarden.co.uk

HEREFORD CATHEDRAL
Garden visits for groups by prior appointment
5 College Cloisters
Cathedral Close
Hereford
Herefordshire HR1 2NG
Telephone: (01432) 374200
E-mail: office@herefordcathedral.org
www.herefordcathedral.org/garden-tours

HERTERTON HOUSE
Check opening by telephone
Cambo, Morpeth
Northumberland NE61 4BN
Telephone: (01670) 774278

HILBOROUGH HOUSE
Private
Norfolk

KNIGHTSHAYES COURT
Open to visitors as part of the National Trust
Bolham
Tiverton
Devon EX16 7RQ
Telephone: (01884) 254665
E-mail: knightshayes@nationaltrust.org.uk
www.nationaltrust.org.uk

THE LASKETT
Prebooked groups by appointment only
Laskett Lane
Much Birch
Herefordshire HR2 8HZ
Telephone: (07989) 338217
E-mail: info@thelaskettgardens.co.uk
www.thelaskettgardens.co.uk

LEONARDSLEE
Regularly open to visitors
Brighton Road
Lower Beeding, Horsham
West Sussex RH13 6PP
Telephone: (0871) 333 89
E-mail: info@ leonardsleegardens.co.uk
www.leonardsleegardens.co.uk

LOWDER MILL
Open one or two days only, as part of the National Garden Scheme
Bell Vale Lane
Haslemere
West Sussex GU27 3DJ
Telephone: (01428) 644822
www.lowdermill.com
www.ngs.org.uk

MUNSTEAD WOOD
Private but open to specialist groups by appointment
Heath Lane
Godalming
Surrey GU7 1UN
E-mail:
contact@munsteadwood.org.uk
https://munsteadwood.org.uk

NORWICH CATHEDRAL, THE BISHOP'S GARDEN

Open to visitors on several charity days
Bishops Office
Saint Martin at Palace Plain
Norwich
Norfolk NR3 1SB
Telephone: (01603) 614172
E-mail: bishops.chaplain@
dioceseofnorwich.org
www.dioceseofnorwhich.org/gardens

THE OLD RECTORY, NAUNTON

Private
Naunton
Gloucestershire

ORPHEUS, BOUGHTON HOUSE

Limited opening on selected days and to groups by prior appointment
Kettering
Northamptonshire NN14 1BJ
Telephone: (01536) 515731
E-mail: info@boughtonhouse.co.uk
www.boughtonhouse.co.uk

OUSDEN HOUSE

Private, but open for a charity day as part of the National Garden Scheme
Ousden, Newmarket
Suffolk CB8 8TN
www.ngs.org.uk

PAINSHILL PARK

Regularly open to visitors
Portsmouth Road
Cobham
Surrey KT11 1JE
Telephone: (01932) 868113
E-mail: info@painshill.co.uk
www.painshill.co.uk

PARHAM HOUSE

Open on selected days through the season
Pulborough
West Sussex RH20 4HS
Telephone: (01903) 742021
E-mail: enquiries@parhaminsussex.co.uk
www.parhaminsussex.co.uk

PERRYCROFT

Private but open to group visits by appointment
Jubilee Drive
Upper Colwall
Malvern
Herefordshire WR13 6DN
Telephone: (07858) 393767
E-mail: info@perrycroft.co.uk
www.perrycroft.co.uk

ROYAL BOTANIC GARDENS, KEW

Regularly open to visitors
Kew
Richmond
London TW9 3AE
Telephone: (020) 8332 5655
E-mail: info@kew.org
www.kew.org

RYCOTE PARK

Private
Oxfordshire

SCAMPSTON HALL

Regularly open to visitors and prebooked groups but check for restricted dates
Malton
North Yorkshire YO17 8NG
Telephone: (01944) 759111
E-mail: info@scampston.co.uk
www.scampston.co.uk

SISSINGHURST CASTLE

Open to visitors as part of the National Trust
Biddenden Road
Cranbrook
Kent TN17 2AB
www.nationaltrust.org.uk

SOUTH WOOD FARM

Private, but open to visitors on one or two charity days as part of the National Garden Scheme and to groups by prior appointment
Cotleigh, Honiton
Devon EX14 9HU
www.ngs.org.uk

STANBRIDGE MILL

Private, but occasionally open for a charity day via the National Garden Scheme
Gussage All Saints
Dorset BH21 5EP
www.ngs.org.uk

TEMPLE GUITING MANOR

Private but lodging available as a boutique hotel
Temple Guiting
Cheltenham
Gloucestershire GL54 5RP
Telephone: (07748) 118288
E-mail: reservations@
templeguitingmanor.co.uk
www.templeguitingmanor.co.uk

TRESCO ABBEY GARDENS

Regularly open to visitors
Tresco Estate
Tresco
Isles of Scilly
Cornwall TR24 0QQ
Telephone: (01720) 422849
E-mail: contactus@tresco.co.uk
www.tresco.co.uk

UPTON GREY, THE MANOR HOUSE

Regularly open to visitors
The Manor House
Hampshire RG25 2RD
Telephone: (01256) 862827
www.gertrudejekyllgarden.co.uk

VILLAGE GARDEN

Private
Greater London

WARNELL HALL

Private
Cumbria

WEST PROMENADE, BEXHILL

Regularly open to visitors
Bexhill-on-Sea
East Sussex

WEST WOODHAY

Private but sometimes open to prebooked groups; contact the estate office
West Woodhay House Estate Office
Newbury
Berkshire RG20 0BS

WISLEY ROYAL HORTICULTURAL SOCIETY GARDENS

Open to visitors and rhs members year-round
Wisley Lane
Wisley, Woking
Surrey GU23 6QB
Telephone: (01483) 224234
E-mail: wisley@rhs.org.uk
www.rhs.org.uk

WOOLBEDING HOUSE

Open by prior appointment only, on selected days, via the National Trust
Midhurst
West Sussex GU29 9RR
Telephone: (03442) 491895
E-mail: woolbedinggardens@nationaltrust.org.uk
www.nationaltrust.org.uk

WORCESTER COLLEGE, OXFORD

Regularly open but check access times on website. Groups by appointment.
Walton Street
Oxford OX1 2HB
Telephone: (01865) 278300
www.worc.ox.ac.uk

WRETHAM LODGE

Private, but open to visitors by prior arrangement, via the National Garden Scheme
East Wretham
Norfolk IP24 1RL
www.ngs.org.uk

SELECTED BIBLIOGRAPHY

ANDERTON, Stephen. *Christopher Lloyd: His Life at Great Dixter.* London: Chatto & Windus, 2010.

ANDERTON, Stephen. *Lives of The Great Gardeners.* London: Thames & Hudson, 2016.

ASLET, Clive. *The Arts and Crafts Country House from The Archives of* Country Life. London: Aurum Press, 2011.

AUSTIN, David. *The Rose.* 2nd ed. Woodbridge, Suffolk, England: Garden Art Press, 2012.

BECKER, Robert. *Nancy Lancaster: Her Life, Her World, Her Art.* New York: Alfred A. Knopf, 1996.

BETTEY, J. H. *Estates and The English Landscape.* Londo   sford, 1993.

BISGROVE, Richard. *William Robinson: The Wild Gardener.* London: Frances Lincoln, 2008.

BLOMFIELD, Reginald, and Thomas F. Inigo. *The Formal Garden in England.* Facsimile ed. London: Waterstone, 1995.

BOWE, Patrick. *Gardens of The Roman World.* London: Frances Lincoln, 2004.

BRADLEY-HOLE, Christopher, with Mark Griffiths. *Making The Modern Garden.* London: Mitchell Beazley, 2007.

BRADLEY-HOLE, Kathryn. *Lost Gardens of England: From The Archives of Country Life.* London: Aurum Press, 2004.

BROOKES, John. *Room Outside: A New Approach to Garden Design.* London: Thames & Hudson, 1969.

BROWN, Jane. *Eminent Gardeners: Some People of Influence and their Gardens, 1880–1980.* London: Penguin, 1990.

BROWN, Jane. *Gardens of a Golden Afternoon: The Story of a Partnership: Edwin Lutyens and Gertrude Jekyll.* London: Penguin, 1985.

BUCHAN, Ursula. *The English Garden.* London: Frances Lincoln, 2006.

BUCHAN, Ursula. *Garden People: Valerie Finnis and The Golden Age of Gardening.* London: Thames & Hudson, 2007.

CANE, Percy S., ed. *Garden Design 1936.* London: Offices of Garden Design, 1936.

CARTER, George. *Setting The Scene: A Garden Design Masterclass from Repton to The Modern Age.* London: Pimpernel Press, 2018.

CHATTO, Beth. *Beth Chatto's Garden Notebook.* London: J. M. Dent, 1988.

CHATTO, Beth. *Beth Chatto's Gravel Garden: Drought-Resistant Planting Through The Year.* London: Frances Lincoln, 2000.

COMPTON, Tania, ed. *The Private Gardens of England.* London: Constable & Robinson, 2015.

COURTIER, Jane. *Gardening as It Was: From The Pages of* Amateur Gardening *1884–1945.* London: Batsford, 1995.

DARWIN, Bernard. *Fifty Years of* Country Life. London: Country Life, 1947.

DEVONSHIRE, The Duchess of. *The Garden at Chatsworth.* London: Frances Lincoln, 1999.

EDWARDS, Ambra. *Head Gardeners.* London: Pimpernel Press, 2017.

EDWARDS, Ambra. *The Story of The English Garden.* London: National Trust Books, 2018.

ELLIOTT, Brent. *The Country House Garden from The Archives of* Country Life, *1897–1939.* London: Mitchell Beazley, 1995.

ELLIOTT, Brent. *The Royal Horticultural Society: A History 1804–2004.* Chichester, West Sussex, England: Phillimore, 2004.

ELLIOTT, Brent. *Victorian Gardens.* London: Batsford, 1986.

FESTING, Sally. *Gertrude Jekyll.* London: Viking, 1991.

FISH, Margery. *We Made a Garden.* London: Collingridge, 1956.

FLEMING, Laurence, and Alan Gore. *The English Garden.* London: Spring Books, 1988.

GLENDINNING, Victoria. *Vita: The Life of V. Sackville-West.* London: Penguin, 1984.

GRIFFITHS, Mark, ed., with Anthony Huxley, editor in chief, and Margot Levy, managing editor. *The New Royal Horticultural Society Dictionary of Gardening.* London: Macmillan, 1992.

HALL, Michael. *The Victorian Country House, from The Archives of* Country Life. London: Aurum Press, 2009.

HAMILTON, Jill Duchess of, Penny Hart, and John Simmons. *The Gardens of William Morris.* London: Frances Lincoln, 1998.

HIBBERD, Shirley. *Rustic Adornments for Homes of Taste.* Facimile ed. London: Century/The National Trust, 1987.

HOBHOUSE, Penelope. *Plants in Garden History: An Illustrated History of Plants and Their Influences on Garden Styles— From Ancient Egypt to The Present Day.* London: Pavilion, 1992.

HUDSON, Jules. *Walled Gardens.* London: National Trust Books, 2018.

HUXLEY, Anthony, and Maurice Michael. *An Illustrated History of Gardening.* New York and London: Paddington Press, 1978.

HYAMS, Edward. *Capability Brown and Humphry Repton.* London: J. M. Dent, 1971.

JEKYLL, Gertrude. *Colour Schemes for The Flower Garden*. 8th ed. London: Country Life, 1935.

JEKYLL, Gertrude. *Colour in The Flower Garden*. London: Country Life, 1908.

JEKYLL, Gertrude. *Flower Decoration in The House*. London: Country Life, 1907.

JEKYLL, Gertrude. *Home and Garden*. London: Longman, Green and Co., 1900.

LACEY, Stephen. *Gardens of The National Trust*. London: National Trust Books, 2005.

LAIRD, Mark. *The Formal Garden*. London: Thames & Hudson, 1992.

LE LIEVRE, Audrey. *Miss Willmott of Warley Place*. London: Faber & Faber, 1980.

LEWIS, Pam. *Making Wildflower Meadows*. London: Frances Lincoln, 2003.

LLOYD, Christopher. *In My Garden*. Edited by Frank Ronan. London: Bloomsbury, 1993.

LLOYD, Christopher. *The Well-Tempered Garden*. London: Collins, 1970.

LOUDON, John Claudius. *In Search of English Gardens*. London: Century, 1990.

MACLEOD, Dawn. *Down to Earth Women*. Edinburgh: William Blackwood, 1982.

MAYNARD, Arne. *The Gardens of Arne Maynard*. London: Merrell, 2015.

McDOWELL, Marta. *Beatrix Potter's Gardening Life: The Plants and Places That Inspired The Classic Children's Tales*. Portland and London: Timber Press, 2013.

MORRIS, Christopher, ed. *The Illustrated Journeys of Celia Fiennes 1685-c.1712*. Stroud, Gloucestershire, England: Alan Sutton, 1995.

MUSGRAVE, Toby, Chris Gardner, and Will Musgrave. *The Plant Hunters: Two Hundred Years of Adventure and Discovery Around The World*. London: Ward Lock, 1998.

NICOLSON, Harold. *Diaries and Letters 1930–1939*. London: Collins, 1966.

OTTEWILL, David. *The Edwardian Garden*. New Haven and London: Yale University Press, 1989.

PAGE, Russell. *The Education of a Gardener*. London: Harvill Press, 1994.

PAVORD, Anna. *The Tulip: The Story of a Flower That Has Made Men Mad*. London: Bloomsbury, 1999.

PLUMPTRE, Geoge. *The English Country House Garden*. London: Frances Lincoln, 2014.

POWERS, Alan. *The Twentieth Century House in Britain: From The Archives of Country Life*. London: Aurum Press, 2004.

QUEST-RITSON, Charles. *The English Garden: A Social History*. London: Penguin, 2003.

RICHARDSON, Tim. *The Arcadian Friends: Inventing The English Landscape Garden*. London: Bantam, 2007.

RICHARDSON, Tim. *English Gardens in The Twentieth Century: From The Archives of Country Life*. London: Aurum Press, 2005.

RICHARDSON, Tim. *The New English Garden*. London: Frances Lincoln, 2013.

ROBINSON, Barbara Paul. *Rosemary Verey: The Life and Lessons of a Legendary Gardener*. Boston: David R. Godine, 2012.

ROBINSON, William. *The Wild Garden*. 5th ed. London: John Murray, 1903.

ROTHSCHILD, Miriam, Kate Garton, and Lionel de Rothschild. *The Rothschild Gardens*. London: Gaia Books, 1996.

SACKVILLE-WEST, V. *Country Notes*. London: Michael Joseph, 1939.

SCOTT-JAMES, Anne. *Sissinghurst: The Making of a Garden*. London: Michael Joseph, 1975.

SIMMS, Barbara. *John Brookes, Garden and Landscape Designer*. London: Conran Octopus, 2007.

STRONG, Roy. Country Life *1897–1997: The English Arcadia*. London: Boxtree, 1996.

STRONG, Roy. *The Laskett: The Story of a Garden*. London: Bantam, 2003.

STRONG, Roy. *The Renaissance Garden in England*. London: Thames & Hudson, 1979.

STRONG, Roy. *Small Traditional Gardens*. Reprint. London: Conran Octopus, 1995.

STROUD, Dorothy. *Capability Brown*. 5th ed. London: Faber & Faber, 1984.

STROUD, Dorothy. *Humphry Repton*. London: Country Life, 1962.

TAIGEL, Anthea, and Tom Williamson. *Parks and Gardens*. London: Batsford, 1993.

TANKARD, Judith B. *Gardens of The Arts and Crafts Movement*. New York: Abrams, 2004.

TANKARD, Judith B. *Gertrude Jekyll and The Country House Garden: From The Archives of Country Life*. London: Aurum Press, 2011.

TANKARD, Judith B., and Martin A. Wood. *Gertrude Jekyll at Munstead Wood*. Stroud, Gloucestershire, England: Alan Sutton, 1996.

TAYLOR, Jane, and Andrew Lawson. *The English Cottage Garden*. London: Weidenfeld & Nicolson, 1994.

TAYLOR, Patrick, ed. *The Oxford Companion to The Garden*. Oxford, England: Oxford University Press, 2006.

THACKER, Christopher. *The History of Gardens*. Reprint. Beckenham, Kent, England: Croom Helm, 1985.

THOMAS, Graham Stuart. *The Gardens of The National Trust*. London: Weidenfeld & Nicolson, 1979.

THOMAS, Graham Stuart. *Recollections of Great Gardeners*. London: Frances Lincoln, 2003.

TURIN, Luca. *The Secret of Scent: Adventures in Perfume and The Science of Smell*. London: Faber & Faber, 2006.

VEREY, Rosemary. *Rosemary Verey's Making of a Garden*. London: Frances Lincoln, 1995.

WALLINGER, Rosamund. *Gertrude Jekyll's Lost Garden: The Restoration of an Edwardian Masterpiece*. Woodbridge, Suffolk, England: Garden Art Press, 2000.

WEAVER, Sir Lawrence. *Cottages: Their Planning, Design and Materials*. London: Country Life, 1926.

WEAVER, Sir Lawrence. *Houses and Gardens by Sir Edwin Lutyens RA*. London: Country Life, 1925.

WHITSEY, Fred. *The Garden at Hidcote*. London: Frances Lincoln, 2007.

WILLIAMSON, Tom. *Polite Landscapes: Gardens and Society in Eighteenth-Century England*. Stroud, Gloucestershire, England: Alan Sutton, 1995.

WORSLEY, Giles. *England's Lost Houses: From The Archives of Country Life*. London: Aurum Press, 2002.

ACKNOWLEDGMENTS

I would like to thank Charles Miers at Rizzoli and Mark Hedges at *Country Life* for inviting me to write this book and Klaus Kirschbaum for his considerate editing. Robert Dalrymple has designed *English Gardens* with great sympathy for the subjects and photographs. Also grateful thanks to Melanie Bryan, Paula Fahey, and Sarah Hart at the *Country Life* picture archive.

Particular thanks to my former colleagues at *Country Life* with whom I had the pleasure to work for many years, and the specialist writers who all brought their own individual styles and observations to the original features we prepared. They include: Tom Coward, Steven Desmond, Mark Griffiths, Jacky Hobbs, Tim Longville, Non Morris, George Plumptre, Charles Quest-Ritson, Roy Strong, Tim Richardson.

Likewise, it has been the greatest pleasure to work down the years with such talented photographers as the late Paul Barker, Clive Boursnell, Val Corbett, Jerry Harpur, the late Marcus Harpur, Andrew Lawson, Marianne Majerus, Clive Nichols, and Julian Nieman. Their ability to capture the special atmosphere of any garden or the textured richness of a single flower, despite vagaries of weather and season, has greatly enriched our appreciation and understanding of the English garden as a genre.

Which leads me on to the gardens themselves and their dedicated owners who invest in and create these green paradises and often generously open them for others to see the work in real life. Gardens change day by day, hour by hour, and I have also gained much insight and knowledge through talking with the talented gardeners who tend these places on a day to day basis.

Special thanks to the Duke of Devonshire for his extremely thoughtful foreword. English gardening is flourishing and leading in several interesting directions and therefore, grateful thanks to the garden designers whose work is featured here. Their inspiration and knowledge ensure that English gardens will continue to delight and inspire the world.

KATHRYN BRADLEY-HOLE

INDEX

First published in the United States of America
in 2019 by Rizzoli International Publications, Inc.
300 Park Avenue South New York, NY 10010

www.rizzoliusa.com

Publisher: Charles Miers
Editor: Klaus Kirschbaum
Designer: Robert Dalrymple
Editorial Coordinator: Jennifer Duardo
Production Manager: Kaija Markoe
Managing Editor: Lynn Scrabis

Set in Jeremy Tankard's, Kingfisher type
Printed in Spain

2024 2025 2026 / 10 9 8 7 6

ISBN: 978–0–8478–6579–6
Library of Congress Control Number: 2019938524

Visit us online:
Facebook.com/RizzoliNewYork
Twitter: @Rizzoli_Books
Instagram.com/RizzoliBooks
Pinterest.com/RizzoliBooks
Youtube.com/user/RizzoliNY
Issuu.com/Rizzoli